Committees and Commissions in India
1980

Concepts in Communication
Informatics & Librarianship-56

General Editor : **S.P. Agrawal**

Committees and Commissions in India 1980

Volume 18

PART A

A Concept's Project

Compiled by a team of professionals
under the guidance of
VIRENDRA KUMAR

CONCEPT PUBLISHING COMPANY, NEW DELHI 110059

ISBN 81-7022-510-8 (Vol. 18, Part A)

First Published 1994

Published and Printed by
Ashok Kumar Mittal
Concept Publishing Company
A/15-16, Commercial Block, Mohan Garden
NEW DELHI 110059 (India)

Lasertypeset by
Printing Express
H-13, Bali Nagar
NEW DELHI 110015

GENERAL EDITOR'S INTRODUCTION

In the context of the changing world, the role of the government – be it at central, state or local level – is becoming more pervasive in the modern society. Everyday, it has to encounter new problems and face new issues which demand quite a new thinking and novel strategies to overcome them. Thus, the increasing role of the government in every sphere of people's life has broadened its functions and responsibilities tremendously and enlarged its activities to such an extent that the government machinery of its own can hardly manage its affairs. Moreover, its functions are becoming more complicated and complex requiring the assistance of outside specialists, technocrats and specialized agencies.

In view of this, the modern government has to set-up committees and commissions and working or study groups on various problems and issues from time to time. In the light of the recommendations of these committees and commissions, the government take decisions on key issues and problems. Often the government is obliged to seek the assistance of a committee to evaluate some of its schemes in operation so that on the basis of the evaluation reports of the committee, it may either continue, modify or scrap the on-going schemes. In other words, the committees or commissions, etc., exercise a great deal of pivotal force in shaping the policies and programmes of the government and for this purpose submit a large number of reports.

In these volumes of *Committees and Commissions in India*, now being published under the *Concepts in Communication Informatics and Librarianship (CICIL)* series, an attempt has been made to cover the period from 1974 onwards. The volumes include the vital data about only those reports of the committees and commissions which have been constituted by the Central Government. We have made every endeavour to include the digest of all the important reports on various vital issues of great importance and on major areas of national development.

We have also an ambitious plan to publish the digests of the important reports of the committees and commissions appointed by different state governments, the semi-government organisations and the learned bodies as also the reports published during the period of the British Government.

The publication has been brought out under the guidance of Shri Virendra Kumar, specialist in his own right with vast experience of working in Government Documents Section in the Central Secretariat Library and having the privilege of the blessings of Dr. S.R. Ranganathan – the father of Indian Library Science. I also put on record the collaborative help provided by Shri M.W.K. Sherwani.

We are sure that this compilation will prove a very useful reference tool for researchers, serious students and scholars of the public administration and political science, administrators, policy-makers, educationists and historians.

S.P. AGRAWAL

PREFACE

This volume of *Committees and Commissions in India* attempts to understand the activities of the various Committees and Commissions during the period 1974.

A 'Commission' is a governmental agency created to perform a particular function such as special investigations or on governmental regulations of business. It is appointed mainly when it is thought that a matter involves some financial questions. There are other reasons for which a Commission is appointed, e.g., in matters pertaining to welfare of the State and its citizens and/or improving the efficiency in an administration. The status of a 'Committee' is also the same as that of a 'Commission', but it does not possess as wide powers as are enjoyed by a Commission and has to limit itself to specific work assigned to it under its terms of reference. While arriving at decisions in the form of recommendations, a Commission or Committee ensures that such decisions are representative of interests of various types of people and also a safeguard against abuse of power.

A Committee or a Commission comprises a Chairman, the Members and Member Secretary (sometimes there is also an Assistant Secretary). In some cases, there are even One-man Commissions and the enquiry in such Commissions is entrusted to an Officer-on-Special Duty.

The Chairman of a Commission is a person well-versed mostly in legal matters and is often a retired judge of a High Court or the Supreme Court of India. Occasionally, a Member of Parliament is also appointed as the Chairman of a Commission. On the other hand, the Chairman of the Committee is mostly a specialist in the subject of the Committee. He can be a Leader or a Convenor also, if he heads a Panel, a Study Group or a Delegation, etc.

The Members of a Commission, Committee, Panel, Study Group etc., are specialists in their respective fields and provide valuable guidance to the Commission or the Committee in making recommendations.

The Member-Secretary or Secretary is generally nominated from among the experienced officials who have the requisite competent knowledge of the subject on which the Commission or the Committee is appointed.

Committees and Commissions in India provides in chronological order vital information about Committees and Commissions appointed by the Government from time to time. Information for each Committee or Commission is presented in a compact form in four parts, namely; Constitution; Appointment; Terms of Reference and Recommendations.

CONTENTS

PART A

PART B

1

GODAVARI WATER DISPUTES TRIBUNAL UNDER SECTION 5(3) OF THE INTER-STATE WATER DISPUTES ACT, 1956, 1979 — FURTHER REPORT[1]

Chairman Shri R.S. Bachawat
Members Shri D.M. Bhandari; Shri D.M. Sen

Appointment

The Godavari Water Disputes Tribunal investigated the matters referred to it under Sections 5(1) of the Inter-State Water Disputes Act, 1956 and forwarded its unanimous decision and Report to the Government of India on the 27th November, 1979. The Government of India and the States of Andhra Pradesh, Madhya Pradesh and Maharashtra field references under Section 5(3) of the said Act by the 26th February, 1980.

Terms of Reference

The Government of India filed its reference on the 25th February, 1980 and replies there were field by the States of Andhra Pradesh, Maharashtra, Karnataka, Orissa and Madhya Pradesh.

The State of Andhra Pradesh filed its reference on the 25th February, 1980 and replies thereto were field by the States of Maharashtra, Karnataka, Orissa and Madhya Pradesh.

The State of Madhya Pradesh filed its reference on 25th February, 1980 and replies thereto were filed by States of Andhra Pradesh Maharashtra, Karnataka and Orissa.

The State of Maharashtra filed its reference on the 25th February, 1980 and replies thereto were filed by states of Karnataka Orissa and

1. Delhi, Controller of Publications, 1980, 68 p.

Madhya Pradesh.

The Government of India did not filed any replies on the references made by the States of Andhra Pradesh, Madhya Pradesh and Maharashtra but reserved its right to make appropriate oral submission on those references.

The States of Karnataka and Orissa did not file any separate reference on their part. Their cases are stated in the replies filed by them.

The main subject-matter of all the references and replies filed by the Government of India and the Party States, as mentioned above, relates to the decision of the Tribunal on the Polavaram Project of the State of Andhra Pradesh.

Contents

Letter of Transmittal; Representatives of the Government of India and the State Governments; Preliminary; Polavaram Project; Reference of the Government of India relating to matters other than the Polavaram Project; Section I — Reference of the State of Madhya Pradesh relating to matters other than the Polavaram Project; Section II — Certain Corrections; Direction for Costs; Concluding Remarks; Final Order of the Tribunal.

Concluding Observations

Before parting with the case finally, we place on record our appreciation of the persistent efforts of the party States to arrive at a settlement of all the points of disputes arising in the matter of sharing the waters of the inter-State river Godavari and the river valley thereof. In retrospect it becomes manifest that the foundation of such a settlement was laid by the Agreement dated the 19th December, 1975 when by showing exemplary spirit of accommodation, the parties took the momentous decision of settling an important part of the dispute. Thereafter, the parties took slow but sure steps to reach the ultimate destination of a full and final settlement of the entire dispute. This task was not easy and the parties took their own time to arrive at a settlement on the remaining matters.

At times, to break the stalemate in the negotiations, the case was listed for arguments. But every time the parties evinced an earnest desire to settle the entire controversy in a most amicable manner. As the stakes were high, the negotiations for settlement took a long time specially when the parties devoted themselves to a thorough examination of all the areas in which waters of the river Godavari and its tributaries could be beneficially utilised. For this, they had to take into consideration all the small and big rivers flowing in their territories and contributing water to the river Godavari and also to examine the possibilities for undertaking joint projects.

It gave the Tribunal immense satisfaction when the parties filed the Agreements annexed to our Final Order in the Original Report. But still, in spite of best efforts, the parties could not reach a satisfactory settlement of the question of diversion of the waters of the river Godavari into the Krishna through the Polavaram Dam. At this stage we took this matter in our hands and decided the case as mentioned in the Original Report.

The Government of India and some of the party States filed references under Section 5(3) of the Inter-State Water Disputes Act, 1956. During the course of the hearing of these references, the Government of India came to our assistance in resolving this dispute to the satisfaction of all the party States by making the statement annexed to the Final Order and marked Annexure "H". We are sincerely thankful to the Government of India for this.

We need not reiterate what we have already said in the Original Report about the devoted services rendered by the Assessors and the Secretary of the Tribunal and other members of the staff. We record our appreciation of their services.

To the inhabitants of the Godavari basin and to those beyond the basin who would be utilising the waters of the river Godavari, we wish all happiness and prosperity. It is our earnest hope that while making its use they will take all possible steps to prevent wastage and pollution of the waters of this holy river. We are confident that the party States will take appropriate and effective steps in this direction.

The Godavari basin is rich in forests. It is our sincere desire that the party States should preserve this national wealth with utmost care so that its usefulness and beauty remain unspoilt.

The Final Order set forth in Chapter VII of Vol. I of the Original Report as modified in accordance with the explanations given by the Tribunal under Section 5(3) of the Inter-State Water Disputes Act, 1956 is given below:

Final Order of the Tribunal

The Tribunal hereby passes the following Order:

Clause I

All the States can make use of underground water within their respective State territories in the Godavari basin and such use shall not be reckoned as use of the water of the river Godavari.

Clause II

Use shall include any use, made by any State of the waters of the river Godavari and its tributaries for domestic, municipal, irrigation, industrial, production of power, navigation, pisciculture, wildlife protection, recreation purposes and evaporation losses from the storages created for the above purposes.

Clause III

(A). The uses of water mentioned in column (1) below shall be measured in the manner indicated in column (2):

Use	Measurement
(1)	(2)
(i) Irrigation use	100 per cent of the quantity diverted or lifted from the river or any of the tributaries or from any reservoir, storage or canal and 100 per cent of evaporation losses in there storages.
(ii) Power use	100 per cent of evaporation losses in the storage.
(iii) Domestic and municipal water supply within the basin	20 per cent of the quantity of water diverted or lifted from the river or any of its tributaries or from any reservoir, storage or canal.
(iv) Industrial use within the basin	2.5 per cent of the quantity of water diverted or lifted from the river or any of its tributaries or from any reservoir, storage or canal.
(v) All uses outside the basin	100 per cent of the quantity diverted or lifted from the river or any of the tributaries or from any reservoir, storage or canal.

(B) Except as provided in sub-clause (A) or in the Agreements between the parties a use shall be measured by the extent of depletion of the waters of the river Godavari in any manner whatsoever including losses of water by evaporation and other natural causes from man made reservoirs and other works without deducting in the case of use for irrigation the quantity of water that any return after such use to the river.

(C) The water stored in any reservoir across any stream of the Godavari river system shall not of itself be reckoned as depletion of the water of the stream except to the extent of the losses of water from evaporation and other natural causes from such reservoir. The water diverted from such reservoir by any State for its own use in any water year shall be reckoned as use by that State in that water year.

(D) If in any water year any State is not able to use any portion of the water allocated to it during that year on account of the non-development of its projects or damage to any of its projects or doses not use it for any reason whatsoever, that State will not be entitled to claim the unutilised water in any subsequent water year.

(E) Failure of any State to make use of any portion of the water allocated to it during any water year shall not constitute forfeiture or abandonment of its share of water in any subsequent water year nor shall it increase the share of any other State in any subsequent water year even if such State may have used such water.

Clause IV

Each of the States concerned will be at liberty to divert any part of the share of the Godavari waters allocated to it from the Godavari basin to any other basin.

Clause V

The following Agreements so far as they relate to the Godavari river and Godavari river basin be observed and carried out:

A. Agreement dated the 19th December, 1975 between the States of Karnataka, Maharashtra, Madhya Pradesh, Orissa and Andhra Pradesh annexed hereto and marked Annexure "A" agreeing to the clearance of projects for the utilisation of waters of the Godavari river and is tributaries in accordance with:

(a) Agreement between the States of Karnataka and Andhra Pradesh on the 17th September, 1975—Annexure I.

(b) Agreement between the States of Maharashtra and Andhra Pradesh on the 6th October, 1975—Annexure II.

(c) Agreement between the States of Madhya Pradesh and Andhra Pradesh on the 7th November, 1975—Annexure III.

(d) Agreement between the States of Orissa and Madhya Pradesh on the 9th December, 1975—Annexure IV.

B. Agreement dated the 7th August, 1978 between the States of Maharashtra, Madhya Pradesh and Andhra Pradesh annexed hereto and marked Annexure "B", subject to the provisions of the Agreement dated the 2nd April, 1980 mentioned below.

C. Agreement dated the 4th August, 1978 between the States of Andhra Pradesh and Karnataka annexed hereto and marked Annexure "C".

D. Agreement dated the 15th December, 1978 between the States of Andhra Pradesh and Karnataka annexed hereto and marked Annexure "C".

E. Agreement between the States of Karnataka and Maharashtra evidenced letters dated the 29th January, 1979, 30th January, 1979 and 31st January, 1979 annexed hereto and marked Annexure "E".

F. Agreement dated the 11th July, 1979 between the States of Orissa and Madhya Pradesh annexed hereto and marked Annexure "F".

G. Agreement dated the 2nd April, 1989 between the States of Andhra Pradesh, Madhya Pradesh and Orissa annexed hereto and marked Annexure "G".

Clause VI

(1) In accordance with the statement dated the 3rd April, 1980 submitted on behalf of the Government of India, annexed hereto and marked Annexure "H", we direct that—

(i) the Polavaram Project shall be cleared by the Central Water Commission as expeditiously as possible for FRL/MWL + 150 feet;

(ii) the matter of design of the dam and its operation schedule is left to the Central Water Commission which it shall decide keeping in view all the Agreements between the parties, including the

Agreement dated the 2nd April, 1980 as far as practicable; and

(iii) if there is to be any change in the operation schedule as indicated in the Agreement dated the 2nd April, 1980 it shall be made only after consultation with the States of Andhra Pradesh, Madhya Pradesh and Orissa. The design aspects shall, however, be left entirely to the Central Water Commission.

(2) The State of Andhra Pradesh shall observe all safeguards, including the safeguard mentioned in sub-clause (1) above, regarding the Polavaram Project, as directed by the Central Water Commission.

Clause VII

Nothing in the Order of this Tribunal shall impair the right or power or authority of any State to regulate within its boundaries the use of water or to enjoy the benefit of waters within that State in a manner not inconsistent with the Order of this Tribunal.

Clause VIII

In this Order:

(a) Use of the water of the river Godavari by any person or entity of any nature whatsoever within the territories of a State shall be reckoned as use by that State.

(b) The expression "Godavari waters" with its grammatical variations and cognate expressions includes water of the main stream of the Godavari river, all its tributaries and all other streams, contributing water directly or indirectly to the Godavari river.

(c) The sub-basins of the Godavari basin mean the sub-basins described in the statement annexed hereto marked Annexure "I".

(d) Use of quantities of water specified in the Agreements is for a water year commencing on 1st June and ending on 31st May.

Clause IX

Nothing contained herein shall prevent the alteration, amendment or modification of all or any of the foregoing Clauses by agreement between the parties or by legislation by Parliament.

Clause X

(A) The Governments of Maharashtra, Karnataka, Andhra Pradesh, Madhya Pradesh and Orissa and shall bear their own costs of appearing before the Tribunal. The expenses of the Tribunal shall be apportioned and paid by the Governments of Maharashtra, Karnataka, Andhra Pradesh, Madhya Pradesh and Orissa in equal shares. These directions relate to the reference under Section 5(1) of the Inter-State Water Disputes Act, 1956.

(B) The Government of India and the Governments of Maharashtra, Karnataka, Andhra Pradesh, Madhya Pradesh and Orissa shall bear their own costs of appearing before the Tribunal in the references under Section 5(3) of the said Act. The expenses of the Tribunal in respect of the aforesaid references shall be apportioned and paid by the Governments of Maharashtra, Karnataka, Andhra Pradesh, Madhya Pradesh and Orissa in equal shares.

RAILWAY ACCIDENT INVESTIGATION REPORT ON ACCIDENT TO 11 DOWN BARAK VALLEY EXPRESS TRAIN AT KM 51.863 BETWEEN DIHAKHO AND MUPA STATIONS ON LUMDING-BADARPUR SINGLE LINE METRE GAUGE SECTION IN LUMDING DIVISION OF NORTHEAST FRONTIER RAILWAY AT 0.5.05 HOURS ON 20TH MARCH, 1980 — REPORT[1]

One Man Commission	Shri K. Ganapati, Commissioner of Railway Safety, Eastern Circle, Calcutta
Officers Present	Shri R.K. Sabharwal, Shri G.S. Koppikar, Shri A.K. Malakar.

Appointment

The Commission was appointed under Ministry of Tourism and Civil Aviation (Commission of Railway Safety) in accordance with Rule 4 of the Statutory Investigation into Railway Accidents Rules, 1973 on March 20, 1980.

Terms of Reference

To inquire into the Accident to 11 Down Barak Valley Express Train at km 51.863 between Dihakho and Mupa Stations on Lumding-Badarpur Single Line Metre Gauge section in Lumding Division of Northeast Frontier Railway at 05.05 hours on 20th March, 1980.

1. Ministry of Tourism and Civil Aviation (Commission of Railway Safety), Government of India, New Delhi, 1983, iii + 24 p.

Contents

Inspection and Inquiry; The Accident; Casualities Relief Measure; The Train; Local Conditions; Summary of Evidence; Tests and Observations; Discussion; Conclusions; Remarks and Recommendations; Annexures I and II; Railway Board's Comments on Various Paras of the Report.

Conclusions

Cause of Accident

On careful consideration of the factual, material and circumstantial evidence, I have reached the conclusion that the accident to 11 Down Barak Valley Express train at km. 51.863 between Dihakho and Mupa Stations on Lumding-Badarpur Single Line M.G. Section in Lumding Division of N.F. Railway at 05.05 hours on 20-3-1980 was caused by overturning of the 7th coach No. 1552 due to the excessive speed of the train at 65 kmph far beyond the safe maximum permissible speed of 32 kmph and booked speed of 28 kmph prescribed by the Railway on this Hill Section.

Responsibility

(a) The Driver of the train, Shri Rakhal Chandra Dey, is held solely responsible for rash and negligent driving and exceeding the maximum permissible speed prescribed by the Railway. He violated G.R. 89 (a) and (b) reproduced below:

> "89. *Limits of speed generally.* – (a) Every train shall be run on each section of the railway within the limits of speed sanctioned for that section by approved special instructions. The sectional speed sanctioned shall be shown in the Working Time Table, a copy of which shall be supplied on issue to the Additional Commissioner of Railway safety; and
> (b) The Driver shall regulate and control the running of his train as accurately as possible, according to the Working Time Table, so as to avoid either excessive speed or loss of time, he shall not make up between any two stations more time than is allowed in this behalf by special instructions, and shall observe all temporary speed

restrictions."

(b) Shri Rakhal Chandra Dey, Driver of the ill-fated train is further held responsible for destroying the vital evidence relevant to the accident, viz., VDO Speed Chart.

Service Record

Shri Rakhal Chandra Dey was born on 25-5-1924 and was appointed as a Cleaner in the Railway on 3-7-1944. He was promoted as Driver 'C' grade on 1-12-1962, as a Driver 'B' grade on 8-7-1978 and as Driver 'A' grade on 8-11-1979. He passed the Diesel conversion course on 16-6-1971. He passed the Refresher course on 13-12-1978 at New Bongaigaon. He passed the Diesel Refresher course at Siliguri on 15-3-1976. He passed the last Medical examination on 18-7-1979. There are no punishments in the service record.

Relief Arrangements and Medical Attention

I am satisfied with the relief arrangements and medical attention given. The Magistrate, Haflong, however, brought to my notice that there was some complaints from passengers regarding inadequate supply of water, refreshments and delay in clearing the uninjured passengers. The site conditions were somewhat unusual and difficult and the arrangements made by the Railway appeared to have fallen short of the expectations of the passengers. The Railway may bear this in mind for future.

Recommendations

9.1 *Monitoring of VDO Speed Chart*

The present system of monitoring VDO Speed Chart in the Loco Shed and tracking down errant drivers is far from satisfactory. The condition of working of speed recorder is also far from satisfactory. The N.F. Railway Administration may take further action and ensure that –

(a) Speedometer and Speed recorder are properly calibrated and work accurately;
(b) The speed charts are inserted and removed promptly at ap-

propriate places;

(c) The speed charts are checked, scrutinised and monitored by responsible staff;

(d) Errant drivers who are prone to overspeeding are properly and promptly warned and brought to book; and

(e) An officer at appropriate level is specifically nominated to ensure the above.

9.2 *String-lining of curves not done at prescribed intervals*

It came to notice during the enquiry that the versines of the curves under PWI, Lumding were not recorded at intervals of 6 months as per extant rules during the years 1977, 1978 and 1979. When the PWI failed to perform his duties over a period of 3 years the matter was not detected by any official of the Administration above him till it came to light in the Accident Enquiry. N.F. Railway may evolve a suitable procedure whereby it is ensured that the PWIs carry out the prescribed duties within the time limit and in case of their failure the matter is detected promptly and appropriate corrective and punitive action taken by the Railway Administration.

9.3 *Drivers to be checked for intoxication*

In the accident under reference, for reasons which could not be ascertained the Driver of the train was not checked for intoxication after the accident. The Medical Officers were so busy in rendering first aid that it did not occur to any one that the Driver of the train should be examined for intoxication. Recently the Railway Board under their letter No. 76/Safety-I/20/24 dated 22-12-1979 have issued orders for supply of Breath Analyser Testing equipment at various points. The instructions do not appear to be insufficient detail and the Railway has not taken any action so far, for implementing the Board's orders. It is no doubt very important that the Railway staff like Driver as in the present case who are directly involved or who could possibly be connected with the cause of accident be examined for intoxication after the accident. It would appear that the easiest way to ensure the same is to introduce an appropriate S.R. under G.R. 182 prescribing the manner in which the Railway staff suspected are to be examined for intoxication after the accident.

9.4 *Slack working in many respects*

The following minor irregularities came to notice:

(a) The Guard of 203 Up Passenger did not carry portable telephone, fire extinguisher, emergency train lighting equipment and fusee;
(b) The Guard of 11 Down Barak Valley Express did not carry portable control phone, emergency train lighting equipment and fusee; and
(c) The V.C.D. on the loco was not functioning.

The above irregularities in train working do not have a direct bearing on the cause of the present accident. They only show slack supervision at various levels and poor procurement of stores. The Railway may take necessary action to tighten the supervision and ensure better compliance to the safety rules.

9.5 *Marshalling order violations*

The marshalling order of 11 Down Barak Valley Express involved in the accident revealed violations of standing marshalling orders, which it is understood is due to non-availability of AT SLRs. The same position was noticed in the case of collision of 26 Down with 1 Down on 23rd December, 1979 on the same Railway. The Railway should either procure more number of AT SLRs to enable them to conform to the marshalling order rules or take measures to keep down the percentage of sick SLRs.

9.6 *Check rails*

It was noticed that the check rail on the curve at the site of accident was fixed to the sleepers by dog spikes. The normal practice is to connect the check rail by check blocks to the running rail to make the track more rigid. The N.F. Railway may profitably adopt the standard method of fixing check rail to the running rail with check blocks to make the track more rigid. The check rail clearance prescribed for 10° curves on the N.F. Railways was 2-3/4". With the above clearance it was noticed that there was no wheel mark on the check rail indicating that the wheel was not touching the check rail. The outer rail was however badly worn out to the extent of 3/16". Thus the provision of the check rail though it prevented the wheel from mounting the outer rail, did not help in reducing the wear on outer rail. N.F. Railway may re-examine the issue and suitably reduce the check rail clearance profitably to lessen the side wear on the outer rail.

9.7 *Guard to be taken up for giving false evidence*

The enquiry has established beyond reasonable doubt that the train was running at a speed of 65 kmph at the time of the accident. Even before the commencement of the enquiry the Guard was specifically informed that as the General Rules stand at present, he had no responsibility regarding the overspeeding of the train and that therefore he should speak out the truth. In spite of this warning the Guard had chosen to give false evidence regarding the speed of the train. It should be clear to any one who has gone through the report that the evidence of the Guard on a vital issue regarding the speed of the train was false and motivated. The Railway should therefore take up the matter suitably with the Guard for tendering false evidence in the C.R.S. Enquiry.

9.8 *Track to be monitored by mechanical track recording*

Even though an Express train is running on this section it is seen that the track is not being periodically monitored by any mechanical track recording equipment. It is considered necessary and desirable that tracks on which Express trains are run should be periodically monitored by mechanical track recording cars/equipment at suitable periodical intervals.

Railway Board's Comments on Various Paras of the Report

Para 9.1: Necessary action has been taken by the Railway Administration in compliance with the recommendation made by the CRS. Instructions with regard to proper maintenance and calibration of speedometers, insertion/removal and scrutiny of speed charts *vis-a-vis* the action to be taken against the Drivers who are prone to overspeeding have been reiterated to the Railways, vide circular letter No. 77 M(/M&P)/467/7 dated 22-4-1980. Five copies of the said circular are enclosed for information.

As regards CCRS's Memorandum No. RS. 22-T (15)/77 dated 7-5-1980, the matter has already been considered and reply sent to the

CCRS vide this Ministry's letter of 11-9-1980.

Para 9.2: The matter has been taken up with the Northeast Frontier Railway.

Para 9.3: Instructions with regard to introduction of Breath Analyser Test on the Railways, have already been issued vide circular letter No. 76/Safety-I/20/24 dated 22-12-1979. These are still in experimental stage. Further instructions have been sent to the Railways that Medical Officers, attending the site of accident, should consider the necessity of subjecting alcohol test to Motormen/Drivers or any other staff connected with the safe running of trains, involved in the accident.

Para 9.4: As regards non-availability of portable telephones, emergency lighting equipment and fire extinguishers in the brakevans of 203 Up passenger and 11 Down Express, the matter has been taken up suitably by the Railway Administration. The non-supply of fusee to the Guard of 11 Down was due to the limited stock of the fusee and the Railway has since placed the indents to obtain fresh supply of fusees. As regards non-functioning of the Vigilance Control Device, this was due to non-availability of spare parts. Railway administration is being advised to make good these omissions expeditiously.

Para 9.5: As explained by the Railway, 11 Up/12 Down Barak Valley Express are "end-on-generation rakes". There is shortage of anti-telescopic/steel bodied SLRs, and 14 Nos. of newly built SLRs have since been allotted to the Northeast Frontier Railway on replacement account. Non-anti-telescopic/steel bodied SLRs in the Barak Valley Express will now be gradually replaced after converting them into end-on-generation system. In the meantime, all out efforts are being made by the Railway to keep down the inefficient percentage to the minimum.

It is seen that CCRS has noted the position explained by the Railway.

Para 9.6: The matter is under consideration in consultation with the RDSO.

Para 9.7: Disciplinary action is being taken against the Guard for tendering false evidence.

Para 9.8: As advised by the Railway, the testing of the track on this section by Hallade Track Recorder was programmed earlier last year but could not be taken up because of difficult law and order situation in the area. However, such an inspection would be taken up as soon as feasible.

3

LAW COMMISSION OF INDIA: EIGHTY-FOURTH REPORT ON RAPE AND ALLIED OFFENCES — REPORT[1]

Chairman P.V. Dixit, Justice
Members Shri S.N. Shankar; Gangeshwar Prasad
M. Secy. P.M. Bakshi

Appointments

By his letter No. PS/LS/LA-80 dated 27th March, 1980,addressed by the Law Secretary to Shri P.M. Bakshi, Secretary of the Law Commission, the desire of the Government that the Law Commission should make a special study of the law relating to rape and assaults on the modesty of women and related matters was communicated to the Commission.

Terms of Reference

A Special study of the law relating to rape and assaults on the modesty of women and related matters.

Contents

Introductory; Rape and indecent assault: the substantive law; Arrest and investigation; Medical examination of the accused and the victim; Procedure for trail, including trial *in camera* and publication of court proceedings; Publicity on conviction; Evidence; Conclusion; Appendices I & II.

1. Controller of Publications, Government of India, Delhi, 1980, iii + 42 p.

Recommendations

8.1 *Effect of our proposals*: We have come to the end of the task committed to us. We believe that we have made proposals to secure that no person who has committed rape escapes punishment, that women who become victims of rape are not harassed during the course of investigation and trail in the Court and that the trail of persons charged with rape is speeded up, to ensure that the police discharge efficiently and promptly the manifold and complex problems that confront them in rape cases, and to assure the free movement of women by giving them protection when they move cut, as also to the inmates of women's lodgings and hostels.

8.2 *Changes whether going for enough or too far*: There may be some who feel that the changes recommended by us are likely to be for the worse. Such persons are too complacent for our taste. There may be still others, who may regard our recommendations as nothing more than an attempt to patch-up the system of criminal justice, which, according to them, is so defective as to be beyond redemption. We do not delude ourselves into thinking that our proposals will bring into the investigation and trial of cases of rape a state of perfection. Sometimes one's best endeavours go away. What we have attempted is to strike a balance between the interests of the accused and those of the victim in a case relating to rape, and thus to protect the interests of the society.

8.3 *Effect of films and the real challenge*: During the course of discussion with us, a lady Member of Parliament pointed out the pernicious influence of Indian films highlighting rape and its attendant violence. The real challenge, therefore, in dealing with the problems of rape and its horrors lies in rousing public consciousness against it, and in preventing the publication and exhibition in any form of that trash material, which only corrupts the minds of the youth and of the depraved. To this problem we commend Government's earnest and immediate attention.

4

COMMITTEE ON FOREST AND TRIBALS IN INDIA, 1980 — REPORT[1]

Chairman Dr. B.K. Roy Burman
Members Shri S.A. Shah; Shri N.J. Joshi; Shri Ranjit Singh; Shri J.N. Pandey; Shri K.S. Chandrasekharan; Shri Munawar Hussain; Shri D.N. Tiwari
M. Secy. Dr. Bhupinder Singh

Appointment

At the Conference of the State Forest Ministers and Ministers incharge of Tribal Development held in July, 1978 it was resolved that:

(a) the development of forests, instead of being planned in isolation, should form an integral part of the comprehensive plans of integrated tribal development;
(b) the Forest Department should constitute better organised forest labour co-operative societies within a time-bound programme of two to three years to undertake all forestry operations replacing intermediaries;
(c) the right of collection of minor forest produce of collection of minor forest produce by tribals and its marketing for remunerative price to the tribals should be ensured; and
(d) the forest villages should be abolished and be converted into revenue villages.

Guidelines have to be prepared to enable States to orient these resolutions into practice. For drawing up the guidelines, it has been decided to constitute a committee on forest and tribals in India by the Government of India, Ministry of Home Affairs, Tribal Development Division, vide its office Memorandum No. 12023/2/79-TD dated April 9, 1980.

---

1. New Delhi, Ministry of Home Affairs, Tribal Development Division, 1982, 122 p.

Terms of Reference

(a) Appraisal of the nature of rights of tribals in respect of land and forest.

(b) Review of integrated forestry development programmes with particular reference to social forestry.

(e) Review of horticulture, agro-forestry and other productive programmes with particular reference to satisfaction of the basic consumption needs of tribals, generation of employment and creation of incremental income for the tribal and the non-tribal segments of the indigenous population.

(d) Review of the activities of the various bodies concerned with forest and tribal economy with reference to their role in promotion of interest of tribal economy.

(e) Concrete suggestions for guidelines to be laid down to re-orient forest policy so that, *inter alia*, it serves the interests of tribal economy.

Contents

Introduction; Forest in India; Tribals and Forests; Recommendations of Commissions, Committees and Working Group; Resume of States Scene; Summing Up; Summary of Conclusions and Recommendations Annexure 1.

Recommendations

Background

India has a total geographical area of about 328.8 million hectares with about 683.81 million population (15% of the world population), the majority of whom reside in about 6 lakh villages. The forest area in the country is reported to be 74.74 million hectares (22.7% of total land area of the country) which works out to 0.109 hectares per capita which is far below the world average of 1.04 hectares.

2. During 1951-75, the forest area in India receded by 4.134 million hectares, a loss of 0.161 million hectares every year or 441 hectares per day. The stocking of existing forest has gone down appreciably; it is estimated that only 10 per cent of the country's forest areas are capable of performing protective, productive and ecological

functions. The consequence of destruction of tree groves from the forest area as well as outside has created a situation where:

- there may be now enough food but not energy-fuel to cook it with;
- there may be large number of cattle and sheep but not enough fodder to feed them;
- there is vast area under agricultural crop but not enough organic fertiliser to keep the soil in a healthy condition;
- crop lands have become devoid of protective cover from dessicating and soil eroding winds;
- rivers have increased surface discharge of more than 10 times within the last 70 years, causing floods and damage, destruction and misery;
- with silt eroding away millions of tonnes of top soil every year reducing fertility of the crop land; and
- mountains have become sensitive and prone to landslides at the slightest disturbance causing untold misery and loss to the local residents and the plains are in constant danger of devastating floods.

3. We, therefore recommend that:

(i) For the existing 10 per cent stocked forest area of the country, measures for protection, conservation and regulated working should be stringent.

(ii) Restocking of the existing 13 per cent degraded forest area should be taken up quickly and at a rapid pace.

(iii) Afforestation of 10 per cent of the country's wasteland scattered as well as in strips alongside roads, railway lines, canals, river banks should be undertaken with public participation.

(iv) Forest should be strengthened by rational operations, large investments and use of new technology so that it can yield a higher surplus to be shared locally, regionally and nationally as against rapid disappearance of trees and vegetation.

(v) The symbiosis between the tribal community and the forest management should be established through imaginative forestry programmes and conservation and reorganisation of traditional skills of the tribals.

Forest Policy

4. Tribal communities in India largely occupy forested regions, where for long periods in their history they have lived in isolation. They draw their sustenance from forests. Forests not only provide them food, material to build houses, fuel for cooking as well as for light and warmth, fodder for their cattle, but also satisfy the deep-rooted tribal sentiments connected one way or the other with forests, right from birth to death. In time of distress such as famine, forests are their last succour. Forests occupy a central position in tribal economy.

5. The significant role that forests play in tribal economy has to be clearly recognised and forest policy under formulation should have appropriate orientation. We recommend that:

(i) Forest policy and forest system should be directed towards managing a renewable endowment of vast potential for subserving national, regional as well as local developmental goals. In fact, the individual tribal, the local tribal community and national interest should be regarded as three corners of a triangular forest policy.

(ii) Forest policy must fulfil three sets of needs (a) ecological security; (b) food, fruit, fuel, fodder, fibre, timber and other domestic needs of particularly the rural and tribal population; (c) cottage, small, medium and large industries including the requirement of defence and communications.

(iii) A national forest policy should recognise the positive role of the people in maintaining forests and environment in unambiguous terms and not merely in its implication.

(iv) Wherever community rights exist on forest land, they should be recognised and adapted to serve the urgent needs of soil and water management and re-afforestation of denuded tracts by suitable species.

(v) Conjoint efforts of government, cooperative, community and private sectors are necessary to increase production of fuelwood, fodder, fruit and industrial wood.

(vi) It is necessary to build up broad-based approach at the State level involving officials, technological personnel, academics as also leaders of the public (particularly tribal) opinion which can transcend narrow sectional interests for environment and resource management.

(vii) There should be a standing National Commission to coordinate State Plans, frame national goals and generally to ensure pursuit of a wholesome land use policy in the country, keeping technological advances in view.

(viii) Social forestry, farm forestry, community, agro-forestry, should be encouraged as multi-use land resource pattern in the context of national land-use policy and for increased production of fodder, fuelwood, fertiliser, generating employment, improving environment, and relieving rural women from drudgery and hardship of finding fuelwood.

(ix) A programme of large-scale plantation should be taken up with the help of tribals giving them rights on the trees planted by them in assigned areas and their usufruct. Possibilities of short-term subsidy programmes for implementing forestry programmes may be concretised.

(x) The State Plans and Tribal sub-Plans should portray long-range and short-term perspectives clearly in terms of financial resources and physical targets under three broad heads — reserve forestry, social forestry and farm forestry. Progress should be monitored annually in physical and financial terms. Agencies for implementation should be clearly identified.

(xi) Tribal and local organisations, may be made use of it in good shape and after revitalisation if not in good shape, for management of protected and village forests for commercial, social and farm forestry purposes.

(xii) Considering that forestry is coming to be recognised more and more important in the economy energy, ecology, employment, poverty, alleviation, etc., contexts, higher financial and physical effort is called for.

(xiii) For achieving employment targets, like that of 20 MSPY, intensive forestry, better collection of minor forest produce, local processing of forest produce, etc., are necessary.

(xiv) There needs to be deliberate and conscious shift in the orientation and approach of the foresters towards public perspective policy.

Forestry and Tribal Development Programmes

6. Forests occupy a vital position in tribal economy. In regions having a substantial area under forest. Planning for tribal development

or forest development in isolation has no meaning; the two must reinforce each other. While the management of forests and vegetal resources should be such as will provide for maximum goods and services for the well-being of all sections of the country's population, there has to be judicious balance between the national and the local, particularly the tribal, needs.

7. We, therefore, recommend that :

(i) In forest-rich regions (forest area 30 per cent or more) forestry-oriented tribal development programmes should be framed. For such Integrated Tribal Development Projects (ITDPs), separate working (management) plans would be necessary for linking forestry programmes with economic development of tribals.

(ii) In forest-rich ITDPs landless people should be provided gainful employment in forest industries so that tribal migration is prevented.

(iii) Through selection of suitable technology and production pattern, land about a hectare or so can make a family economically viable. Hence, choice should be made from capital-intensive coffee plantation, plantation of fruit-bearing tree, host plants for tussar, plantation of fodder trees linked to animal husbandry, fuel-wood plantation, etc. Tussar cultivation with plantation of host trees is important since the tribal area has good potential for sericulture.

(iv) On the pattern of Gujarat Social security plantation schemes, tribal families may be involved in plantation work. They may be paid wages during the gestation period and subsequently profits from the usufruct may be shared on fifty-fifty basis between them and the Forest Department.

(v) Tribal farmers should be encouraged to take up farm-forestry and agro-forestry under which production and fertility of soil and environment improve.

(vi) Some of the cottage, small and medium forest-based industries, e.g., saw-milling, furniture-making, toy-making, etc., should be locally established to generate employment for tribals.

(vii) Bullock-carts should be provided to individuals assigning them transportation work of forest produce on an average for 150 days in a year. These bullock-carts may also be engaged in transportation of seedlings from nursery to the planting sites and consumer goods from market to tribal areas.

(viii) Beneficiary-oriented programmes in forestry sector should be identified for tribals and they should be executed under IRDP, NREP, DPAP, DDP, Hill Area Development Plan, Tribal sub-Plan, etc.

Shifting Cultivation

8. Shifting cultivation has become a way of life of the tribals. As such, change from shifting cultivation to settled cultivation has to be gradual, so that they are able to adjust themselves. The problem has social and cultural overtones and, therefore, motivational approach through introduction of alternative programmes is recommended. Integrated programmes of forestry suitably harmonised with proper landuse practices may form the backbone of such strategy.

9. We, therefore, recommend that:

(i) Special comprehensive projects for each concerned micro-situation, with problem of shifting cultivation as their focus, should be prepared. The project should induce in the shifting cultivators the desire for a switch-over to settled cultivation as a result of hope of better economic return from the same piece of land.

(ii) The settlement of shifting cultivators should primarily be within the area of their traditional habitat.

(iii) There should broadly be a programme of developing valley lands for permanent cultivation (with provision of irrigation wherever possible), horticulture in moderate slopes and forestry plantation on hill tops. Animal husbandry, poultry and piggery should be provided as subsidiary occupations.

(iv) The broad approach of family-based programme should be followed in these areas, the aim being individual economically-viable schemes with a suitable mix of economic activity and choice of tree cops. Each shifting cultivators group may be accepted as a unit so that suitable leadership can emerge from within for sustaining the programme.

(v) Comprehensive micro-plans for each group of cultivators should be prepared by inter-disciplinary teams which may be constituted exclusively for this purpose. Funds for implementation should be available from the Agriculture Ministry, Tribal sub-Plan, Hill Area Development, State and Union Territory

Plan funds, institutional finance, etc.

(vi) Pilot rehabilitation schemes may be instituted including rubber, coffee, tea, cashew and horticulture (*in situ* or otherwise) plantations. Such schemes should be prepared on a small regional area basis keeping a mini-catchment or water-shed as the area of operation.

(vii) Lands set free from shifting cultivation should be put under alternative use without any time-lag so that individuals in the group are not attracted again to shifting cultivation.

(viii) There should be effective evaluation and monitoring of the programme. For this purpose adequate staff should be provided in the forestry Division of the Ministry of Agriculture.

Forest Villages

10. Forest villages were originally created for supply of manpower requirements for exploitation of forest resources. In these villages, a tribal does not have a right to the land which he cultivates.

11. We, recommend that:

(i) The forest villages may be converted into normal revenue villages, enabling tribals to acquire inalienable rights to land and benefits of development plans. The Forest Department should continue to play a special role in development of these villages in view of their physical location.

(ii) All social and economic development programmes should be extended to these villages on the same lines as for residents of revenue villages.

Social Forestry

12. Social forestry is designed to meet the primary needs of tribal and rural population as opposed to the needs of industry and the urban elite. The desiderata are: (a) a mixed production system including fruit, fodder, grass, fuel-wood, fibre and small timber, etc., (b) involvement of beneficiary right from the planning stage, (c) minimal government control, (d) financial or labour contribution by local bodies, voluntary contributions, government subsidies and (e) use of communal and government lands. Social forestry envisages creation of wood-lots or pastures on government, communal and private marginal, sub-marginal

waste-land as per a predetermined land-use pattern, afforestation of degraded forests, block, plantation along road-side, canal banks, railways, etc.

13. Several elements relevant to the success of social forestry with community participation are:

- strong commitment at Government as well as at communal levels;
- substained technical support;
- full range of development services;
- tangible benefits for the participating community;
- community organisation for planning work and benefit allocation; and
- the right community attitude towards tree and forests.

14. We recommend that:

(i) Comprehensive approach be evolved for village wood-lots or urban tree plantations where there is an active pattern of communal land holdings or communal activities. Involvement of women of the community (who usually gather and utilise fuelwood) in the identification, design and implementation of such project will be helpful.

(ii) Steps to be taken for planning materials, technology and trained people for a variety of forestry activities which can be locally initiated and controlled, viz., tree plantation, agro-forestry, wood-lots and, private holding tree-planting.

(iii) Assistance be given for developing income-generating programmes based on managing and marketing of forest products, on a sustainable basis so that there is local interest in maintaining natural and planted forests.

(iv) Financial allocations for social forestry should be commensurate with the role in can play. Flow of institutional finance from commercial banks and cooperatives may be ensured by evolving forms and procedures for extending loans for forestry projects.

(v) The cooperative sector should wholeheartedly participate in this programme.

(vi) Action for initiating, supporting and expanding existing programmes of applied research in agroforestry to identify, screen and evaluate trees and plants useful for solving socio-economic problems of the rural poor. This should include multi-purpose species (yielding wood, forage, fertilisers, soil fertility improvements), and food.

(vii) Action research should be planned on an adequate scale with a view of harnessing traditional skills of the tribal and indigenous population, keeping in view the objective of optimisation of production and reduction of hazards of environmental degradation.

Forest-based Industries

15. The importance of forest-based industries in the nation's economy directly and indirectly generating rural employment and upgrading tribal economy is being realised increasingly. After agriculture, these industries have the largest potential for generating employment in rural areas. In the higher capital-intensive industry like paper, while the interests of the State, the entrepreneur and the labourers in the organised sector are adequately taken care of, the forest labourers have to be satisfied with casual employment which is generally seasonal in character. A fair deal can be given to the forest labourers (mostly tribal) if a programme for training them for higher skill/job is taken up.

16. Forest industries are finding it difficult to meet their requirement of raw materials. Further, since raw materials are required to be hauled over, the national transport system has been under strain. Immediate action is called for improving the resource base, both in its extent and location. In many areas, non-use of raw material due to the absence of industrial demand and non-supply of raw material due to distant location, have caused low employment potential in both public and private sectors. This calls for the closest coordination between raw material production and forest-based industries.

17. We, therefore, recommend that:

(i) More and more industrial units should be set-up in cooperative sector so that there is sharing of benefits among the raw material grower, the forest labourer and the processing unit employee.

(ii) A forest-based industry could also be a joint venture of three parties, i.e., the concerned corporation, the entrepreneur and the tribal producer and collector of raw-material.

(iii) Leases for supply of forest raw material should be assigned to cooperatives who should organise its production, harnessing transportation and undertaking delivery to forest-based industries.

(iv) Industrial raw material production may be planned by ensuing inputs, technical know-how and financial support. Tribals should be encouraged to grow industrial raw material by providing them seedlings, technical know-how, selected subsidies and other incentives.

(v) The industry should assure takeover of all the raw-material grown by the tribals as per schedule. The concerned extension workers should work for adherence of schedule by the tribals.

(vi) The industry-linked plantation should not be located close to the tribal habitation and it should not be more than 300 hectares in extent at any one place to enable the local people to get their Nistar without difficulty.

(vii) For developing cottage and small industry, beneficiaries should be identified among tribals. They should be trained and tools, machines and financial support should be provided to them.

(viii) Public financing bodies should play a positive role in providing filip to plantation-industry nexus and for forestry and industry should to make use of public finance.

Minor Forest Produce (MPF)

18. Minor Forest Produce includes all items of forest produce other than wood. According to the National Commission on Agriculture, various items of MFP have the potential to bring about an economic revolution for tribals and other rural people in the country. During drought and adverse climatic conditions, the tribals depend mainly on MFP collection. A large number of MFP items are not collected and are wasted because tribals do not find their collection remunerative. A big percentage of tribal population is at present being forced to eke out their subsistence by cultivation of marginal lands, shifting cultivation, overgrazing of forest areas and exploitation of trees. It is necessary to provide economically viable schemes of MFP collection, processing and marketing which can ensure for tribals reasonable sustenance. MFP collection generates employment largely during the non-agricultural season when unemployment and under-

employment problems are acute. MFP collection and processing can employ not only the able-bodied workers but also old and infirms, women and children in their traditional environment.

19. We, recommend that:

(i) Item-wise resource inventory survey of MFP should be carried out for each State by involving the Forest Survey of India. Botanical Survey of India and Resource Survey units. Project report should be prepared amenable to economic appraisal for organising collection, procurement, transport, storage, grading, local processing and marketing of each item of MFP. The project report might be State-wise, division-wise, according to the local conditions.

(ii) The right of collection of tribals of MFP without restriction, wherever this is lacking should be ensured. This should be followed by organised collection and marketing. In fact, the most crucial problem is marketing of MFP. The question of realisation of royalty of MFP by the Forest Department from individuals, cooperatives or corporations engaged in MFP collection should be reviewed for exemption or rationalisation in the interest of remunerative price to be made available to the tribal.

(iii) Cooperativisation of MFP should be accorded priority since this will give some additional income to the tribal and will also be in the interest of development of MFP. Adequate attention should be paid to LAMPS and other primary cooperatives, secondary and apex cooperatives as well as federating tribal development corporations, forest development corporations and other corporations.

(iv) Cooperatives and private marketing channels, operating parallel to each other, should set up healthy economic forces in the interest of tribals.

(v) Performance audit of Tribal Development Corporations and Forest Development Corporations is called for to enable assess the extent of their objectives – achievement and their reorientation.

(vi) Improved storage techniques should be employed using scientific methods. Warehouses and other facilities should be built in interior areas to avoid deterioration of MFP items.

(vii) First-stage processing of MFP should be organised within tribal areas, particularly through cooperatives. The main objective should be to enable local retention of the maximum benefit from the activity to benefit the primary collector.

(viii) In forest-rich States, MFP corporations may be created connected with procurement, marketing and processing at the State level.

(ix) An All India level organisation (TRIFED) may be created federating the Forest Development Corporations, Tribal Development Corporations, and MFP Corporations for tackling different matters connected with MFP and for coordinating with the National Cooperative Development Corporation (NCDC), the State Trading Corporation (STC), the National Agricultural Cooperative Marketing Federation (NAFED) and other national organisations concerned with processing and marketing development of MFP.

(x) Research and Development efforts are required to meet the needs of genetically improved species, better techniques of collection, semi-processing, processing, storage, etc., new uses of MFP and associated technology.

(xi) Regeneration of MFP be given special attention. Plantation of MFP be taken up on individual or community lands by associating tribals in management and protection under the technical guidance and supervision of the forest department.

Forest Labour Cooperative Society (FLCS)

20. Serious efforts need to be made to ensure that the entire working of forest should be planned and executed through cooperatives. So long as the individual tribal remains a casual forest wage-earner, he is bound to seek a base in agriculture or other activity. Further, forestry management should be able to resolve the problem of seasonal employment against the desiderata of sustained regular employment through practice of intensive forestry through cooperatives.

21. We, therefore, recommend that –

(i) Forestry operations should be executed through cooperatives of forest labourers. The agency of contractor should be eliminated. Cooperative may be organised and encouraged by the Forest Department both for economic benefit of the tribal and as a protective device for the existing forest. They should be given share in profits from those operations.

(ii) Cooperatives should organise labour teams for working in regions which may be outside the reach of an individual. Regularity and predictability of wage employment should help stabilise local economy. Cooperatives should ensure reasonable wage for their labour.

(iii) FLCSs should venture into the field of haulage of forest material making it over to the Forest Department in depots located on the periphery of the forests. As much as possible, haulage in forest area should be done through animal-powered vehicles rather than through automobiles to provide employment to tribals and effect POL saving.

Biosphere Reserve

22. For affording strict protection to wild-life germplasm and gene pools facing the danger of extinction, attempts have been made to establish biosphere reserves, national parks, sanctuaries. In the process in some areas tribal interest is said to have been disregarded. We recommend that:

(i) Virgin forest areas rich in flora and fauna should be declared as biosphere reserve for germ-plasm, gene-pools and other purpose over a limited area without displacing the tribal on a large scale. For the purpose, speedy, administrative, scientific and legislative action is necessary.

(ii) Tribal families having been displaced by national parks and sanctuaries should be suitably rehabilitated by providing them alternative source of habitation and livelihood.

(iii) There is no need of creating tribal reserves on the mainland on the analogy of some in the Andaman and Nicobar Islands.

Management System

23. (i) The crux of the problem of forest management lies in the need for integration of tribal and forest economies. The relationship between forest managers and tribals should be one of partnership. This will be possible if an identity-interest between the forest department and tribals is created.

(ii) Forestry development programmes should aim at internalising its components into the rural production system as a whole.

(iii) The management should ensure strong backward and forward linkages between forestry and other development sectors on the local, regional, State and national levels.

(iv) Tribals should be inducted into a more constructive role of forestry. They should be employed in forest service at different levels imparting specialised training.

(v) Forest management practices need to be modulated to be able to generate employment all the year round for prevention of migration and sustained supply of raw materials for the requirements of agriculture and industry.

(vi) The role of the forester needs to be reappraised. The new emphasis should be on forester as an extension agent advising the owners or the management personnel of village, communal private and other forests for undertaking scientific forestry.

(vii) The transformation from conservation to development forestry should be induced through community forestry. Forestry activities should be carried out by many, often local institutions, rather than by a single forest department. In other words, meta-management system should be applied rather than super-management.

(viii) The course from departmental production forestry to broad-based community forestry can be made smoother through public participation. At the State-level, a broad-based body comprised of officials, technical experts, academics, leaders of public (particularly tribals) opinion should be built up. At the forest, divisional and ITDP levels, advisory committees representing forest interest such as government departments, statutory bodies (like the TDC, FDC, banks, etc.) and forest dwellers to review, formulate programmes and over-see their implementation should be set up. Similar Committees should be set up at development block level.

(ix) The respective roles of the forest department, the Forest Development Corporations, the Tribal Development Corporations should be clearly spelt out. The forest department might be the apex agency for formulation of policies and programmes as well as for supervision of their implementation. Execution of programmes may be entrusted to field-level corporate organisations like the Forest Development Corporations as well as local representative institutions.

Legislation

24. Forest legislation dates back to 1965 when the Indian Forest

Act was passed. This Act was reformulated in 1927. New revised draft is under consideration in the Ministry of Agriculture which should take into consideration the necessary legislative provisions which will strengthen the symbiotic relationship between forests and tribals.

25. We, therefore, recommend that:

(i) The traditional rights, concessions and privileges of tribals in respect of all forest produce, grazing and hunting should not be abridged. They should be freely allowed to visit places of their worship inside the forests. Further, they should be suitably recorded.

(ii) In the forest villages, they should be given heritable and inalienable right over the land which they cultivate.

(iii) There should be restriction on deforestation of the area vulnerable to soil erosion, landslide, desertification, etc. Felling of fruit trees should, ordinarily be prohibited.

(iv) Association of tribal should be ensured in a large scale plantation programme giving them the right to usufruct.

(v) Ownership right on the trees growing in the holding allotted to a tribal in a forest village should vest in him.

(vi) National parks, sanctuaries, biosphere should normally be not located close to the tribal villages. Persons displaced on account of their creation should be properly rehabilitated.

(vii) There should be attempt at simplification of laws and procedures so that tribals can comprehend them.

(viii) Relevant laws should be modified so that the village councils can obtain term-loan against standing tree-stock in forests.

(ix) If necessary, the State might assume the right to provide guidelines about land-use and resource-mobilisation on communal, clan and private lands. The operation of the Bill framed by the Government of Orissa aimed at restriction of sale of timber trees belonging to tribals might be watched for adoption by other State Governments.

5

COMMITTEE ON FINANCING OF TEA INDUSTRY, 1980 — REPORT[1]

Chairman Shri K.B. Chore
Chief Officer, Department of Banking Operations and Development, Reserve Bank of India, Central Office, Bombay.

Members Shri V.M. Sundar Raj; Shri S.P. Chandavarkar; Shri S.C. Khanna; Shri K. Margabanthu; Shri C.R. Mukherjee; Shri R. Barua; Shri Y.S. Borgaonkar; Shri R.C. Mody; Shri A.N. Roy; Shri K.K. Misra.

Alterations

Shri S.P. Chandavarkar resigned from the membership of the Committee with effect from 3rd April 1981 consequent upon his resignation from the service of the Union Bank of India. Shri R. Barua retired from the service of the Assam Co-operative Apex Bank Ltd., on 28th February 1981 and in his place Shri G.C. Khound, the new Managing Director, was appointed on the Committee on 13th April 1981.

Appointment

The Working Group on Finance for Tea Industry (Dutt Working Group) had reviewed the credit requirements of the tea industry in 1972 and recommended certain norms/guidelines for providing working capital and development credit to the industry. In the context of the continuous rise in cost in production and a downtrend in the auction prices of tea, the tea industry has been representing to the Reserve Bank of India that the norms for providing working capital credit recommended by the Dutt Working Group do not adequately meet the

1. Reserve Bank of India, Bombay, 1981

requirements of the industry and have, therefore, to be revised. There is also the need to expand tea production substantially in the coming years to cope with the sustained rise in domestic consumption without impinging on the exportable surplus. The Reserve Bank of India, therefore, constituted a Committee in October 1980 to examine the problems relating to the financing of the tea industry.

Terms of Reference

(i) To review the existing norms for providing working capital to the tea industry recommended by the Reserve Bank of India to scheduled commercial banks in March 1972 on the basis of the Report of the Working Group under the Chairmanship of Shri B.K. Dutt, and to suggest suitable modifications in the present changed circumstances;

(ii) To examine the credit requirements of the tea industry (both working capital and term loans) in the wider context of the need to expand output to meet the sustained rise in domestic consumption without impinging on the exportable surplus;

(iii) To enquire into the problems faced by the industry in obtaining finance (both working capital and term loans) from commercial banks, other financial institutions, and the Tea Board;

(iv) To consider other problems faced by the commercial banks in providing credit to the tea industry; and

(v) To make recommendations on these and any other related matters which the Committee may consider germane to the subject.

Contents

Introduction; Position and Problems of Tea Industry; Working Capital Finance; Term Finance; Summary of Recommendations; Appendices I to III.

Recommendations

1. The tea industry has represented that it is facing many problems other than those relating to availability of credit, such as, increasing cost of production, inadequate price realisation, low cash generation compared to other industries and high rates of taxation. Also, there is a large difference between the prices realised by the producers in auctions and the prices charged by the retail outlets to the ultimate

consumers in the domestic market. The effect of these problems, in their totality, on the tea industry may be examined by an appropriate agency (Para 2.42).

2. The method of assessing credit requirements on the basis of cash budgets should be made applicable to all tea units with their own processing factories, irrespective of the size of their holdings, as well as to the units which do not have processing factories but whose holdings are above 100 hectares (250 acres). The cash credit limits for these borrowers may be fixed on the basis of a detailed monthly cash budget for the entire season/year obtained from them in advance before the commencement of a particular season/year, at the level of the peak deficit reflected in the cash budget. Variations from the projected drawing schedules as per cash budget may be allowed, within the overall cash credit limit, with flexibility at the discretion of the Branch Managers on the basis of periodical review of the actual operations (Paras 3.13 and 3.14).

3. It is necessary for banks to ensure that the larger borrowers in the tea industry meet at least a part of their working capital requirements from their owned funds and long-term resources. For this purpose, while considering credit proposals for the next season/year, banks should insist on these borrowers furnishing a *pro forma* balance sheet as on 31st October of the current year. The surplus available with the borrowers (i.e., excess of owned funds and long-term resources over investments in fixed and non-current assets), as revealed by the *pro forma* balance sheets, should normally be equal to at least 25 per cent of the limits proposed to be fixed. Where the borrowers' own contribution is found to be less, banks should lay down suitable covenants while sanctioning the limits so that the borrowers achieve the level of minimum contribution over a period not exceeding five years. Where it is observed that the surplus available with the borrowers is more, banks should not normally allow a slip-back in the following years unless warranted by factors like loss or low profitability of the borrowing unit or its need to make matching contribution for development finance (Para 3.15).

4. Banks and co-operatives should make sustained efforts to institutionalise the borrowings of tea planters so as to make them less dependent for their credit requirements on bought leaf factories. The Lead Banks in the concerned tea growing districts should take initiative in this direction and ensure that the small planters are provided adequate short-term credit (Para 3.17).

5. The method of fixing scales of finance per acre may be adopted for providing short-term credit to tea planters with holdings up to 100 hectares (250 acres) and who do not have processing factories of their own. Area committees (referred to in para 22 below) could fix scales of finance for different areas periodically. They may also determine the cash and kind components of the scales of finance. The limits may be allowed on cash credit basis to be adjusted by the and of each season/year. Banks should ensure that in working out the credit requirements of these borrowers, the amount of owned funds that could be brought in by the more affluent among them, is taken into account in determining the size of the limits. If any of these borrowers is prepared to project his requirements of working capital finance on the basis of detailed cash budgets, banks should allow the borrower the choice to do so instead of adopting the scale of finance (Para 3.19).

6. Short-term credit granted by banks to very small planters with holdings of less than 8.09 hectares (20 acres) may be treated as agricultural advances and included in the category of priority sector advances. There is also a strong case for including short-term credit granted to planters with holdings between 20 acres and 250 acres without having processing factories under priority sector advances, which in effect would mean that the borrowers in this category would be able to obtain adequate credit from banks more easily at rates of interest applicable to agricultural advances. Such help to this sector is well deserved and would not be misplaced, particularly as these borrowers would be engaged in purely agricultural operations and economics of tea leaf production, as it exists currently, does call for some help to such planters (Paras 3.23 and 3.26).

7. The guarantee cover of the Deposit Insurance and Credit Guarantee Corporation of India, under its Small Loans Guarantee Scheme, may be extended to short-term credit facilities granted to the small tea planters with holdings up to 20 acres (Para 3.28).

8. Where there are exceptional circumstances, e.g., natural calamities, fall in prices or other contingencies such as port strike, warehouse strike, etc., banks may consider sympathetically requests from tea units for temporary limits in excess of the regular cash credit limits. Such limits should be allowed only for predetermined short durations and given through separate demand loan or 'non-operable' cash credit account. In view of the uncertainties faced by the tea industry, banks should view the deviations from the projected cash budgets more leniently than in the case of other industries and charge

additional interest of one per cent per annum over the normal rate on such ad hoc or temporary additional limits only in exceptional cases (Para 3.29).

9. There may be occasions when additional credit may have to be provided without delay to tea producers to tide over temporary difficulties. To facilitate granting of such credit, banks should delegate adequate discretionary powers to the Regional Managers/Branch Managers. Financing of tea producers by brokers for such purposes should be discouraged by banks and they should desist from accommodating brokers for the purpose of re-lending to the producers (Para 3.30).

10. Short-term credit facilities granted to tea units are basically self-liquidating and banks should maintain separate accounts for each season/year so that the expenses and realisations for each season/year are reflected in the same account (Para 3.31).

11. The demand of the tea industry for automatic conversion of the deficits in working capital accounts at the end of a season/year into term loans cannot be conceded. Deficits in working capital accounts may arise due to bad management or diversion of sale proceeds for liquidation of past liabilities, financing of capital expenditure, etc. In such cases, banks should take necessary corrective steps to ensure that the borrowers tone up their management and bring in funds from outside sources to cover the shortfalls. However, where banks are satisfied that the deficits in working capital accounts represent losses incurred by the units due to price fluctuations or natural calamities or other factors beyond their control, the deficit may be kept in a separate account to be adjusted over a period of time which may be determined taking into account the financial position and projected future cash generation of the individual borrower. Normally, such period should not exceed three years (Para 3.32).

12. According to the information received by the Committee, 51 private bought leaf factories (out of 80) and nine industrial co-operative tea factories (our of 11) in the Nilgiris district, Tamil Nadu, have been issued registration certificates as small-scale industrial (SSI) units by the concerned authority of the State Government on the basis that the value of their plant and machinery does not exceed Rs. 20 lakhs. These factories are accordingly eligible for financial assistance as available to SSI units. Advances to the bought leaf units in Nilgiris as well as in other areas (both in the private and cooperative sectors), holding registration certificates as SSI units, should be eligible for

classification as priority sector advances. The position regarding the classification of advances granted to bought leaf units as priority sector advances is not clearly understood by some bank officials at branch level. The Reserve Bank of India, in consultation with Government of India, may issue suitable clarificatory instructions to the banks in this regard (Para 3.36).

13. Tea traders have represented for larger bill purchase limits, and for grant of limits against-pledge of delivery orders issued by the registered broker-firms covering auctioned teas, in view of the expected increase in the quantities of teas offered for sale through auctions. The banks should consider granting of increased bill or other working capital limits to their trader clients on the merits of each case (Para 3.40).

14. While there should be no objection to the tea companies maintaining accounts at Calcutta or other metropolitan/urban centres for managing the sales of teas through auctions, etc., where the financing bank has branches in the tea growing areas, a part of the sanctioned working capital limits may be transferred to the branches nearest to the tea gardens so that the Branch Managers can exercise adequate supervision over the operations in the accounts. This will also facilitate the control of drawings in the accounts as well as the grant of *ad hoc* credit to the gardens to get over temporary difficulties in exceptional circumstances (Para 3.42).

15. To avoid delays, banks should delegate adequate discretionary powers to their Regional Offices in the tea growing regions so that decision-making on tea proposals is decentralised to the extent possible (Para 3.43).

16. Banks which have a substantial stake in the tea industry and which do not have a separate Tea Department or Tea Cell, should set up Tea Cells in their head Offices or in Regional Offices in the tea growing regions, manned by officers with adequate knowledge of the tea industry, to closely guide and monitor the financing of the industry (Para 3.44).

17. The gross requirement of funds for development of the tea industry during the Sixth Plan period from 1980-81 to 1984-85, according to the Plan prepared by the Tea Board, is estimated at about Rs. 300 crores. The Committee is assured that funds to the extent of Rs. 240 crores would be made available by the existing institutional set-up comprising the Tea Board, ARDC, IDBI and banks. This would leave a gap of Rs. 60 crores to be met by the tea industry itself out of

its own resources. Normally, the tea industry should provide margin on the projected development finance at the rate of 25 per cent. However, where it is not possible for individual units to do so, relaxation may be allowed on merits, particularly in the case of small planters and deserving weak units (Para 4.18).

18. There may be cases where a tea unit requires finance for purposes not covered by the existing schemes of ARDC or the Tea Board, such as, purchase of balancing equipments or renovation of factory building. It should be the endeavour of banks to provide term loans for such purposes on merits. Time is of essence in such cases and banks should avoid delay in meeting such genuine requirements (Para 4.19).

19. The Tea Board, ARDC and IDBI should make a review of their existing financing schemes so that term loans for essential purposes not covered by the existing schemes are made available to tea units (Para 4.20).

20. There is no special merit in setting up a new financing institution for meeting the growing financial needs of the tea industry as the required finance can be provided from within the existing institutional framework (Para 4.22).

21. The implementation and monitoring of the development plan for the tea industry should be the responsibility of the Tea Board. The representatives of the Reserve Bank of India, ARDC, IDBI and banks may be, formally or informally, associated with the statutory Development Committee of the Tea Board. This enlarged Committee would attend to various aspects relating to the implementation and monitoring of the plan and co-ordination between the different financial institutions (Para 4.23).

22. Standing Area Development Committees may be constituted for the tea industry by the Tea Board for the various tea growing areas, consisting of representatives of the Tea Board, Reserve Bank of India, ARDC, IDBI, tea producers, State Governments and banks. The more important functions of these area committees would be preparation of sub-plans for the respective areas out of the total plan, preparation of specific schemes out of the area plans, particularly for small planters, co-ordination between different financial institutions and development agencies in the areas, and fixing of scales of finance for small planters in the different areas periodically. The area committees should also look into the special problems of the concerned tea growing areas which need special attention and suggest suitable solutions (Para 4.24 and 4.29).

23. A sum of Rs. 10 crores has already been earmarked in the plan for development of small tea planters with holdings up to 25 acres. Similar arrangement is necessary for other small planters with holdings between 25 acres and 250 acres. The allocation of plan outlay for them should at least be proportionate to their holdings in relation to the total area under tea. The Tea Board should organise a regular information system for reviewing the implementation of the schemes for small planters (Para 4.30)

24. It is necessary to organise the activities of clusters of small planters in each area into groups, either on co-operative basis or otherwise. The area committees should draw up schemes for small planters coming together for development programmes. The Lead Bank in each tea growing district should take the initiative and ensure that such development schemes for small tea planters do not suffer for want of adequate and timely finance. ARDC should also consider extending refinance in respect of small tea planters with holdings up to 20 acres at the same concessionary rate of interest as applicable to small farmers (Para 4.31).

25. The small tea planters in Nilgiris district, Tamil Nadu, have a problem of providing security to banks, because they are holding joint *pattas* in respect of their lands. The State Government should take urgent steps for revising the land records so that this impediment to the flow of institutional finance to them could be removed (Para 4.32).

26. The Tea Board and UPASI are providing technical advice to the small tea planters at present; but there is still considerable scope for enlargement of this service (Para 4.33).

27. Banks should monitor the performance of tea producing units according to the definition of sick units as applicable to the other industries and adopt suitable measures for rehabilitation, where necessary (Para 4.35).

28. The problem of sharing of security between the Tea Board and tea financing banks arises in the case of the Tea Board's assistance under the Plantation Finance Scheme. The Tea Board may review its lending arrangements and consider adopting either a consortium approach or refinance approach. Meanwhile, banks may concede pari passu charge in favour of the Tea Board on merits of each case. the Tea Board may take into account the methods adopted by various Government departments for routing subsidy through banks and consider the merits of adopting this approach (Para 4.37).

29. The gross requirement of funds for research and training

during the next five years has been estimated by the Tea Board at Rs. 12.57 crores, of which the Tea Board's involvement would be Rs. 3.21 crores (Rs. 1 crore under Plan expenditure and Rs. 2.21 crores under non-Plan schemes). According to the Tea Board, the gap of Rs. 9.36 crores is expected to be provided by the tea industry and other agencies such as Council of Scientific and Industrial Research. ARDC (NABARD when set up) and IDBI may also consider providing some assistance for this purpose (Para 4.38).

30. The Tea Board may examine the suggestion made by the Tocklai Research Institute for setting up a 'Plantation Crop Research Institute' at Jorhat for training of managerial cadres in the tea industry (Para 4.39).

RAILWAY ACCIDENT INVESTIGATION REPORT ON OCCURRENCE OF CASUALTIES TO 352 DOWN GUA-KHARAGPUR PASSENGER TRAIN AT KM. 264/4-8 BETWEEN SINI AND GOMHARRIA STATIONS ON THE DOUBLE LINE ELECTRIFIED CHAKRADHARPUR-TATANAGAR SECTION IN THE CHAKRADHARPUR DIVISION OF S.E. RAILWAY AT ABOUT 17.25 HOURS ON APRIL 13, 1980 — REPORT[1]

One Man Commission	Shri K. Ganapati, Commissioner of Railway Safety, South Eastern Circle, Calcutta.
Officers Present	Shri M.K. Gangopadhyay; Shri J. Sharan; Shri P.S. Choudhury.

Appointment

The Commission was appointed under Ministry of Tourism and Civil Aviation (Commission of Railway Safety) in accordance with Rule 4 of the Statutory Investigation into Railway Accidents Rules, 1973 vide its Notification No. RS.13-T(8)/71 dated April 19, 1973 on April 13, 1980.

Terms of Reference

To investigate into occurrence of Casualties to 352 Down Gua-Kharagpur Passenger Train at km 264/4-8 between Sini and Gomharria Stations on the Double line electrified Chakradharpur-Tatanagar section in the Chakradharpur Division of South Eastern Railway at about 17.25 hours on April 13, 1980.

1. Ministry of Tourism and Civil Aviation (Commission of Railway Safety), Government of India, Delhi, 1984, ii + 10 p.

Contents

Summary; Relief Measures; The Train; Local Conditions; Summary of Evidence; Tests and Observations; Discussion; Conclusion; Remarks and Recommendations; Railway Board's Comments on Various Paras of the Report.

Conclusions

8.1 *Cause of the Accident*

On careful consideration of the factual material and circumstantial evidence, I have reached the conclusion that the occurrence of the casualties to passengers of coach No. 1177 of 352 Down at Km. 264/4-8 between Sini and Gomharria stations on the double line electrified section of Chakradharpur-Tatanagar Section of Chakradharpur Division of South Eastern Railway at about 17.25 hours on 13-4-1980 was caused due to striking by the top side steel sheet of coach No. LVPR 2857 eighth from the engine of 321 Up which worked loose and got detached, while this train crossed 352 Down between Gomharria and Sini stations.

8.2 *Responsibility*

(a) Sri P.N. Choudhury, Head Train Examiner, Tatanagar who examined the rake of 321 Up at Tatanagar and issued the fit certificate is held responsible for the accident. He violated Clause Nos. 2.2.1. and 4.3 of Conference Rules Part IV.

(b) The coach came out of the Shop after POH on 28-12-1979 and the accident happened within 3-1/2 months after the POH. In view of para 7.5 of the report the Kharagpur Workshop is held fully responsible for the accident. The Railway Administration may probe further and fix responsibility for the accident at various levels including workshop officers in addition to the Chargeman and the two Stage Inspectors who were entrusted with the work.

8.3 *Service Record*

Shri P.N. Choudhury was born on 18-1-1940 and was appointed on the railway on 18-1-1957 as Trade Apprentice. He was absorbed as Fitter in March 1959, promoted at TXR in April 1962, and was promoted as Head TXR on 3-6-1978. There are no punishments in his record during the last five years. He was given a cash award of Rs. 50 in April 1970 for maintenance of rake at Tatanagar in good condition. He was also given a Merit Certificate in January 1969 for making significant improvement of coaching stock based at Tatanagar. He is a Matriculate.

8.4 *Relief Arrangements and Medical Attention*

I am generally satisfied with the relief arrangements and medical attention given.

Recommendations

9.1 *Immediate Recommendation*

To avoid a recurrence of an accident of the same type an immediate recommendation was made with the Preliminary Report asking the South Eastern Railway to undertake urgent intensive examination of all coaching vehicles with wooden panels and steel side sheets. Proper repairs should be carried out to ensure that steel side sheets do not work out when the train is in motion specially while crossing another train on the adjoining track and where this is not possible the coaches should be withdrawn from service and sent to shops for periodical overhaul (POH).

9.2 *No Alarm Chain Apparatus Provided in Coach No. 1177*

The alarm chain apparatus was not functioning in coach No. 1177 and there was no authorisation for its removal or non-functioning. The Railway may fix responsibility for the same.

9.3 *Violation of Marshalling Orders*

The marshalling of non-AT LVPR as last coach of 352 Down violates standard marshalling orders for which responsibility may be fixed.

9.4 *No Change in Sick Line Procedure*

The accident was not caused due to any lacuna or deficiency in Indian

Railway Conference Association (IRCA) rules, departmental manuals and circular instructions. The accident has been caused due to improper and perfunctory inspection of an individual TXT. Therefore no modifications are suggested to IRCA rules or any departmental manuals. The Railway may however bring this case to the notice of the TXRs high-lighting the importance of proper examination of steel side sheeting of wooden body coaches on sick lines and issue such instructions as they deem fit.

9.5 *No changes required in Workshop in Workshop Procedures*

The accident reveals the improper and perfunctory manner in which the coach was POHed in the Kharagpur Workshop. Neither sophisticated technology nor complicated instrumentation work is involved in finding out that screw holes on wooden panels of coaches are elongated and that these should be properly rectified. It is, therefore, not necessary to suggest any improvement to the workshop practice. Nevertheless the Railway Administration may bring this case to the notice of workshop staff and also issue such instructions as they deem fit.

9.6 *No First-aid Box or Stretcher with the Guard of 321 Up*

The Guard of 321 Up did not carry first-aid box or stretcher and he stated that these were not supplied to him. Responsibility of this lapse may be fixed.

9.7 *No Speed Recorder or VCD on WAGI Locos*

It was seen that there was no Speed recorder or Vigilance Control Device on WAGI locos hauling 352 Down and 321 Up Passenger trains. Since these are accepted as standard equipment the same may be provided.

Railway Board's Comments on Various Paras of the Report

Paras 9.1 and 9.4: Suitable instructions for attending to all such coaches under close supervision with strict quality control have been issued by the Railway Administration. A preventive maintenance programme has also been drawn up and all the Divisions advised for attention to the panels being given in the sick lines alongwith the repacking of axle boxes of IRS coaches. Instructions have also been issued to other Railways for necessary action.

Para 9.2: The Train Examiner, Kharagpur has been suitably taken up for the lapse.

Para 9.3: In terms of Marshalling instructions in force, LRs, VPs or WLRRMs, i.e., coaches which have no passenger accommodation, can be marshalled as rear-most vehicles. Attaching of non-A.T. LVPR as the last coach of 352 Down is, therefore, not a violation of the existing marshalling instructions.

Para 9.5: Necessary instructions in this regard have already been issued by the Railway Administration as early as 17-4-80. Instructions to other Railways in this respect have also been issued.

Para 9.6: The first aid box and stretcher could not be provided in 321 UP due to acute shortage. Arrangements have since been made to guard against the recurrence. However, the responsibility for the acute shortage of these essential items in Chakradharpur Division is being fixed.

Para 9.7: The recommendations, insofar as it relates to provision of speed recorders on the electric locos, has been circulated to the Railways for guidance. As regards provision of Vigilance Control Device keeping in view the fact that two crew members are available on the diesel and electric locomotives and the operation of the Vigilance Control Device was found to detract the attention of the drivers from Safety functions, the recommendation of RAEC-78, for not pursuing the installation of VCD, has been accepted. It was found that the VCD also served as an irritant to the drivers. However, the need for developing a suitable design which may be an improvement on the existing design, has been accepted for use if and when Indian Railways adopt single crew operation of locos.

7

RAILWAY ACCIDENT INVESTIGATION REPORT ON DERAILMENT OF NO. 156 UP VILLUPURAM-KATPADI PASSENGER TRAIN AT KM 52/0-2 BETWEEN TANDARAI AND VELANANDAL STATIONS ON THE VILLUPURAM-KATPADI METRE GAUGE SINGLE LINE SECTION OF TIRUCHCHIRAPALLI DIVISION OF SOUTHERN RAILWAY AT ABOUT 13.46 HOURS ON APRIL 19, 1980 — REPORT[1]

One Man Commission Shri A.S. Rego, Commissioner of Railway Safety, Western Circle, Bombay

Appointment

The Commission was appointed under Ministry of Tourism and Civil Aviation (Commission of Railway Safety) in accordance with Rule 4 of the Statutory Investigation into Railway Accidents Rules, 1973 vide Notification No. 13-T(8)/71 dated April 19, 1973 on April 19, 1980.

Terms of Reference

To require into the Derailment of 156 Up Villupuram-Katpadi Passenger Train at Km 52/0-2 between Tandarai and Velanandal Stations on the Villupuram-Katpadi Metre Gauge single line section of Tiruchchirapalli Division of Southern Railway at about 13.46 hours on April 19, 1980.

Contents

Summary; Inspection and Inquiry; Relief Measures; The Train; Local

1. Delhi, Controller of Publications, 1983, 50 p.

Features; Summary of Evidence; Observation and Tests; Discussion; Conclusion; Service Record of the PW1 held primarily responsible; Extenuating Circumstances; Relief Measures; Remarks and Recommendations; Annexures from I to X.

Conclusions

8.1 *Cause of Accident*

(a) On full consideration of the factual, material and circumstantial evidence, I have come to the conclusion that the derailment of 156 Up Villupuram-Katpadi Passenger train at Km. 52/0-2 at the approach to Turingee Bridge between Tandarai and Velanandal Passenger train at km 52/0-2 at the approach to Turingee Bridge between Tandarai and Velanandal stations on the Villupuram-Katpadi Metre Gauge single line section of the Tiruchchirapalli Division of Southern Railway at about 13.46 hours on 19-4-1980 was due to the progressive distortion of theft running rail and gauge widening under the passing train.

(b) The variation in wheel diameters in two axles of the 5th coach No. GSY 9914 and broken/weak coil and laminated springs and variation in the wheel gauge in one axle of the 6th coach No. SYLR 9647 contributed to unsteady running of the 5th and 6th coaches and this assisted in the gauge widening of the left running rail that took place under the passing train.

8.2 *Responsibility*

(a) Shri R. Doraiswamy, PWI/Gr. II Tiruvannamalai is primarily responsible for this accident. There was gross negligence on his part in that he did not adjust the creep and expansion gaps in the kilometre before the first point of drop and did not ensure that the second Keyman sanctioned was deputed to patrol the gang length for 5 days before and on 19-4-80 when the accident took place. He had trollied over the section on 16-4-80 when this should have come to his notice. He violated the provisions contained in para 204(a), 638(c) and (f) of the Way and Works Manual and General Rule 198(a).

(b) The following persons have to share responsibility in this case:

(i) Shri C. Mathrubootham, ex-PWI Tiruvannamalai for his failure to comply with his AEN's instructions on 29-8-79 (recorded in the

Creep Register) to pull back creep immediately in km. 52. No action was taken by him on his instruction till he relinquished charge of his post as PWI Tiruvannamalai on 12-3-1980. The pulling back of rails in km. 51-52 said to have been done by PWI Grade III Tirukoilur on 30-1-1980, was not actually done as noted by Shri Mathrubootham on 8-2-1980 (as per entries made in the Creep Register) and as admitted by the PWI Gr. III Tirukoilur Shri A. Kolandairaj during the Inquiry. He violated the provisions contained in paras 204(a) and 638(f) of the IRW & WWM and General Rule 198(a).

(ii) Shri P. Kumaraswamy, Acting Mate of Gang No. 8 for his failure to depute the second Keyman for 4 days before the accident when the Mate was on leave. He violated the provisions contained in para 502 of the Way and Works Manual and General Rule 205(c).

(iii) Shri A. Lakshmanan, Acting Keyman of Gang No. 8 for his failure to drive/replace the loose/missing keys between sleeper Nos. 83 to 98, if his statement that he patrolled over the zone of derailment just before 156 Up is to be accepted. He violated the provisions of para 502 of the Way & Works Manual. I believe that he did not patrol this zone on 19-4-80 before 156 Up and gave evidence to the contrary without realising its implications. Even if the latter surmise is accepted, he should be taken up for giving false evidence.

(c) The following persons of the Engineering Department are blame-worthy for lapses noted against each:

(i) Shri S. Vedanta Ramanujam, AEN Villupuram for his slack supervision and failure to take note of the extent of creep prevailing between Km. posts 51 and 52 when he measured the creep at Km. post 52 on 22-3-1980.

(ii) Shri A. Kolandairaj, PWI Gr. III Tirukoilur for not pulling back rails and adjusting creep between Km. 51/1 to 52/1 as per the message issued by him and instead only adjusting the gaps at km. 52/1 to replace a rail which had been damaged after the accident on 27-1-80.

(iii) Shri K. Pattu, Gangmate of Gang No. 8 for not regularly deputing the second Keyman for several days on and prior to 14-4-80 though he was required to do so. This is evident from the record maintained from 1-1-80 in the Mate's diary.

(d) (i) I do not hold any individual staff in the train examining branch of the Mechanical Department responsible for the accident as it was not possible for any of them to have detected the broken/weak coil/elliptical springs and variation in wheel gauge and wheel diameters of the 6th and 5th coaches of 156 Up at the time of the last primary/secondary maintenance.

(ii) There has however been a lapse on the part of Shri B.M. Santhanakrishnan, HTXR and his staff at Thanjavur in permitting 2 inner coil springs of smaller diameter to remain in the 6th coach SYLR No. 9647 while carrying out equalisation beam examination of this coach at Thanjavur on 3-11-79. They violated the provisions in Rule 2.24.2 of the Conference Rules – Part IV.

(iii) There has also been a failure in permitting wheels with a variation in tread diameters of 6 and 5 mm on the same axle of the front and rear bogie of the 5th coach GSY No. 9914 and variation in wheel gauge exceeding – 3 mm in one axle of the 6th coach SYLR No. 9647. As such defects are not checked at the time of primary/secondary maintenance, responsibility for allowing these defects rests with the Workshops/Maintenance Depots where these 2 coaches were last attended to. The Southern Railway may look into this and fix responsibility as due.

Note – All the rules are extracted in Annexure XI.

8.3 *Service Record of the PWI held Primarily Responsible*

(a) Shri R. Doraiswamy, PWI Gr. II Tiruvannamalai aged 51 years, was first appointed as a Lascar on 1-10-50 on Quilon-Ernakulam Railway Survey and after working in various capacities was promoted as a Mistry on 10-8-53 on the Quilon-Ernakulam Railway Construction. He was promoted to officiate as APWI on 1-5-61 and as PWI on 9-11-62 in the Construction Branch before he was promoted as PWI Gr. II, Tiruvannamalai on 26-2-80.

8.4 *Extenuating Circumstances*

Shri R. Doraiswamy PWI took over charge of the Tiruvannamalai length on 12-3-80, i.e., just 5 weeks prior to the accident. The Villupuram-Tiruvannamalai section, under his charge, was due complete track renewal as the steel trough sleepers had elongated holes and dropping of keys was a chronic problem. The Tiruchchirapalli Division had, year after year, been pressing for Complete Track Renewals (CTR) of the Villupuram-Katpadi section but for various reasons even the CTR from km. 137/4 to km. 159/1 sanctioned in the track renewal programme of 1973-74 and the CTR from km. 129/9 to km. 134/2 sanctioned in the track renewal programme of 1974-75 could not be progressed. The complete track renewal of these kilometrages has been taken up just 6 months earlier and about 1.5 kms only completed, due to non-availability of track materials, till the time of the accident. The supply of liners to arrest creep was by no means satisfactory and it was left to the PWIs to make local arrangements for the supply of liners till January 1979, from which date only 5000 moon-washers were supplied in January 1979, 5000 in September 1979, 5000 in January 1980 and 5000 in April 1980. This number is insignificant when compared to the requirements of a PWI holding charge of 76 km. of track where moon-washers/liners are required at the minimum rate of approximately 2600 per kilometre of track laid on ST sleepers. The supply of released materials to replace unserviceable sleepers was also slow. In fact, only 135 CST 9 sleepers, 700 wooden sleepers and Nil ST sleepers were supplied to this PWI during 1979-80. Apparently all concerned were hopefully waiting all these years for the expected supply of released P. Way materials because of CTR which has been sanctioned but which never materialised till very recently.

8.5 *Relief Measures*

(a) While I am satisfied that the medical aid and relief measures were prompt and adequate, I would like to particularly commend the zeal and enthusiasm displayed by Dr. R.P. Buden ADMO/Tiruvannamalai, a young Doctor with just 2 years and 7 months service on the Railway before this accident. He was the first Railway Doctor to arrive at the site of the accident and for quite sometime single handedly saw to the treatment of the injured passengers and their expeditious despatch from site to the Tiruvannamalai Civil Hospital.

(b) Though this did not affect the medical aid and relief measures taken after the accident, there was undue delay in the ordering and despatching of the Medical Van and Accident Relief Train from Pakala, South-Central Railway. The accident took place at 13.46 hours and first information was conveyed to the Control at 14.06 hours. Nevertheless the Medical Van and Breakdown Specials were ordered from Pakala only at 14.25 hours. There were further delays in the despatch of these Specials, e.g., Medical Relief Van left Pakala at 16.00 hours and the Breakdown Train followed it at 16.40 hours. The delays at Pakala were attributed to the non-availability of engines according to a message received from the Guntakal Division of South-Central Railway. It is considered that the delay in ordering the specials and in starting them from Pakala needs looking into as the time taken was unduly excessive.

Recommendations

9.1 There is need to tighten up the machinery for measuring and adjustment of creep and rail joint gaps and scrutiny of Creep Registers maintained by PWIs. The measurements of creep recorded by PWI only at rail posts fixed opposite kilometre stones suffer from the disadvantage that PWIs can got away with adjustment of creep only at these posts without bothering about the situation prevailing in the rest of the kilometre. It is recommended, therefore, that besides recording the creep measurements at kilometre stones, another column should be maintained in the Creep Register showing the maximum creep in that kilometrage. Surprisingly, the Southern Railway did not have any detailed circular instructions on the adjustment of creep and gaps and scrutiny of Creep Registers. No local instructions in this regard could be produced during the Inquiry except letters issued by the Board. Southern Railway may therefore issue necessary instructions and tighten up the machinery for measurement and adjustment of creep and scrutiny of Creep Registers maintained by PWIs. During the inspections, Officers from the Divisions and Headquarters should check to ascertain whether Creep Registers are maintained properly and whether creep has been adjusted.

9.2 Urgent steps should be taken to arrest creep in Katpadi-Villupuram section. If complete track renewals of the section cannot be undertaken in the near future, the insertion of liners/moon-washers to arrest the falling of keys should be undertaken on war-footing and the supply of liners/moon-washers made commensurate with the needs of the prevailing situation. RDSO may also be asked to design an Anti-creep Anchor suited to sleepers.

9.3 Besides engaging a second Keyman, the hours of patrolling by the Keymen should be staggered, as falling of keys is taking place on a large and alarming scale in the Villupuram-Katpadi section. It is suggested that the two Keymen employed in this section should come on duty at day-break and having patrolled over their respective lengths in the morning session, they should take a long lunch break and do their second patrolling in the late afternoon hours till dusk. The present practice of both Keymen patrolling during normal working hours suffers from the disadvantage that the entire stretch will not receive attention from 17.30 hours to 07.00 hours the next day in summer or 17.00 hours to 0.7.30 hours the next day in winter instead of from dusk to dawn the next day. While the danger of keys falling is not eliminated, the risk can be some what reduced by resort to this suggestion.

9.4 Coach No. SYLR 9647 was found to be badly corroded when it was seen in a twisted and damaged condition in the bed of Turingee River after the accident. I therefore had the coach examined by the Shop Superintendent of Golden Rock Workshops. While his report would appear to indicate that the corrosion observed was not abnormal as the coach was shortly due another periodical overhaul (POH) in May 1980 after its last POH in November 1978, it appears to me that due to the atmospheric conditions in this coastal areas, corrosion of coaches is quite severe and therefore calls for a review of the anti-corrosion measures currently adopted at the time of POH in the Golden Rock Workshops to enable a passenger coach to remain in good service for 18 months.

9.5 The bio-data of Engineering staff submitted indicates a heavy backlog of staff to be deputed for Refresher Courses. Shri S. Vedantha Ramanujam AEN of the section, who is an *ad hoc* promotee from the works cadre, had not been given any training in P. Way and last attended a P. Way refresher course way back in 1964. Lower down the ranks, PWI Gr. III Shri A. Kolandairaj had last attended a refresher course in March 1972, Mate Shri K. Pattu had last attended a refresher course in 1969 and Keyman Shri P. Kumaraswamy in 1962. The Southern Railway would do well to have this matter reviewed and ensure that staff attend refresher courses at regular intervals to update their knowledge in the latest practices and advances made in P. Way Engineering. In particular, it may be ensured that staff, before promotion as AENs, undergo a refresher course in subjects on which they have no background knowledge and experience. In fact, the passing of pre-promotional refresher courses should be a pre-requisite qualification before promotion of any category of staff to gazetted ranks in the Indian Railways.

9.6 The length of pit lines at Villupuram is inadequate for the proper maintenance of passenger stock to be done at this station. Whereas the rakes of passenger trains are of atleast 6-coach lengths as in the case of 156 Up, one of the pit lines had a pit of only 5-coach length with the result the 6th coach had to be inspected outside the pit. The extension of this pit line to 6-coach length should therefore be expedited. The Railway may examine and take similar action if this situation exists at other stations as well.

9.7 Guard Shri R. Polaish of 156 Up was not provided with a first-aid box though he had been working as a passenger train Guard for the last 2 years. I was told that this was because there was no stock available at Villupuram. Although this shortage has since been made good, it is surprising that this situation was not detected earlier. Responsibility may therefore be fixed for this lapse.

9.8 The photographs taken after an accident generally highlight the gruesome features of damage to the coaches after the accident. In the case of a derailment, it is more important, from the point of view of determining the cause, to take photographs of the track near the first marks of derailment. Fortunately in this case and at my instance, very clear and good photographs were taken of the accident site, which enabled me to get a complete picture of the track conditions prevailing after the derailment. Where the cause of a derailment is in doubt, it would be a great help if in serious accidents, photographs of the track and other conditions near the first marks of derailment are taken, as a matter of course, under the directions of a Senior Railway Officer.

9.9 It came to light that on 14-4-80, a report of bad running, due to what appeared to be a distortion of track, had been received by the SM Velanandal. While he brought this matter to the notice of PWI, neither the AEN nor DEN was made aware of this incident till after the matter came to my notice during the Inquiry. All reports of rough running are to be advised to all concerned in terms of para 4(b)(i) of the Southern Railway's Rules for Reporting and Investigating Accidents. The failure of staff concerned to advise the AEN and DEN may therefore be suitably taken up.

9.10 The rake link of 156 Up consisted of passenger coaches with one SYLR in front and one SYLR in rear as indicated at page 80 of Booklet Number 23 Appendix 'L' to the Working Time Table. This composition of two SYLRs on a MG Passenger train also exists on may other MG trains, e.g., 102, 106, 119, etc., shown in same Booklet. Both SYLRs of 156 Up had been marshalled with the guard's portion trailing, presumably taking advantage of the relaxation permitted under para 3 of Board's letter No. 76-Chg. II/14/1 dated 4-6-77 due to the difficulty of MG coupler arrangements. Since 156 Up and the other MG trains normally run with set rakes, there should be no difficulty in suitably altering the existing couplings or providing universal couplings so that the guard's portion is always leading in the SYLR next to the engine and trailing in the SYLR in rear. This will give maximum protection to passengers in collision accidents as in whichever direction the train travels, the rearmost portion will always be the guard's portion. Southern Railway may consider this suggestion. The Board may also consider advising all railways to adopt this suggestion for set MG rakes and only permit relaxation in exceptional cases.

9.11 A derailment, which was attributed to tampering of track, had occurred at Turingee Bridge on 27-1-80. This finding was arrived at by a Committee of four Senior HODs, i.e., CE, CME, CSS and CSO. The report of this Committee was accepted by the General Manager and the Commission advised of the Railways acceptance on 19-3-80. Yet the Superintendent of Railway Police and the CSO informed me that the Railway Police had registered at case only under 'derailment'. During my Inquiry in the last week of April 1980 and again in the first week of June 1980, I was informed by the SRP that Police investigation were still going on the the level of the Investigating Officer, who is the Inspector of Railway Police, Villupuram. The CSO, who was a member of the Enquiry Committee, should be able to convince his counterpart in the State Railway Police of the reasons which led to the Railway's finding and get the investigation finalised one way or the other at appropriate levels as quickly as possible as a deterrent against a possible recurrence in this apparently disturbed areas.

9.12. The two derailed right wheels of the trailing bogie of the 5th coach ICF GSY. 9914 had many clear indentation marks of the loose jaws of the steel trough sleepers on the tread of the tyres of the right wheels. The Brinell Hardness Number of these tyres was therefore checked from the Shore Hardness. Number, after a Sclerscope Test. This gave a Brinell Hardness at places at the lower ranges of 210-225. It was quite an unusual sight to find such clear impressions of the curved shape of loose jaws on the tyre of wheels and that too on an ICF coach. This needs looking into. I was informed that as per specifications, only C&W tyres can be either normalised or oil hardened and tempered during Heat Treatment at the option of the manufacturer, but no such option is given for tyres of Engines and motor and trailer coaches of EMU Stock, which shall only be oil hardened and tempered. Southern Railway may also apprise the ICF and RDSO of this phenomenon so that their specification of heat treatment of Carriage and Wagon tyres can be reviewed.

Railway Board's Comments on Various Paras of the Report

Para 9.1: It seems the accident has been caused due to non-implementation of instructions already existing. The recommendation of the Chief Commissioner of Railway Safety is accepted. All the Railways have been instructed vide circular No. 80/Safety (A & R)/1/6 dated 5-6-81 to lay down supplementary instructions for measurement of creep at intervals closer than one kilometre on sections where the rails are known to creep and to ensure that not more than six consecutive jammed joints are permitted in such lengths. A copy of the circular is attached.

Para 9.2: Steps have been taken by the Railway Administration to arrest creep in Katpadi-Villupuram section and to procure supplies of necessary liners and moon-washers from EWS, Arakkonam who have been asked to give top priority for manufacture of these items. The RDSO has also been advised to design an anti-creep device to suit ST sleepers.

Para 9.3: Instructions have been issued by the Railway Administration for taggering the hours of patrolling by the Keymen to ensure that continuous attention to the loose fitting is available from sun-rise to sun-set. This has been noted by Chief Commissioner of Railway Safety.

Para 9.4: Instructions for examining and attending corroded coaches have been clearly laid down in RDSO's instructions contained in pamphlets Nos. 6905, 7602 and 75003. In addition suitable local instructions have also been issued to Golden Rock Workshops. The Addl. Chief Mechanical Engineer (Carriage & Wagon), Golden Rock has again been advised to look into this aspect and tighten inspection and repair procedures during POH so that the coach turned out after POH can be safety in service till the next POH. Chief Commissioner of Railway Safety (CCRS) has also noted the same.

Para 9.5: The Railways have been instructed to review the position of refresher courses for officers and staff connected with safety and maintenance of permanent way and to pull up arrears. A copy of the instructions issued is attached.

Para 9.6: The carriage maintenance pit line at Villupuram has been extended and commissioned in May, 1980. This can now accommodate six coaches. The Railway have also confirmed that it is extending pit line facilities at stations where required, on a regular programmed basis.

Para 9.7: Necessary action has been taken by the Railway against the staff at fault.

Para 9.8: Suitable instructions have been issued by the Railway Administration to all concerned.

As for CCRS's remarks against this para, it may be mentioned that instructions with regard to taking of photographs of the scene of serious accidents already exist vice Board's letter No. 80/WI/TK/3 (P. clues) dated 6-7-80 (copy enclosed).

Para 9.9: Necessary action has been taken by the Railway Administration. This has been noted by CCRS.

Para 9.10: The question of marshalling of M.G. SLRs has been examined afresh. As universal coupler are not available on the MG, Railways have been advised to marshal MG SLRs in train formation a operationally convenient.

Para 9.11: The police investigated the case and came to the conclusion that it was a case of derailment not due to tampering of track. They, therefore, closed the case. At this late stage re-opening of the case at a higher level would not serve any useful purpose. However, Chief Security Officer, Southern Railway has been advised to bring this to the notice of the concerned Police authority.

Para 9.12: The heat treatment to be given for carriage and wagon tyres as stipulated in IRS specification R-15 has been reviewed by RDSO, who have since advised that the present stipulation of allowing normalising also (as an alternative to hardening and tampering) is considered adequate to give the required hardness of the tyre surface. This view of RDSO has been accepted.

Southern Railway have been instructed to accurately assess the actual hardness of the particular wheel which has been commented upon by CRS to determine whether the actual hardness of the affected wheel was lower than the value stipulated in IRS specification R-15 and if so, the reason for the same. Further action will be taken by the Railway in this regard.

Relief Measures

South Central Railway have already been asked by the Southern Railway to fix the responsibility for the delay in ordering and despatching of Medical Relief Van and Accident Relief Train and to take suitable disciplinary action.

8

RAILWAY ACCIDENT INVESTIGATION REPORT ON FIRE ACCIDENT TO 319 UP HOWRAH-MUGHALSARAI PASSENGER TRAIN AT KIUL STATION ON JHAJHA-DANAPUR MAIN LINE SECTION IN DANAPUR DIVISION OF EASTERN RAILWAY AT 13.03 HOURS ON APRIL 24, 1980 — REPORT[1]

One-Man Commission Shri K. Ganapati, Commissioner of Railway Safety, South Eastern Circle, Calcutta

Appointment

The Commission was constituted under Ministry of Tourism and Civil Aviation (Commission of Railway Safety) in accordance with Rule 4 of the Statutory Investigation into the Railway Accidents Rules, 1973 on April 24, 1980.

Terms of Reference

To enquire into the fire accident to 319 up Howrah-Mughalsarai Passenger Train at Kiul Station on Jhajha-Danapur Main Line Section in Danapur Division of Eastern Railway at 13.03 hours on April 24, 1980.

Contents

Summary; Inspection and Inquiry; Relief Measures; The Train; Local Conditions; Summary of Evidences; Tests and Observations; Division; Conclusions; Remarks and Recommendations; Annexure I; Railway Board Comments on Various Paras of the Report.

---

1. Delhi; Controller of Publications; 1983; 13 p.

Conclusions

Cause of Accident

On careful consideration of the factual, material and circumstantial evidence, I have reached the conclusion that the Fire accident to coach No. FCS 1994 of 319 Up Howrah-Mughalsarai Passenger train at 13.03 hours of 24.4.1980 was caused by inflammable Materials catching fire in the middle first class coupe compartment of the coach accidentally or due to misadventure.

Responsibility

(a) No Railway servant can be held responsible for this accident.

(b) In all probability, the fire was started due to the personal clothing of Hameeda Begum an occupant of the middle first class couch compartment aged 74 years catching fire from the stove either accidentally or due to misadventure, for which she had paid dearly with her life.

Relief arrangements and medical attention.

I am satisfied with the relief arrangements and medical attention given.

Recommendations

Screening of Annular Space

9.1 Under letter No. SL/SX/l dated 5-2-1972 the RDSO advised all Railway Administrations to carry out modifications to arrest large size sparks which may passes through the annular space between the spark arrest or plate and conventional blast pipe cap. Inspite of this advice it is seen that in large number of locomotives including WP locomotive No. 7029 which hauled the ill-fated 319 Up, this annular space has not been protected by standard mesh. In the case of Fire accident to 37 Up Howrah-Madras Janta Express on the South Eastern Railway on 2-3-1979, the CRS, South Eastern Circle has concluded that live cinders escaping from the chimney of the locomotive was the cause of the accident. He has also requested Railway Board to review the action taken by the Railway to arrest the escape of large size sparks through the annular space between the spark arrestor plate and the blast pipe-cap. Even though the spark from the locomotives has been ruled out as the cause of fire in the present case it is necessary that urgent action be taken to protect the annular space by means of suitable mesh. The Railway Board may arrive at a quick decision in the matter.

No synchronising arrangements in the locomotive

9.2 Locomotive No. 7029 hauling the ill-fated train did not have synchronising arrangement between the steam and vacuum brakes. In the evidence, Loco-Foreman, Jhajha Shed accepted that more than 25 per cent of the locomotive are not fitted with this arrangement. The synchronising arrangements is normally accepted as a safety aid and working of large number of engines without this arrangement is to say the least unfortunate. The immediate consequence of the absence of such an arrangement is an increase in the emergency braking distance. Railway Board may take notice of this fact and issue suitable instructions to the Railway as deemed fit.

Guard did not have Fire Extinguisher

9.3 The evidence showed that the Guard of 319 Up did not carry Fire Extinguisher. Responsibility may be fixed for this lapse.

No fans in First Class Compartment

9.4 The evidence showed that there were no fans in the first class compartment of the train. The absence of fans during day time in mid-summer in first class compartment is bound to cause great inconvenience to passengers. The reply of the Administration that fans are out of stock is hardly tenable.

Alarm chain blanking off-Guard and Driver ignorant

9.5 Even though alarm chain apparatus was blanked off under proper authority in the train involved in the accident, no caution order was issued to the Guard/Driver of the train as per the rules. The Railway may comply with Board's orders in this connection.

Violation of rules regarding carriage of inflammable goods

9.6 The present rules viz. 505 and 506 Coaching Tariff Part I regarding the prohibition of carriage of inflammable articles in the compartment are more than adequate. However, their actual implementation in practice is far from satisfactory. After the present accident an immediate recommendation was made along with the Preliminary Report suggesting that the Eastern Railway may organise intensive checks by special squads of staff consisting of TTEs. Coach Attendants and RPF staff at strategic and vulnerable points and trains depending on past history of fire cases and incidence of marriage and other parties travelling in trains with a view track down violations of rules 505 and 506 of Coaching Tariff Rules.

Fire accidents—Is there is a solution ?

9.7 One redeeming feature of the present accident was that the fire started only few minutes before the train reached Kiul. Had the fire started somewhere in between stations, there being no alarm chain apparatus in this train, more than one coach would have been gutted in no time and casualties would have been correspondingly more. The provision of fire fighting facilities at each station may not help as the fire may take place in the mid-section, and before the train reached the station a number of bogies would be gutted. Even if, the Railway were to produce a coach out of non-inflammable materials, the problem would not be solved satisfactorily as seen from the present case as the fire emanated from the personal clothing and the inflammable goods brought in by the passengers. The possibility of providing auxiliary water tanks at strategic points on the roof of the coach has also been considered. Even if such tanks are provided considerable damage would have taken place before the fire can actuate discharge of water from these tanks. The casualties due to jumping out from the running train would also be correspondingly more. Even if the passengers do not carry inflammable articles like kerosene stoves etc. still a fire accident could take place by careless throwing of lighted cigarette butts etc. The loose clothing available in an occupied coach coupled with strong wind always obtaining at the time of running of trains are factors which facilitate quick spread of fire. In the circumstances no reliable method of eliminating fires in running trains appears in sight. Nevertheless the Railway has to do its share to work by tracking down carriage of inflammable goods in compartments and educating passengers to be more careful. Strong action like prosecution launched on a few offenders may have a salutary effect.

Railway Boards Comments on Various Paras of the Report

Para 9.1: Instructions have been issued to the Railways, vide Board's wireless No. 78/M (L)/467/4KW dated 1-7-80, asking them to confirm that the modifications as suggested in RDSO's letter No. SL/SX/1 dated 5-2-72, have been carried out on all WP/WG and YP/YG locomotives. If not, immediate action may be taken to carry out the proposed modifications.

Para 9.2: As advised by the Railway Administration, normally arrangements for the synchronisation of steam and vacuum brakes exist on the locomotives. Reasons for non provision of this arrangement on the locomotive involved in the accident are being investigated by the Railway who would also take suitable remedial action in the matter.

Instructions with regard to the provision of synchronising arrangements between steam and vacuum brakes on the locomotives were reiterated to the Railways vide Board's circular letter No. 78/M(L)/467/8 dated 20-3-79. These are again being emphasized.

Para 9.3: The responsibility for non-provision of fire extinguisher in the Guards' Brakevan is being fixed by the Railway.

Para 9.4: The replacement of electric fans in the coaches on the Eastern Railway is a continuous process, as thefts of electrical fittings on branch line passenger trains are quite considerable. Instructions have been issued to the Railways vide letter No. 80/Sec/Cr/184/14 dated 16-2-80 to tighten up the security measures for preventing thefts of train lighting equipment.

Para 9.5: The Railway is being asked to investigate the reasons as to why no caution order was issued to the Driver and the Guard and take up with the defaulting staff.

Para 9.6: The railway administration has re-circulated the provisions contained in Rules 505 and 506 of the IRCA Coaching Tariff and has also conducted systematic checks on selected trains originating from Howrah and Sealdah stations with a view to ensuring compliance of these provisions. In addition, suitable local publicity has also been arranged.

Para 9.7: Instructions already exist vide Board's letter No. 74/Tkt. Checking/54 dated 23-4-75 enjoining on the Railways to exercise vigilance through the staff, particularly Ticket Checking Staff, to prevent carriage to inflammable and explosive materials in the train by the travelling public. Although, the powers for search of baggage exist, it is not practicable to exercise these powers effectively. The need to publicise the relevant provisions of the Indian Railway Act and IRCA Coaching Tariff and to educate the public against the hazards of carrying such materials in their luggage, through notices and public address, system, has also been indicated. These instructions have been reiterated vide Board's letter No. 80/Tkt. Checking/5/5 dated 17-7-80.

Regarding replacement of cushions and other furnishings with suitable non-fire excitable materials. RDSO have been directed to do the needful and this matter will be pursued in due course.

TASK FORCE ON EXPORT PROMOTION OF ENTERTAINMENT GOODS, 1980 — REPORT[1]

Chairman Shri A.K. Dutt

Members Shri C. Venkataraman; Dr. V.L. Kelkar; Shri N. Sivasubramanian; Shri G.P. Sippy; Shri B.R. Chopra; Chairman, National Film Development Corporation; Shri S.C. Hira; Shri Gul Anand; Shri L.V. Prasad; Shri Adoor Gopalakrishnan; Shri B.N. Sircar; Shri A.K. Sud; Shri Rama Nand Sagar.

Convenor Shri S.L. Kapur.

Appointment

In view of the rising import bill consequent to rise in prices of petroleum, oils and lubricants, and world inflation, growth of exports has become as one of the top priorities in the emerging situation. In this connection it is necessary to diversify and to explore new markets and new products.

It is felt that the export of cinematographic films and other items of entertainment such as cassettes, radios, tapes, gramophone records, etc., have high export potential. Accordingly, it has been decided to constitute a Task Force on Export of Entertainment Goods, to study the various aspects and recommend suitable measures to increase the export of entertainment goods vide Government of India, Ministry of Commerce and Civil Supplies, Department of Commerce Office Order No. 4(8)/80-EPL dated May 9, 1980.

Terms of Reference

(i) To review the present trend in world trade and India's exports

1. New Delhi, Ministry of Commerce, 1980, 83 + 25 p.

in entertainment goods.

(ii) To identify major productwise export potential and recommend export targets and identify marketwise export strategy.

(iii) To identify productwise measures necessary to remove production and capacity constraints.

(iv) To make recommendations on the matters relating to existing procedures, regulations, etc., in order to promote these exports.

(v) To make recommendations about institutional arrangements that may be considered necessary for improved marketing of entertainment goods.

Contents

Introduction; Review of Exports and the Potential; Policy Considerations and Recommendations; Summary of Recommendations; Annexures from 1 to 13.

Recommendations

FILMS

National Film Development Corporation (NFDC)

1. National Film Development Corporation should play a predominant role in the promotion of export of films. In particular it should take special interest in exporting low budget quality films and regional films. Development of non-traditional markets and exploration of TV Circuits should also be given a high priority. The Corporation should also promote export of short films and documentaries. It should have the status and authority of an Export Promotion Council.

2. NFDC should be the nodal institution for collection and dissemination of market intelligence regarding projects, films and services. For this purpose, it should have a regular division with competent research oriented staff. A data bank to store and disseminate relevant statistics/information may also be set up.

3. The Corporation may also consider setting up of business offices abroad for collection and collection of relevant information and data and to serve as show-windows.

4. NFDC may also publish a regular periodical journal to keep the film industry acquainted with necessary export information.

5. Significant taste oriented adaptation is necessary in order to enter new markets. The Corporation should play a meaningful role in the matter of such adaptations. It can also finance on a somewhat liberal terms, films meant for export only. NFDC could also take up for initial incentive financing certain special types of films required abroad by some countries. NFDC may also consider helping in the promotion of a special effects studio.

6. The recommendations of the Working Group on Film Policy to continue the present scheme of canalising exports through NFDC is endorsed. The existing rate of canalisation fees, viz., 20.5 per cent may also be continued. The scheme may however be reviewed to permit levy of canalisation fees on exports of films after deducting the costs incurred on account of prints, freight and insurance.

7. The quantum of additional commission levied (15%) on exports to countries with which it has exclusive agreements may reviewed keeping in view the services rendered by the Corporation and the effect it has on the volume of exports.

Video Transferring Facilities/Sub-titling

8. Immediate action to be taken up by NFDC to implement its scheme for the setting up of a modern sub-titling facility within the country. Similarly Video transferring facilities should also be set-up in the country within the shortest possible time. If no private party is willing to set these up, the same may also be taken up by NFDC.

Imports of Equipments

9. It is recommended that imports of equipments required for upgradation and modernisation of shooting/processing of films be permitted freely, i.e., placed on O.G.L. Such imports be treated at par with the imports of capital goods/equipment for industrial projects and charged duty at the reduced rate of 25 per cent to encourage modernisation. Duty reduction may also be considered for tele-cine cameras and sub-titling machines.

Sales on Profit-sharing basis

10. Export of films on the basis of minimum guarantee and shared receipts may be permitted in respect of non-traditional areas.

Export of Negatives

11. Export of negatives may be permitted in exceptional cases with a view to generating additional earnings and improving the quality of films, particularly for TV circuits (16 mm) and non-traditional sophisticated markets. Such exports may also be permitted where because of local regulations and customs duties our exports will otherwise be outpriced.

Import of Raw Stock

12. The existing schemes of (i) advance licensing without payment of duty and (ii) duty free REP imports to restore the necessary competitive edge to our exports. A limited quantity of Cine Sound also be permitted to be imported against REP licences to enable producers to prepare export quality final prints. For this purpose utilisation of 10 per cent of the REP licences i.e. 5 per cent of the export value may be permitted.

13. At present, packing materials are permitted to the imported against REP Licences to the extent of 15 per cent. As the industry does not require packing materials, it is recommended that this be utilised for importing cinematograph film (unexposed) to the extent of 5% and cine sound to the extent of 10 per cent.

TV Films Export

14. To encourage production of a new genre of TV films for the export market a domestic market for this type of films has to be developed. In this Doordarshan can and should play a very important and pioneering role.

Sale of Video Rights

15. Video cassettes can generate sizable exports within a short period. In this connection the recommendations are:

(i) as a general policy, there should be no objection to the assignment of video rights of Indian feature films to the foreign buyers;
(ii) these rights should be sold to a single buyer for the entire over-

seas territories under a separate contract;

(iii) sales may be on outright or on the basis of minimum guarantee and shared receipts;

(iv) the registration of contracts for the sale of video rights be subjected to the approval of the price by the consultative committee of NFDC;

(v) the foreign buyer be permitted to make his own arrangements for transferring the films to the video cassettes; one of the members dissented and insisted that the transfer should be made by the units located within the country (including those in SEEPZ); and

(vi) sales of video rights should be canalised through NFDC.

16. Esquire Video Services Ltd., a unit of SEEPZ, may be treated at par with any other foreign based buyer of video rights with no special restrictions of any kind. Sales of films to them may also be canalised through NFDC and should qualify for various export promotion incentives.

Censorship

17. The censorship guidelines for films meant for export should be on a somewhat liberal basis.

Co-production and Joint Ventures

18. The existing rules, regulations and laws relating to co-productions, joint ventures and shooting of films in India should be revised with a view to encouraging such activities. An Inter-Ministerial group be set-up for doing this and from laying down fresh comprehensive guidelines.

Processing Facilities as Export Earners

19. A small committee consisting of the representatives of the Ministries of Information and Broadcasting, Finance (Department of Revenue) and Film Laboratories be set-up to re-structure the existing procedures to cut down delays and reduce the formalities regarding import, processing and re-export of foreign short films.

Incentives for Exports to Non-traditional Markets

20. Cash assistance and freight subsidy at liberal rates be given to encourage exports to non-traditional markets for a period of five years.

Consortia to Promote Exports

21. Government of India and the Indian Missions abroad should help in the setting up of business offices and distribution networks abroad by film producers and exporters' consortia. Such offices and facilities may also be partly funded by NFDC and the Market Development Fund of the Ministry of Commerce.

Accepting Deferred Payments

22. Acceptance of deferred payments and grant of long-term credits on Government to Government basis may be tried to penetrate few selected non-traditional markets. NFDC can play a pioneering and a pivotal role of a catalyst in this behalf.

Exchange of Films

23. NFDC may try buying some films of Sri Lanka, Pakistan and Bangladesh in exchange of our films. This will have to be done in close co-ordination and cooperation with the producers exporters and with the overall objective of promoting exports of Indian films to these countries.

Film Festivals and Special Film Weeks

24. NFDC should co-ordinate an increasing Indian participation in the market sections of film festivals. Film producers and exporters may also be directly assisted by NFDC for this purpose. Extra foreign exchange may also be provided to them by Reserve Bank of India to participate effectively in such festivals.

Film Weeks for Export Promotion

25. Indian film weeks abroad should also be availed of for pushing exports of our films. Besides, special film weeks be organised with

help of the Government of India, NFDC and the Indian Missions abroad for this purpose. During these special film weeks visits of film delegations may also be sponsored to explore and open up non-traditional markets.

Short Films, Documentaries and TV Films

26. Purchase of short films from independent producers by Films Division has to be increased substantially to provide a suitable domestic market for short film producers and to give them the necessary strength and support for attempting exports. Short-film makers may also be encouraged to produce films for TV in colour and these may be purchased by the Government for use in the Cultural Exchange programmes. NCERT and other similar agencies should also be encouraged to produce scientific and educational films for exports.

Incentives for Export of Short Films and TV Films

27. A liberal cash-cum-freight assistance be given for five years to promote exports of short films. This assistance may also be available for short TV films not exceeding one hour playing time.

Revision of RBI Procedures

28. The Reserve Bank of India procedures regarding (a) export of films for sub-titling; (b) export of additional prints and (c) export of trailers and other publicity materials be reviewed and restrictions relaxed with a view to generating more exports.

29. The standard format for export contracts be revised suitably by NFDC in consultation with the various interests involved to permit for sales of films in terms of payment of royalty only and to enable separate payment on account of supply of prints in accordance with the lab rates prevalent at the time of delivery.

Incentives to Boost Cine-equipment Export

30. Liberal cash support be given to units manufacturing cine equipment for promoting their exports. REP Licences of at least 10 per cent be also given to them. This may be given for a period of five years. The Engineering Export Promotion Council should help such

units in gathering necessary market intelligence and assisting them in sending delegations abroad and participating in various fairs and markets.

Musical Instruments

31. Imported raw-materials for such instruments could be procured, stored and provided by STC under its IRMAC scheme. Institutional arrangements may also be made for displaying our musical instruments in all trade fairs abroad. Cash assistance at the rate usual for such instruments for five years is also recommended.

Entertainment Troupes

32. Government may consider the possibility of advancing loans and giving assistance for organising a few cultural bodies which could sponsor such entertainment troupes for earning more foreign exchange. The new provision in the income-tax laws treating foreign exchange earnings of a sportsman differently for purposes of tax may also be extended to entertainers. A new incentive oriented scheme which would enable such entertainers to claim exemption in respect of 50 per cent of their foreign exchange earnings abroad and be taxed only on the remaining 50 per cent may also be considered.

ELECTRONIC ENTERTAINMENT GOODS

Radio and Radio Parts

33. In order to promote exports in price sensitive markets the rate of cash assistance be restored to 20 per cent which was the rate prevalent until two years ago. This rate be maintained for atleast five years. Components should be allowed to be imported free of duty subject to their re-export in equipments with a minimum value addition of 20 per cent.

34. For export to developed countries which are brand sensitive foreign collaborations may be allowed to our manufacturers if in their view it is necessary to do so to be able to export to such countries. Foreign collaborations may also be permitted provided a reasonably high percentage of the manufactured products is likely to be exported. However, where 100 per cent of the manufactured product is ear-

marked for exports with a minimum of 20 per cent value addition, foreign collaborations should be allowed liberally. In such cases duty-free import of components may also be permitted.

35. Export opportunities involving foreign collaborations should be fully exploited within the framework of the existing guidelines and norms prescribed.

TV Sets and Components

36. With a view to encouraging our manufacturers of black and white TV sets to exploit the export market, cash assistance available to them be restored to 20 per cent and kept at that level for the next five years.

37. Foreign collaborations may be allowed liberally for manufacture of both black and white and colour TV sets on a 100 per cent export basis. Import of components may also be allowed free of duty, to such units provided the components are re-exported in equipments with atleast 20 per cent value addition.

Tape-recorders and Two-in-ones

38. For making exports of tape-recorders in two-in-one sets competitive, it is necessary to have a sizable domestic market in respect of these products. This market can only develop if excise duty is suitably reduced in respect of the products at the lower and of the price spectrum. The price of a cassette tape-recorder presently available at Rs. 400 should be reduced by a suitable restructuring of the duty/excise to make it available to consumers at Rs. 250. In line with the recommendations regarding Radio and TV, import of components, duty-free, be permitted in respect of these provided the same are re-exported with atleast 20 per cent value addition. All limitations on capacities should be waived to enable the units to grow and fully exploit both the domestic and the export markets.

39. Regarding video tape-recorders the recommendations made in respect of colour TV sets may apply *mutatis mutandis*.

Amplifiers, Public Address Systems, Stereos and Hifi Systems

40. In addition to the package of recommendations for tape-recorders and two-in-one sets which may also apply in the case of

amplifiers, etc. Government should also restore cash assistance to 20 per cent.

Electronic Games, etc.

41. Foreign collaboration should be permitted freely in respect of local manufacture of electronic games and hobbies. Duty free import of components may also be permitted provided these are re-exported with atleast 20 per cent value addition. Cash assistance at 20 per cent may also be restored to assist in their exports.

Gramophones/Audio Tapes

42. Enforcement of the anti-piracy laws be made strict and all audio cassettes sold within the country or exported abroad should carry the names and addresses of the manufacturers. Cash assistance on export of gramophone records and pre-recorded cassettes be increased to 10 per cent for exports to all areas. An additional 5 per cent should be allowed on exports to the Americas on account of higher freight. The enhanced cash assistance be allowed for atleast three years. The industry should also be allowed to import capital equipments which are not now being made in India and the same should be subject to an import duty of 40 per cent as for other project equipments.

43. Foreign exchange earnings arising out of such sale of rights should be entitled for 10 per cent cash assistance. Sale of samples and connected export marketing expenditure should be allowed as weighted deduction under the Income Tax Act.

44. Raw materials and components may be allowed to be imported duty-free for 100 per cent export units.

45. The gramophone record industry should be allowed adequate representation in the Export Promotion Council for Plastics and Linoleum.

General

46. In line with the declared policy of the Government, manufacturers of electronics entertainment goods may be allowed to expand their capacity provided the expansion is exclusively for export production.

47. Our manufacturing units be encouraged to invest in Research

and Development.

48. Facilities enjoyed by wholly export-oriented units and the units located in SEEPZ may also be extended to predominantly export-oriented units in the hinterland.

49. Duty-free import of raw-materials, components and sub-assemblies be allowed under advance licensing and also under *ad hoc* import licences to manufacturers, operating within bonded perimeters and exporting not less than 75 per cent of their products with atleast 20 per cent value addition.

50. Electronic manufacturers/exporters be allowed to utilise their REP licences up to Rs. 15 lakhs for import of essential capital goods, required by them without having to go through the usual formalities of essentiality certificates, etc., including import of electronic goods when the limit of Rs. 5 lakhs fixed in 1971 has not yet been revised upwards.

51. Imports of capital goods including tooling, jigs, etc., for manufacture of entertainment electronics predominantly for exports may be exempted completely from the payment of import duty.

52. Consortium selling on the part of the Indian exporters be encouraged.

53. The present liberal attitude of Government as reflected in the 1980-81 budget, towards electronics industry be maintained throughout the 6th Plan period to ensure speedy growth of this industry. Fiscal incentives be increasingly used to develop this industry and add to the export effort which is sensitive to the price factor at the micro level.

54. Benefits given in the recent budget to new manufacturing investments, viz., exemption of 25 per cent of profits from corporate income-tax, be extended also to units exporting 75 per cent or more of their products in a financial year.

55. Facility of bonded warehouses should be permitted to units located anywhere in the country. The Central Government should also set-up bonded warehouses stocking raw-materials, components and sub-assemblies. This may be done through the ETTDC or the export houses.

56. The attractiveness of the export promotion zone (SEEPZ) for exporters should be enhanced as recommended by the Menon Committee and the Sondhi Committee.

57. Priority be given to electronic industry in the matter of availability of institutional and bank finance and IDBI nominated as the lead bank for electronics industry.

58. A separate Export Promotion Council be set up for this industry.

59. Liberal imports of proto-types and samples over and above the provisions of the import policy should be permitted to exporters of electronic entertainment goods.

60. Government should set up testing and quality assurance centres specifically to assist exporters.

61. Container services be developed and cost on account of movement of export goods to ports be reduced to make our exports competitive.

62. Centralised tool house and common service facilities be developed to provide low cost services necessary for making exports competitive.

63. Fiscal and port procedures be revised to encourage maintenance of bonded warehouses, storing of a wide range of electronic general purpose components at international prices to assist manufacturers in meeting orders quickly.

64. Customs Department should recruit electronic engineers to cut down delays in application of tariff notifications giving concessions, etc.

65. Claims for duty drawbacks and REP licences be settled early. Administrative procedures be re-structured accordingly.

66. Procedures for approval of foreign collaborations have to be restructured to cut delays and introduce an element of flexibility.

67. Delays in licensing of additional capacity or diversification be cut. The general infrastructure regarding transport, power supply, etc., be toned up to gear this industry to meet the challenges of expanding exports.

68. Registration and approval of de-licensed units and small-scale units should be automatic and given for the asking.

69. Capacity as per the industrial licence should have relevance only to production for the domestic market and the export production should be allowed over and above such a capacity limitation.

70. Long-term and large volume exports have to be planned only after ensuring the continued availability of export market. Therefore, they must receive adequate financial, fiscal, diplomatic and political support.

71. Production of simple communication equipment, e.g., citizen band radios, etc., be permitted to predominantly. 100 per cent export oriented units in the private sector.

SECOND PRESS COMMISSION — REPORT[1]
May 29, 1978 – April 3, 1982

Chairman Shri P.K. Goswami, Justice, Retired Judge of the Supreme Court.

Members Sarvashri Abu Abraham; Prem Bhatia; S.N. Dwivedy; Moinuddin Harris; Professor Ravi J. Matthai; Yashodhar N. Mehta; V.K. Narasimhan; Fali S. Nariman; S.H. Vatsyayan; Shri Arun Shourie; Shri Nikhil Chakravarty.

Alterations Shri Justice Goswai and his collagues in the Commission resigned on January 14, 1980 after the formation of New Government at the centre in the wake of the Seventh General Elections to the Lok Sabha.

The Commission was reconstituted. Shri Justice K.K. Mathew, Retired Judge of the Supreme Court, was appointed Chairman by Notification No. 14/5/80-Press, dated 21st April 1980. The names of ten Members were notified on 18th June 1980. They were: Shri Justice Sisir Kumar Mukherjee. Retired Judge of the Calcutta High Court; Smt. Amrita Pritam, poet and novelist; Sarvashri P.V. Gadgil, author and journalist; Ishrat Ali Siddiqui, Editor, *Qaumi Awaz*, Lucknow; Rajendra Mathur, Chief Editor *Nai Duniya*, Indore; Girilal Jain, Editor, *Times of India*, Bombay; K.R. Ganesh, former Union Minister of State; Madan Bhatia, Advocate, Supreme Court; Ranbir Singh, Editor, *Milap*, Delhi; and Professor H. K. Paranjape, Economist and former Chairman, Railway Tariff Inquiry Committee, and former Member, Monopolies and Restrictive Trade Practices Commission.

1. Ministry of Information and Broadcasting, Government of India, New Delhi, 1982, 293 p., Vol. I.

On the resignation of Shri Madan Bhatia, Shri Prem Chand Verma, Chief Editor, *Jagat* and *Ekta Sandesh Weeklies*, President of the All India Small and Medium Newspapers' Association, Member of the Press Council, and former Member of the Lok Sabha, was appointed Member by Notification dated 16th October 1980.

By the same Notification, Shri Justice A.N. Mulla, Retired Judge of the Allahabad High Court and former Member of the Lok Sabha and the Rajya Sabha, was appointed in addition, raising the number of Members to 11 besides the Chairman. With the subsequent resignation of Smt. Amrita Pritam, which was accepted on 29th January 1981, the strength of the Commission remained ten, besides the Chairman.

Appointment

The First Press Commission constituted in 1952 made a comprehensive study of the problems of the Indian Press and submitted a valuable report in July 1954. The present Commission – which is the second of its nature – was constituted by the Government by Notification No. 2/1/77-Press dated 29th May 1978.

Terms of Reference

"The Press Commission shall enquire into the growth and status of the Indian Press since the last Press Commission reported and suggest how best it should develop in future. It shall, in particular, examine:

(1) The present constitutional guarantee with regard to the freedom of speech and expression, whether this is adequate to ensure freedom of the Press, and the adequacy and efficacy of the laws, rules and regulations relating to and affecting the Press.
(2) Means of safeguarding the freedom and independence of the Press against pressures of all kinds from Government, proprietors, advertising, commercial, trade union, political or other sources in a plural and democratic society.
(3) Ownership patterns and the financial structure of organs of the Press with a view to ensuring editorial independence and professional integrity and the readers' right to objective news

and views and comments freely expressed.

(4) The relationship that should exist between the Government and the Press especially with regard to access to information, accreditation, official patronage or subsidies.

(5) The structure and functioning of the existing news and feature agencies and measures necessary for their growth as strong and viable organisations that can cover news monitoring at every level right down to the grassroots and also world news.

(6) Relations that should subsist between different elements of the Press, viz., publishers, managers, editors and other professional journalists, etc.

(7) Measures necessary to raise and maintain high standards of journalism and to inculcate among journalists and newspapers a due sense of public and social responsibility corresponding to the power of the Press, its role in national reconstruction and its obligations to the readers.

(8) Ways and means to promote the growth and development of the language and regional Press as also the periodical Press, specialised journals and syndicated services.

(9) The economics of the newspaper industry, including ways and means of rectifying deficiencies and evolving the basis for a fair price for newspapers keeping in view legal and constitutional requirements.

(10) The adequacy of training in communications journalism, newspaper management, printing technology and newspaper design and graphics as also the desirability and feasibility for high learning in journalism and mass communications."

Reconstitution and Revised Terms of Reference

The Terms of Reference of the reconstituted Commission, which was expected to submit its report by 31st December 1980, were notified on 24th July, 1980. They are as follows:

"The Press Commission shall inquire into the growth and status of the Press since the First Press, Commission reported and suggest how best it should develop in future.
It shall, particular examine and make recommendations on:

(1) The role of the Press in a developing and democratic society;

(2) The present constitutional guarantee with regard to the freedom of speech and expression; whether this is adequate to ensure freedom of the Press; adequacy and efficacy of the laws, rules and regulations for maintaining this freedom;
(3) Constitutional and legal safeguards to protect the citizen's right to privacy;
(4) Means of safeguarding the independence of the Press against economic and political pressures and pressures from proprietors and management;
(5) Role of the Press and the responsibilities it should assume in developmental policies;
(6) The Press as an industry, a social institution and a forum for informing discussion of public affairs;
(7) Ownership patterns, management practices and financial structures of the Press; their relation to growth, editorial independence and professional integrity;
(8) Chain newspapers; links with industry, their effect on competition and on the readers' right to objective news and free comments;
(9) Economics of the newspaper industry; newsprint, printing, machinery and other inputs for newspapers;
(10) Advertising – Government and private educational and commercial;
(11) Government – Press relations and the role of official agencies;
(12) Relations that should subsist between different elements of the Press, namely, publishers, managers, editors and professional journalists and others;
(13) Growth of small and medium papers and of the language Press;
(14) Development of the periodical Press and specialised journals;
(15) News coverage and news values; structure and functioning of news agencies and feature agencies; flow of news to and from India;
(16) Training of professional manpower; steps to improve professional standards and performance; research in journalism and mass communication;
(17) Journalism as a means of better mutual understanding in the context of proposals for a new international information order;
(18) Perspective of newspaper development."

Contents

Vol. I: Introduction; Retrospect : 1952-1982; Role of the Press; Constitution and Laws; Pressures on the Press; Right to Privacy; Freedom and Responsibility : Role of the Press Council; Official Agency and the Press; The Press as an Industry; The Press as a Public Utility; News Flow : Internal and International; Training and Research; Abstract of Recommendations; Minutes of Dissent and Supplementary Notes; **Vol. II** Appendices : Introduction; Retrospect 1952-82; Role of the Press; Constitution and Laws; Right to Privacy; Freedom and Responsibility : Role of the Press Council; Official Agencies and the Press; Press as an Industry; News Flow : Internal and International; Training and Research.

Recommendations

CHAPTER I

INTRODUCTION

I.17 Copies of the various studies initiated by the Commission, and of the Working Papers and General Papers prepared by its secretariat, may be made over to appropriate institutions such as the Indian Institute of Mass Communication and the Research & Reference Division of the Ministry of Information & Broadcasting for future reference.

CHAPTER II

RETROSPECT : 1952-1982

II.14 On account of growth in the circulation of newspapers since 1968 when the Press Registrar began the classification of newspapers as 'big', 'medium' and 'small', the definitions call for reconsideration. The Press Registrar classifies, on the basis of circulation, newspapers as 'small' or 'medium' even if the newspapers belong to newspaper undertakings of very large size, bringing out other dailies and periodicals with big circulations. We are of the view that the Press Registrar should identify clearly, in the statistics presented in his annual reports, the number and names of the newspapers that are classified as 'small' or 'medium' but which belong to big newspaper undertakings.

CHAPTER III

ROLE OF THE PRESS

III.7 The role of the Press in a developing and democratic society should neither be that of an adversary nor an ally of the Government. To be a mindless adversary or an unquestioning ally would be to abdicate judgement. A free Press should be, in our view, a constructive critic.

III.19 Elsewhere in the Report we make a wide range of recommendations to protect small and medium newspapers from unfair competition and to provide assistance for acquiring printing machinery, securing teleprinter services and newsprint at reasonable price, etc. We would like to emphasise that it is not our intention to encourage localism or scandal and blackmail–failings which are not confined to newspapers of any particular category of circulation. While providing information of relevance to readers in the villages and small towns, the district level newspaper should also keep them posted, even if not in detail, with significant national and International news in the fields of politics, science and technology, sports and culture.

III.23 the editors should insist on their right to have the final say in the acceptance of rejection of advertisements, specially those which border on or cross the line between decency and obscenity, legitimate claims for a product or service and the proffering of magical remedies.

III.24-25 Exploitation of the female form in commercial advertising promotes the notion of women as sex objects and runs contrary to the news items and articles which many newspapers carry in support of treating women as equals and respecting their personality as individuals endowed with as much human worth as males. We recommend in Chapter VIII that the Press Council should examine complaints of violation of the codes of ethics governing advertising. However, the editor himself can stop the mischief at the source if he assumes responsibility, as he should, for all the matter published in his newspaper including advertisements.

III.26-27 The editor's authority should extend not only to the contents of advertisements but also to the proportion of space devoted to them. The editor should also have the right to veto a particular positioning of advertisements that he may regard as undesirable.

III.29 The editors of general interest dailies and periodicals who believe in promoting a scientific temper among their readers, and in combating superstition and fatalism, should discontinue the publication of astrological predictions.

III.32 A newspaper's perception of a particular problem of foreign relations may differ from that of the Government, the expression of such a difference should not be regarded as anti-national.

III.33 While the Press should exercise the utmost responsibility and restraint in publishing or commenting on sensitive information of possible value to an unfriendly government in the event of hostilities, it ought to evince a greater degree of interest in defence matters.

III.43-44 We generally endorse the guidelines formulated by the Press Council in November 1968 for avoidance of 'objectionable communal writing'. We are of the view that, on the outbreak of a communal disturbance, newspapers should refrain from sensational presentation of the news and from giving community-wise figures of those killed and injured. However, when the situation gets stabilised, there should be no hesitation in investigating the causes of the rioting and its consequences, with identification of the communities concerned.

III.43-44 Communal tensions have economic, social and political causes. There have even been allegations of foreign money at work. These causes should be investigated and exposed. We are of the view that suppression of truth would worsen rather than improve the atmosphere. However, it is difficult to lay down hard and fast rules, and a newspaper should, so to say, play it by the ear, in accordance with the circumstances of each case and with due sense of responsibility.

III.45 We recommend that there should be stricter enforcement of the provisions in the Indian Penal Code with regard to communal incitement.

III.48 There should be dialogue between the civil administration and local newspapers on norms and procedures for information flow, verification and correction, during periods of tension and crisis. Professional bodies of journalists should arrange for the exchange of experience in this regard in various parts of the country.

III.51 Journalists have to be on guard against attempts by the authorities or by landlords to pass off agrarian revolts against exploitation as Naxalite or other politically motivated violence.

III.53 We are of the view that the positive role of the Press–of bringing together the diverse elements in the nation's life by emphasising those aspects which tend towards unifying the communities–is as important as avoidance of objectionable communal or casteist writing. This calls for a sustained campaign to promote the concept of human brotherhood taught and exemplified by the founders and the saints of all religions.

III.55 Superstitious beliefs which are unrelated to the essence of religions and are inimical to physical and social health must be relentlessly exposed and fought.

III.57 The Press must address itself to the question of what contribution it is making to the strengthening of the moral fabric of society and discouraging the trend towards conspicuous and excessive consumption which a developing country can ill afford.

III.58 If illegitimate actions like insurrection and secessionist activity have their roots in economic neglect or exploitation or apprehension of loss of cultural identity, the Press can play a useful role, on the one hand by bringing those cause to public notice and on the other by advocating adherence to lawful methods of ventilating grievances.

III.61 While the Press should bring to light and extend support to genuine public grievances, it should take a forth-right stand against unconstitutional methods of agitation.

III.63 The Press will have to campaign for judicial reforms to speed up the legal process and continue to resolutely expose and condemn brutal methods of dealing with suspected criminals.

III.75 There is need to give news values a different orientation in the interest of social health and national development. We would urge the organisations of publishers, editors and journalists to pay attention, on a continuing basis, to the question of the values that should govern the selection and display of news items.

III.77 In addition to measures to encourage the growth of newspapers in the interior and border areas, it is in our view that important newspapers in the rest of country should devote more space to news about the progress and problems of people living in such areas.

III.79 Some widely read newspapers in regional language besides English have taken to reporting regularly on developmental topics and major socio-economic issues such as the conditions of the garden labour, problems of drought and irrigation, 'dowry deaths' and the general ill-treatment of women, the plight of under-trail prisoners and the living conditions of urban slum dwellers. This is a welcome trend which should be encouraged and strengthened.

III.81-82 Development reporting should tell the story of what is going well as well as of what is going wrong. It should investigate into the reasons for success as well as for failure, at different places under different conditions, of various development programmes affecting the lives of common people. Most of our newspapers merely carry official handouts. The reporting of non-official initiatives in rural development, etc., is even less extensive than of official development programmes. The free Press in a developing country should be more socially conscious and enterprising.

III.84-85 We welcome the trend towards investigative reporting insofar as it is oriented to social and economic issues. The investigative reporter should not give occasion for the criticism of lack of follow-up which is a widespread failing in the Indian Press.

III.90 We acknowledge that there could be risks in development reporting, as when a reporter exposes local tyranny and oppression. We recommend that the State Governments should see that investigative reporters to not come to harm. Public opinion should assert itself in this matter.

III.93 We recommend that public grievance columns should be more widely offered by newspapers and that the public authorities concerned should take note of the grievances published and take prompt action.

III.95 It is important to that both the Government-owned media and the Press should be conscious of the need for fair and objective presentation of news.

CHAPTER IV

CONSTITUTION AND LAWS

The Constitutional Guarantee of Freedom of Speech and Expression

IV.4 No useful purpose will be served by inserting a separate provision in the Constitution on freedom of the Press as that concept is already embodied in Article 19(1)(a) and by inserting such a provision no particular benefit can be conferred on a non-citizen like a company.

IV.14 Since many newspapers are published by companies and a company is not entitled to the fundamental rights enumerated under

Article 19, being not a citizen, we recommend that all Indian companies engaged in the business of communication and whose shareholders are citizens should be deemed to be 'citizens' for the purpose of the relevant clause of Article 19.

IV.18 The concept of a free market of ideas presupposes that every type of idea will get into the market. If free access is denied to any idea, to that extent the competition of ideas becomes limited. Our constitutional law has been solicitous in protecting an idea when once it comes into the market but has been singularly indifferent in creating opportunities for its expression. We are in the grip of a romantic theory of freedom of speech, viz., the belief that the market place is freely accessible. With the revolution in communication technology on the one hand and the newspapers' development of an antipathy to ideas which are opposed to its commercial interests on the other, the operation of a market place of ideas has ceased to exist. The constitutional issue generally is whether the expression already uttered should be given the shelter of Article 19(1)(a). But what of those ideas which are unacceptable to the media and which to not find access therein? The usual answer is that Article 19(1)(a) guarantees freedom of the owner to do as he chooses with his media. This answer stresses the view that a newspaper in emphatically the private property of the owner who sells a manufactured product at his risk; a newspaper owes nothing to the public which grants it no francise. Thus the constitutional imperative of free expression becomes the very instrument for repressing competitive ideas. The freedom guarantees by Article 19(1)(a) must be reviewed in this light.

IV.20 There is a wrong notion that apart from the reasonable restrictions that could be imposed on the freedom of the Press under Article 19(2), there could be no other interference in the exercise of that freedom. What Article 13(2), forbids is the making of any law which has the effect of 'taking away' or 'abridging' any fundamental right. There can be no ambiguity or controversy when a right is completely 'taken away' and such action would be clearly hit by Article 13(2). In the case of abridgment, however, one has to distinguish between 'abridgment of speech' and 'abridgement of freedom of speech'. Moiklejohn put in rightly when he said that the First Amendment to the U.S. Constitution, though couched in most absolute terms, viz., "The Congress shall make no law abridging freedom of speech or Press", did not forbid "abridging of speech" but that it did forbid 'abridging of freedom of speech'. Difficulty may arise in the application of the term 'abridge' where a law, rule or regulation is designed to accomplish an object other than abridgment of freedom of speech and the impact of such law, rule or regulation upon freedom of speech is secondary, incidental or indirect. In such cases the cardinal principle is that there is no abridgment of the freedom unless the 'content' of speech itself is regulated.

IV.21 Economic and tax measures, legislation relating to social welfare and wages, factory laws, etc., may have some effect upon freedom of the Press when applied to persons or institutions engaged in various forms of communication. But where the burden placed on them is the same as that borne by others engaged in different forms of activity, it does not constitute abridgment of freedom of the Press. The use of such measures, however, to control the 'content' of expression would be clearly impermissible.

IV.22 Article 13(2) does not forbid regulation of the exercise of freedom of speech. No doubt, the freedom enjoys the protection of Article 19(1)(a), but the manner of its exercise or its collatoral aspect is beyond the scope of that sub-article. For example, blaring a speech through a microphone in the dead of the night disturbing the sleep of others or littering the streets with copies of the text of a speech could certainly be prohibited by law in spite of Articles 19(1)(a) and 13(2). Regulation does not hinder or curtail freedom of speech, in fact it can help promote freedom of speech. For freedom of speech to be meaningful in an assembly of persons, regulation of 'speech' is absolutely essential if it were not to degenerate into a cacophony of words. A meeting cannot even be opened unless, by common consent, 'speech' is abridged. If one man has the floor, no one else may interrupt him except as provided by the rules. Freedom of speech does not mean that every individual has an inalienable right to speak whatever, whenever, wherever, however he chooses. The commonsense of any reasonable society would deny the existence of any such unbridled right. Thus general regulatory statutes not intended to control the content of speech but incidentally limiting its unfettered exercise do not infringe Article 19(1)(a) when they are justified by valid governmental or societal interests.

IV.27 Journalism is not merely an industry; it is a public service and a profession. The American Commission on Freedom of the Press likened the newspaper industry to a public utility or a public carrier. As our first Press Commission observed, news and views which newspapers sell, serve not only an informative aspect but also an educational and a propagandist aspect. Newspapers influence opinion, conduct and action in political, social, economic and cultural fields. People have vital interest in the accurate and fair presentation of news and views. The news and views which newspapers purvey carry with them a vital public interest that needs to be safeguarded. Whereas profit motive may operate in the public interest in the case of other industries, it may require regulation in the case of newspaper industry. Taking these factors together, there can be no doubt that a newspaper is essentially a public utility and whatever be the precise form of ownership of newspapers, the exercise of ownership rights has to be subject to some measure or restraint and regulation. Public interest is the criterian that should regulate this activity.

IV.29 Thus the Press has a social responsibility and accountability to the public. The theory that the freedom of the Press knows no restraint is gone. The traditional individualistic theory which has inspired the existing law and social attitude is insufficient to meet its problems. That theory emphasized only the freedom of one party, namely the issuer of the news, and completely ignored the other party, namely the public. In the changed situation, the protection of the freedom of the issuer along is not sufficient, the freedom of the consumer must also be protected.

IV.30 The people are wholly dependent on the Press for the primary data of their political thinking. They are not passive renders of news. It is an entire community of varying minds which the Press must serve with its raw material for thought. Between the right of editors and publishers to express themselves, and the right of the public to be served with a substantial and honest basis of facts for judging public affairs, it is the later which today tends to take precedence in importance. A realistic view of Article 19(1)(a) has to recognize that right to expression is somewhat thin if it can be exercised only at the sufferance of the managers of mass communication. While we recognise that the majority in a democracy may occasionally exercise its power to throttle opportunities for discussion, we do not seem to realise that non-governing minorities who control the machinery of communication can also throttle ideas before their birth.

IV.33 There is no reason why the services of the Press should not be available to citizens for exercise of their fundamental right of freedom of speech and expression on a non-discriminatory basis subject, of course, to availability of space and other relevant considerations. A revised, realistic view of Article 19(1)(a) should permit encouragement of expression by providing not only for its protection 'after publication' but also for its 'emergence by publication'. The Press Council should be empowered to look into complaints of arbitrary and *mala fide* denial of access to the Press, Sarvashri Girilal Jain, Rajendra Mathur, S.K. Mukherjea, H.K. Paranjape and Ishrat Ali Siddiqui are not in favour of this recommendation.

(2) *Pre-Censorship*

IV.38 While we do not think it is proper to say that the power of censorship can be exercised only in circumstances which justify the invocation of the provisions relating to declaration of emergency under Article 352 of the Constitution, we think that the power should be invoked only in cases of extreme necessity in the national interest, while the situation cannot be saved without resort to this power. Dr. H.K. Paranjape, disagreeing with this view, holds that precensorship is justified only in times of emergency as defined in the Constitution. He is further of the view that even if Article 19(2) of the Constitution permits censorship at other times, there should be a convention that the power should not be used.

(3) *Right to Information and Official Secrets Act*

IV.52 Section 5 of the Official Secrets Act, 1923 may be repealed and substituted by other provisions suited to meet the paramount need of national security and other vital interest of the State as well as the right of the people to know the affairs of the State affecting them. It is essential, in our view, to restrict the operation of Section 5 by prescribing the types of information which need protection from disclosure. These types or categories will necessarily be broad, but primarily it will be the task of the executive to determine whether a document falls under any of the specified categories. In this respect we think that the provisions of Part II of the British Freedom of Information Bill may be adopted with appropriate modifications and changes. The other provisions in the Official Secrets Act may be carefully examined by an expert body to see which of them deserve modification and thereafter those provisions could also be incorporated in the new legislation proposed.

IV.53-56 Several countries have enacted legislation to ensure a measure of access to the citizen to official information. It is only appropriate that we should have some provision enacted for this purpose. The legislation can be modelled on the provisions of Part I of the British Official Information Bill with appropriate changes. The suggestion in the Bill is that complaints about rejection of an application for official access will lie only to the Parliamentary Commissioner. We think that it is only proper that we adopt this method instead of entrusting the task to the courts. The draftsmen will have to think of a functionary corresponding to the Parliamentary Commissioner in U.K. for entrusting the work of review. Shri K.R. Ganesh is opposed to any legislation to confer the Right to Information in the present situation in which the country is faced, with internal and external threats to its stability and security.

(4) *Disclosure of Sources of Information*

IV.65 We are of the view that there is no absolute immunity for journalists from disclosing their sources of information. However, we have noted section 15(2) of the Press Council Act, 1978 which provides that no newspaper, news agency, editor or journalist shall be compelled by the Council to disclose the source of any news or information. The public interest in the free flow of information and hence in protecting a journalist's source of information has to receive wide recognition in our country. The strength of the public interest involved will vary from case to case. The court will have to weigh in each case the public interest in doing justice in a case against the public interest involved in the free flow of information through protection of the confidential source of information. Sarvashri Girilal Jain, Rajendra Mathur, S.K. Mukherjea, H.K. Paranjape and Ishrat Ali Siddiqui do not agree with this view. They hold that journalists should be compelled to disclose their sources, if at all, in extreme cases only and that too in confidence to a judge or a judicial Officer, and any changes in a laws that may be necessary for this purpose should be made.

(5) *The Law of Defamation*

IV.69-70 We recommend that provisions in Section 4 of the British Defamation Act, 1952, be introduced in India. This Section provides that in a case where a publisher establishes that he unintentionally published words complained of and that he exercised all reasonable care in relation to the publication, he may make an offer to the claimant which would include an offer to publish a suitable correction and an apology. If the offer is accepted, proceeding in respect of the publication are barred. If the offer is rejected, the publisher can plead the rejection of the offer as a defence, provided he establishes in addition to his innocence that the offer was made as soon as practicable after the defendant received notice that the words were defamatory of the plaintiff.

IV.71 We recommend that the adoption of the principle underlined in Section 6 of the British Defamation Act, 1952, in our law of defamation by the enactment of suitable legislation. This Section says that in an action for libel or slander in respect of words consisting party of allegations of fact and partly of expressions of opinion, a defence of far comment shall not fail by reason only that the truth of every allegation of fact is not proved if the expression of opinion is fair comment having regard to such of the facts alleged or referred to in the words complained of as are proved.

IV.72 Section 8 of the British Defamation Act, 1952, provides that a fair and accurate report in any newspaper of proceedings of cases publicly heard before any court exercising judicial authority within the United Kingdom shall, if published contemporaneously, with such proceedings be privileged provided that nothing in the section shall authorise the publication of any blasphemous or indecent matter. The privilege spoken of here is absolute privilege. We recommend that this provision be incorporated in India but dropping the proviso regarding "any blasphemous or indecent matter".

IV.73 We approve the recommendation of the Law Commission of India which, is its 42nd report, suggested the amendment of section 500 of the Indian Penal Code to read as follows:

(i) Whoever defames another shall be punished with imprisonment of either description for a term which may extend to two years, or with fine, or with both;

(ii) Where the offence has been committed by publishing an imputation in a newspaper, the court convicting the offender may further order that its judgment shall be published in whole or in part, in such newspaper as it may specify; and

(iii) The cost of such publication shall be recoverable from the convicted person as a fine."

We do not, however, favour the adoption of the 'explanation' added to the section as passed by the Rajya Sabha on 23rd November, 1978. That explanation reads as follows:

> "The court may, before passing a sentence under this section, take into consideration the question whether the guilt of the accused is aggravated by the plea and the nature of the evidence adduced to prove or disprove it."

IV.74 We recommended that the schedule to the British Defamation Act, 1952, be adopted in India with certain modifications. Part I of the Schedule gives statements having qualified privilege without explanation or contradiction and Part II gives statements privileged subject to explanation or contradiction. We would favour modification of the entries in the Schedule as follows:

PART I

Statements privileged without explanation or contradiction

(1) A fair and accurate report of any proceedings in public of the legislature of any foreign country.

(2) A fair and accurate report of any proceedings in public of an international organisation of which India is a member, or of organisations recognised by the United Nations or of any international conference to which the Government of India sends a representative.

(3) A fair and accurate report of any proceedings in public of an international court.

(4) A fair and accurate report of proceedings before a court of any foreign country.

(5) A fair and accurate report of or an extract from any register kept in pursuance of any Act of Parliament or State Legislature which is open to inspection by the public or of any other document which is required by the law of any part of India to be open to inspection by the public.

(6) A notice or advertisement published by or under the authority of any court, tribunal or commission of enquiry of committee of investigation constituted by any lawful authority in India or any judge or officer of such a court.

PART II

Statements Privileged Subject to Explanation or Contradiction

A fair and accurate report of:

(7) The findings or decisions of any of the following associations or of any committee or governing body thereof, that is to say,

(a) an association formed in India for the purpose of promoting or encouraging the exercise of or interest in any art, science, religion or learning, and empowered by its constitution to exercise control over or adjudicate upon matters of interest or concern to the association, or the actions or conduct of any person subject to such control or adjudication; and

(b) an association formed in India for the purpose of promoting or safeguarding the interests of any game, sport or pastime to the playing or exercise of which members of the public are invited or admitted, and empowered by its constitution to exercise control over or taking part in the game, sport or pastime.

(8) The proceedings of any meeting in any part of India of:

(a) any local authority or committee of a local authority or authorities;

(b) any justice acting otherwise than as a court exercising judicial authority;

(c) any commission, tribunal, committee or person appointed for the purpose of any inquiry under an Act of Parliament or State Legislature by the appropriate government;

(d) any person appointed by a local authority to hold a local inquiry in pursuance of any Act of Parliament or State Legislature; and

(e) any other tribunal, board, committee or body constituted by or under, and exercising functions under an Act of Parliament or State Legislature, not being a sitting admission to which is denied to representatives of newspapers and other members of the public.

(9) Proceedings at a general meeting of a company of association constituted, registered or certified by or under any Act of Parliament or State Legislature, not being a private company within the meaning of the Companies Act.

(10) Any notice or other matter issued for the information of the public by or on behalf of any Government Department, officer of State, local authority or chief officer of police.

There is one other provision in the British Defamation Act, 1952, which extends the privilege subject to explanation or contradiction, i.e., to a fair and accurate report of any public meeting. We feel that it is not desirable to introduce this provision in India.

IV.77 It has been represented to us that truth should not be a complete defence unless it is accompanied by public interest. This question engaged the attention of the Australian Law Reforms Commission and it was of the view that truth, by itself, should be a complete defence in civil actions as 'public benefit' is a vague term and publishers are entitled to a clear guidance as to the rules binding them. The requirement of public benefit would be adding too much of a burden on journalists. We see no reason for any departure from the present position. Truth alone should continue to be a complete defence.

IV.78 In regard to defences in libel cases, we endorse the following recommendations of the Australian Law Reforms Commission:

"The Commission believes that it should be a defence to the publication of defamatory matter that the matter complained of is true. Matter should be regarded as being true if the matter, and any imputation in the matter relied upon in the action by the plaintiff was in substance true or in substance was not materially different from the truth. In determining the effect of the publication for the purpose of assessing damages, the court should have regard to the whole of the publication and the extent to which the defendant proves the truth of the matter concerning the plaintiff in the publication."

IV.79 *Right of Reply :* The law of defamation in India, in common with the law of England, awards damages to redress the wrong done. It makes no use of *recompense* (droit de reponse) or the "right of reply" which is an important remedy in the Continental legal systems. We suggest elsewhere (in the Chapter on the Press as a Public Utility) a limited right of reply and its enforcement through the Press Council.

IV.80 *Place of Filing of Suit :* On the question where a suit for defamation should be filed, we are of the view that the present position should continue. We do not agree with the view that proceedings for defamation against newspapers and periodicals should be initiated in the first instance in a court, civil or criminal, in the State from where the newspaper is published as it will be discriminatory. We, however, think that unless there is a *prima facie* case of malice the Magistrate should dispense with personal appearance of the accused. Clause (1) of section 205 of the Criminal Procedure Code, 1973, may be suitably amended to provide that in criminal complaints for defamation, unless there is a *prima facie* case of malice, the Magistrate shall dispense with the personal attendance of the accused wherever summons is issued and permit him to appear by a pleader; but the Magistrate may not dispense with the personal attendance of the accused, where the accused is an editor, publisher or proprietor of a newspaper or periodical, if he is satisfied that the accused has unreasonably refused to publish, within a reasonable time, a reply of the complainant to the alleged defamatory publication. However, we are not proposing any interference with the wide discretion of the Magistrate conferred by section 205(2) to direct personal attendance of the accused at any subsequent stages of the proceedings.

The Problem of Multiple Publication

IV.81 Regarding the problem of multiple publication we endorse the following recommendation of the Australian Law Commission: "The rule as to separate publication should be abrogated and a single publication rule adopted. The multiple publication of particular material should give rise to one cause of action only but, in such an action, the plaintiff should have relief appropriate to all publications. This rule could, however, give rise to unsatisfactory results where a plaintiff was unaware of the extent of the multiple publication and therefore, did not seek appropriate remedies. The suggestion of allowing the court a discretion to permit the plaintiff to bring further proceedings in respect of the same matter is a flexible approach but it may result in uncertainty. Even after an action is determined, a defendant may be in doubt whether further proceedings may be brought against him. The position of a plaintiff who discovers that a publication received wider coverage than was first apparent is not entirely clear. Certainty is important to the parties. Moreover, it is desirable that the courts have full information as to the extent of publication in determining relief in the first action. The defendant is likely to know the extent of publication; he should be encouraged to disclose it. Accordingly the plaintiff should be limited to a single action in respect of a multiple publication but only to the extent disclosed in the action. The plaintiff will have a separate right of action in respect of any additional publication. This will automatically cover any further publication after the first trail as well as any publications which the defendant failed to admit. The provision will leave no doubt as to the rights of the parties. A defendant who makes full disclosure will be liable, if at all, for the multiple publication ones for all. A plaintiff who discovers undisclosed material is certain that the court will entertain his action.

Joint Responsibility for Publication

IV.82 About joint responsibility for publication, the following statement of law by Gatley is most appropriate:

> "Where a person has published defamatory words on an occasion of qualified privilege the privilege only will only be defeated so far as he is concerned if he himself is malicious, or if he is liable on the basis of respondent-superior for the malice of a servant or agent."

The incorporation of this principle in our law would mean that:

(1) A published of a newspaper will continue to be vicariously responsible for the malice of his agent;
(2) A published of a newspaper will not be vicariously responsible for the malice of an independent contractor; and
(3) A publisher of a newspaper will not be vicariously liable for the malice of an unsolicited correspondent, whether anonymous or otherwise.

IV.83 On the question of liability of distributors and printers, we suggest that the recommendations of the Faulks Committee in England be incorporated in our law. The Committee said that at present distributors of written publication, e.g., booksellers, news-agents and news-vendors enjoy the special defence of innocent dissemination which is not available to the first or main publishers of a work, namely, that:

(a) they did not know that the book or paper contained the libel complained of;
(b) they did not know that the book or paper was of a character likely to contain a libel; and
(c) such want to knowledge was not due to any negligence.

The Faulks Committee recommended the extension of the above defence of innocent dissemination to printers subject to the same or similar conditions or safeguard as in the case of distributors. The Committee said that the result of this recommendation is that, where printers are put on inquiry as to the potentially defamatory character of the work complained of, or are in any way negligent in failing to inquire in relation to any given work, the defence of innocent dissemination will fail; equally, in the normal course of their business of everyday printing they will have a defence which, if the experience of distributions is any guide, will ensure that they are normally not even joined as defendants.

As regards translations, we are of the view that protection should be given to the translator but not to the publication of offending matter in translation.

(6) *Contempt of Court*

IV.88 We think it is not necessary to adopt the summary procedure in vogue for dealing with all cases falling under Section 2(c)(i) of the Contempt of Courts Act, 1971. In the summary contempt procedure, judges sit as judges in their own cause and the defendant cannot lay claim to all the safeguards provided under the normal procedural law. It is only where the offensive conduct or the offending imputations are made in the face of the court or they relate to particular proceedings which are in progress and give rise to a risk of prejudice to the proceedings on hand that the application of the summary procedure would be justified on the ground of urgency. We therefore, recommend that the application of Section 2(c)(i) should be restricted to such cases only and the Act should be amended accordingly. A new criminal offence should be created to take care of all other cases of contempt falling under Section 2(c)(i). The new offence should be constituted by the Publication in whatever form of matter imputing improper or corrupt judicial conduct with the intention of impairing confidence in the administration of justice. It should be triable only on prosecution. As the offence would be one which struck generally at the administration of justice, prosecution should only be at the instance of the Attorney General/Advocate General. As regards defence for the new offence, we agree with the view of the Phillimore Committee in the United Kingdom that if a defendant were to prove the truth of his allegation and also show that its publication was for the public benefit, he should be entitled to an acquittal. In our view, the creation of the new offence with the defence suggested above would go a long way in removing the complaint that the summary procedure adopted for trying contempt cases inhibits honest and truthful criticism of the administration of justice in public interest.

IV.99 The definition of Criminal Contempt in sub-clauses (ii) and (iii) of Section 2(c) has to be amended. At present, every publication which howsoever minutely interferes or tends to interfere with a pending judicial proceedings technically constitutes 'contempt' under these sub-clauses, although it does not become punishable under Section 13 unless the interference is substantial. We do not see any reason why a publication should constitute a technical 'contempt' unless it is also punishable under the Act. This could lead to unnecessary harassment of newspapers. We recommend that the definition in sub-clauses (ii) and (iii) of Section 2(c) should be tightened by making it clear that it is only a substantial interference that constitutes contempt under the Act. If this change is effected in the definition itself there will be no need to retain section 13 in the Act. The wording of Section 3 will also need consequential changes.

IV.103 Journalists sometimes investigate suspected crimes malpractices and abuses and accumulate evidence. Publication of such material is often in the public interest and also helps in boosting the circulation of the newspaper. The law of contempt does not hinder publication of such accumulated evidence before the accused are arrested and charged. But when once judicial proceedings are set in motion the Press should not publish the evidence. When a person is being tried for an offence, if the Press has evidence that some other person is guilty of the crime, propriety would demand that the evidence in the possession of the Press be placed before the Court. By adopting such a course it will get the credit for its investigative effort though the advantage of increased circulation through publication exclusively in its columns would be lost.

IV.104-105 Publication of comments on or criticism of public utterances of judges is not contempt because the judge sheds his mantle as a judge when he enters the public arena of debate. The Press, however, must at all times act in a responsible manner. The Press should eschew use of immoderate language, the tendency to give a slant to the copy and sensationalising events with a view to increasing circulation or satisfying the sadistic curiosity of the public.

(7) *Contempt of Legislature*

IV.110 From the point of view of freedom of the Press it is essential that the privileges of Parliament and State legislature should be codified as early as possible.

IV.118 We agree with the observations summarised below of the Select Committee appointed by the House of Commons in 1966 on the law of Parliamentary Practice. The Committee said that the use of the word 'privilege, could convey to the public generally the false impression that members were and desired to be a 'privileged class'. It emphasized the fundamental principle that 'privileges' were not the prerogative of members in their personal capacities but were claimed and enjoyed by the House in its corporate capacity and by its members on behalf of the citizens whom they represented. The Committee favoured the discontinuance of the use of the term 'privilege'. Accordingly the Committee preferred to refer to "The right and immunities" of Parliament and its members, rather than their "rights and privileges" to "Contempt of the House" rather than to "breach of privilege"; and to speak generally of the "penal jurisdiction of Parliament" rather than the power to punish for "breach of privilege". The Committee said that regard must be had to the importance of preserving freedom of speech in matters of political controversy. According to the Committee, the law of parliamentary privilege was not, except in the clearest case, to be invoked so as to inhibit or discourage the formation and free expression of opinion outside the House by members equally with other citizens in relation to the conduct of the affairs of the nation. It was of the view that the law of parliamentary privileges should not be administered in a way which would fetter or discourage the free expression of opinion or criticism, however prejudiced or exaggerated such opinion or criticism might be. We endorse the following recommendations of the Committee for adoption by our Parliament and State Legislatures:

(1) The penal jurisdiction of the House should be exercised as

sparingly as possible and only when the House is satisfied that to exercise it is essential in order to provide reasonable protection for the House, its members or its officers, from such improper obstruction or attempt at or threat of obstruction as is causing or is likely to cause interference with the performance of their respective functions.

(2) In the ordinary case where a member has a remedy in courts he should not be permitted to invoke the penal jurisdiction of the House in lieu of or in addition to that remedy.

(3) The penal jurisdiction should never be exercised in respect of complaints which appear to be of a trivial character or unworthy of the attention of the House. Such complaints should be summarily dismissed without the benefit of investigation by the House or its Committee.

(4) In general, the power to commit for contempt should not be used as a deterrent against a person exercising a legal right, whether well-founded or not, to bring legal proceedings against a member or an officer.

(5) It should be open to the Housing in deciding whether or not a contempt has been committed to take into account an honest and reasonable plea in the truth of the allegations made, provided that they have been made only after all investigations had taken place, had been made in the honest and reasonable belief that it was in the public interest to make them, and had been published in a manner reasonably appropriate to that public interest. If the person against whom the complaint has been made is able to satisfy the House of all these matters, he cannot be said to have improperly obstructed or attempted improperly to obstruct the House and ought accordingly to be acquitted of contempt.

(6) The following conduct should not of itself be regarded as being capable of constituting a contempt of the House:

(i) To publish, in advance of the publication of the relevant papers: (a) how any member in fact voted in a division; (b) the content of any parliamentary question or notice or motion which has in fact been tabled; and

(ii) To publish the expressed intention of a member to vote in a particular manner (or to abstain from voting) or to table a particular parliamentary question or notice of motion.

(7) The type of contempt likely to be committed in modern times

can often best be dealt with by a fine. Moreover, it is the only penalty which can be imposed upon a limited company or other corporate body.

(8) The House should enjoy the power to remit, suspend or vary any penalty which it has imposed, upon receiving adequate undertakings from the person found guilty of contempt or for other good cause.

However, Sarvashri P.V. Gadgil, Rajendra Mathur, Girilal Jain, Ishrat Ali Siddiqui and Dr. H.K. Paranjape are of the view that a legislature should not have the penal power of a court of law, and that a person can be punished for contempt of a legislature only by a court of law and after the privileges of that legislature have been codified.

IV.121-122 The protection conferred by Article 361-A inserted by the Constitution (44th Amendment) Act, 1978 extends to news agency reports containing material for publication in a newspaper. The Article, however, does not apply to the publication of any report of the proceedings of a secret sitting. The provision in Article 361-A, being a constitutional provision, overrides section 499 of the Indian Penal Code.

Shri P.V. Gadgil holds that Article 361-A is not valid and its enactment is open to challenge on legal grounds. He has elaborated the point in a separate note. He is of the view that this Article should be repealed because it enables newspapers to indulge in character assassination. We do not, however, share this view. The citizen has a right to know what his representative says in the legislature. It should be noted that a publication with malice is not protected under Article 361-A. We think the remedy for the malady pointed out by Shri Gadgil lies in preventing members from making false and reckless allegations on the floor of the House by the stricter enforcement of procedural rules governing proceedings of Parliament and State legislatures.

IV.128 The rules of business of the Houses of Parliament and State legislatures in India dealing with the procedure for taking action against alleged breaches of privilege, etc., should be reviewed for necessary provisions incorporated therein to provide for a reasonable opportunity to alleged contemners to defend themselves in the proceedings for breach of privilege. While doing so, the principles enunciated by the Supreme Court in *Maneka Gandhi v. Union of India* (1978), particularly those relating to the requirements of natural justice, will have to be kept in view. The rules framed should not violate the fundamental rights. A limitation of one year should be prescribed for taking cognizance of publication of offending material in the newspapers on the ground of breach of privilege. The right of the Press to be present in the legislature, as in the courts, should be recognised.

IV.129-130 About publication of expunged matter we reiterate the view of the First Press Commission that unintentional and unavoidable transgressions of the rulings of the Chair, such as publication of the proceedings of the legislature before the order of the presiding officer expunging those proceedings reached the newspaper offices, should not be regarded as a breach of the privileges of the House. The Press should not publish expunged portions of the proceedings of a legislature. An expunged portion does not form part of the 'proceedings' and its publication is not saved by Article 361-A. A publication of an expunged portion of the proceedings of the house of Commons in U.K. is recognised as a breach of privilege and it should be so in India in view of the latter part of clause (3) of Articles 105 and 194 of the Constitution. However, Dr. H.K. Paranjape is of the view that a newspaper should have the right to publish even those portions which have been expunged, because the citizens of the country have a right to be informed of the activities of their representatives in Parliament and the State legislature.

(8) *The Press and Registration of Books Act, 1867*

IV.137 The terms 'daily newspaper', 'news magazine' and 'periodical' should be separately defined. A printed or cyclostyled work containing public news or comments on pubic news which is published every day or at least six days in a week may come within the category of 'daily newspaper'. Any other printed or cyclostyled periodical containing public news or comments on public news may come within the category of 'news magazine'. All printed periodical publications which do not contain public news or comments on public news to any significant extent may come under the term 'periodical'. We recommend enactment of separate sets of provisions for the registration of these three categories of publication in three separate registers to be maintained by the Press Registrar. Classification of a paper as 'daily newspaper' or 'news magazine' or 'periodical' by the Press Registrar should be done after one month from the date of publication in the case of dailies and after the publication of two issues in the case of other periodicals. When this recommendation is carried out, the entries in the existing register of newspapers will have to be transferred to the appropriate registers.

IV.138 The expression "Registrar of Newspapers for India" wherever occurring in the Act should be substituted by the expression "Press Registrar" which we think is more appropriate.

IV.139 The Act should provide for the appointment of a person with suitable background or experience, and for a tenure of five years as Press Registrar. This will conduce to a professional approach and autonomous functioning.

IV.141-142 The procedure prescribed for making a declaration in respect of a newspaper under the Act requires revision. We suggest that the onus of getting clearance of the title should be thrown on the printer/publisher. The intending printer/publisher should ascertain from the Press Registrar that the title of the newspaper intended to be published is not the same as or similar to that of any other newspaper and make a solemn affirmation in this behalf through an affidavit. The declaration required to be made under Section 5(2) by the printer/publisher could also be made in the form of an affidavit and sent by registered post to the specified Magistrate. We are of the view that there is no need for personal appearance before the Magistrate for this purpose. After sending the declaration and the affidavit regarding title to the Magistrate by registered post, the printer/publisher should be free to commence the publication. Under the scheme of the Act, the requirement of prior authentication for commencing publication has been laid down to enable the Magistrate to ascertain from the Press Registrar whether the proposed title is free. Now, when the intending publisher testifies that the proposed title is free through an affidavit, there will be no reason for insisting on prior authentication for commencing publication. As it is, when once the title is reported to be free, the Magistrate has no discretion in the matter of authentication. We recommend that the District Magistrate should, after authenticating a declaration, send an attested copy to the Press Registrar.

IV.144 The recommended modification of the procedure for making declarations in respect of newspapers will involve amendment of the following provisions of the Act:

(i) Proviso to Section 6 and sub-section (2c) of Section 5 will have to be deleted;

(ii) A new sub-section will have to be inserted in Section 5 with the provision that the intending printer/publisher should inquire and make sure from the Press Registrar that the proposed title of the newspaper is not the same as or similar to that of any other newspaper published either in the same language or in the same State;

(iii) Sub-section (2) of Section 5 will have to be modified by deleting words requiring personal appearance before the Magistrate for making the declaration and inserting the provision for making the declaration through an affidavit and sending it to the specified Magistrate by registered post accompanied by another affidavit solemnly affirming that the proposed title of the newspaper to be published is not the same as or similar to that of any other newspaper published either in the same language or in the same State; and

(iv) The words requiring personal appearance for making the declaration contemplated in section 8 will have to be deleted therefrom and the provision enabling making of the said declaration by an affidavit and sending the same by registered post to the specified Magistrate will have to be inserted in that section.

IV.145 Sub-section (5) of Section 5 which prescribes time limits for commencement of publications, after authentication of the declaration, for newspapers of different periodicities may be amended so as to provide for a uniform time limit of six months in the case of all newspapers irrespective of their periodicity and a discretion in the Magistrate to extend the period for reasons to be recorded in writing. We are recommending the discretion to be vested in the Magistrate in order to take care of situation where there is unavoidable delay in the procurement of machinery, securing power or for other reasons.

IV.146 We recommend amendment of sub-section (7) of Section 5 on the following lines: In the case of a daily newspaper, the declaration should cease to have effect if the publication does not come out (except owing to strike, lock-out, go-slow, power shortage or similar cause) for a month; in all other cases, the time limit should be three months from the due date of the next issue, again excepting reasons beyond the publisher's control. The reasons should be recorded.

IV.147 We recommend deletion of Sections 8B(i) and 15(2) which we consider to be too drastic.

IV.148 Under the existing provisions of Section 8B the Magistrate is not bound to record his reasons for cancelling a declaration. We recommend that the wording of the section should be amended so as to ensure that the Magistrate records his reasons for cancellation of the declaration.

IV.149 The publisher of every newspaper is bound to furnish to the Press Registrar under section 19E read with Sections 19D and 19B(2) such returns, statistics and other information as may be required. We found that information such as the number of persons employed, the capital invested, and the capacity of the machinery in use were not available in the records of the Press Registrar. These can be obtained by adding suitable entries in Form I of the Schedule to the Registration of Newspapers (Central) Rules, 1956.

IV.150 We recommend that, if necessary, the Companies Act and other Acts should be amended to make it obligatory for newspaper companies to maintain techno-economic data including editionwise and publication-wise financial data in proper form and make it available when required. Similarly, if necessary, Section 19B(2) may be amended by addition of entries relating to techno-economic data in the list of particulars mentioned therein. Supply of techno-economic information by the publishers of newspapers to the Press Registrar not only in respect of individual publication but also in respect of separate editions of the same newspaper brought out from different centres, whether by conventional methods of printing or by fascimile reproduction, should be made obligatory.

IV.151 The Act should have a provision under which it should be possible for the Press Registrar to obtain regular information about the volume of advertising revenue of newspapers from the advertising agencies operating in the country.

IV.152 We recommend that the power to impose a fine under Section 19K of the Act for failure to furnish information required by the Press Registrar may be vested in the Press Registrar himself instead of the Magistrate, by a suitable amendment.

IV. 153 A specific provision may be incorporated in the Act providing that whenever a declaration in respect of a newspaper ceases to have effect under any provision of the Act, or becomes void under any provision of the Act, or is cancelled under any provision of the Act, the right to publish under a particular title automatically comes to an end and the title of such a newspaper becomes free. Any intending publisher can file a declaration claiming that title. However, in the case of cessation of publication of a newspaper, its title should not be available to a claimant before the expiry of a period of one year from the date of cessation of its publication.

IV.156 The provisions of the Act should be uniformly referred as "Sections" and not "rules".

IV.157 We recommend that Section 8C of the Act which provides for the constitution by the Central Government of an Appellate Board to consider appeals against the order of a Magistrate refusing to authenticate a declaration under Section 6 or cancelling a declaration under Section 8B may be amended in view of Section 27 of the Press Council Act, 1978. Consequently Section 27 of the Press Council Act, 1978 may be deleted.

(9) *Post and Telegraph Acts*

IV.158-159 Government should continue to have the power of intercepting telegraph messages in a public emergency or in the interest of public safety. Public emergency need not be confined to emergency arising from war or external aggression or armed rebellion justifying the proclamation of an emergency under Article 352 of the Constitution. An emergency may arise in a locality which is likely to have its repercussions in other parts of the country. The power of interception must be vested in the Government to be exercised in appropriate cases in the interest of maintaining and ensuring public safety. In a vast country like India, a power of this nature cannot be exercised solely by Government, i.e., by the responsible Minister concerned. The power will necessarily have to be delegated to local officers. But the delegation of power must be for short periods only and clear instructions should be issued by the Government to the delegated authorities to prevent misuse of the power.

IV.160 The appropriate Government should declare the existence of the public emergency by a notification warranting the exercise of this power and it is only after the issue of such a notification that the power of withholding telegraphic messages should be exercised by the delegated authority.

IV.162 Whenever the power is exercised in the interest of public safety, it should, as far as possible, be exercised by the concerned Minister of the appropriate Government for one month at a time extendable by Government if the emergency continues. However, in exceptional circumstances the power can be delegated to the District

Magistrate.

IV.163 As soon as an order is passed by the District Magistrate withholding the transmission of a telegraphic message, it should be communicated to the Central or State Government, as the case may be, and also to the sender and the addressee of the telegram. The text of the order should be placed on the table of the respective State legislatures after three months. We recommend that, as suggested by the Press Council of India in its annual report covering 1969, the officer in-charge of a telegraph office should maintain a register giving particulars of the time of receipt, the sender and addressee of every telegram which he refers to the District Magistrate with recommendations of its withholding. Similarly, the District Magistrate should maintain a register of the time of receipt, content and addressee of each such telegram and record his decision thereon, together with the time of the decision. Data of this nature will help courts, if called upon, to determine the presence or absence of *mala fide* in the withholding of telegrams.

IV. 166 We recommend that the telephones may not be tapped except in the interest of national security, public order, investigation of crime and similar objectives, under orders made in writing by the Minister concerned or and officer of rank to whom the power in that behalf is delegated. The order should disclose reasons. An order for tapping of telephones should expire after three months from the date of the order. Moreover, within a period of six weeks the order should come up for review before a Board constituted on the lines prescribed in statutes providing for preventive detention. It should be for the Board to decide whether tapping should continue for longer. The decision of the Board should be binding on the Government.

The Minister or his delegate will be competent to issue a fresh order for tapping of the telephone if circumstances call for it. The Telegraph Act should contain a clause to give effect to this recommendation.

IV.167-169 We recommend that insertion of the words "in the interests of the sovereignty and integrity of India, the security of the State, friendly relations with foreign States or public order or for preventing incitement to the commission of an offence "in Section 26 of the Post Office Act. The exercise of the power under this section should be subject to the safeguards recommended by us with regard to the exercise of the power under Section 5(2) of the Telegraph Act. Appropriate amendments may be made in the provisions of Section

5(2) of the Telegraph Act and Section 26 of the Post Office Act.

(10) *Industries (Development and Regulation) Act, 1951*

IV.170-171 The Act gives the Central Government power to take over industrial undertakings included in the First Schedule of the Act without investigation under certain circumstances. An amendment to the Act in 1979 included a number of additional industries in the First Schedule, among them "Printing including litho printing industry". We recommend an addition after this of the words: "other than printing presses used mainly for printing newspapers".

CHAPTER V

PRESSURES ON THE PRESS

V.4 We are of the view that public opinion should assert itself to restrain misguided elements among the public from exercising their disagreement with newspaper reports through physical violence against the premises or property of the newspaper or its editor or employees rather than sending a rejoinder for publication or making a complaint to the Press Council or availing of a remedy provided under the law of the land.

V.6 Political parties and trade union leaders should not for political reasons utilise their following among newspaper employees or hawkers to hinder the publication and/or distribution of any newspaper. We do not refer here to the normal processes of collective bargaining.

V.14 We are of the view that editorial functioning should be insulated from proprietorial pressure irrespective of whether such pressure is exerted on behalf of private business interests or on behalf of governmental authorities.

V.15 There have been allegations of governmental inaction during outbreak of mob violence against newspaper offices and staff, e.g., during the *gherao* of Bangalore newspapers in September 1980. All such allegations have to be investigated by the Press Council and appropriate action recommended against those found guilty of inaction. Public opinion should assert itself, in the legislatures and through the press, to impress upon all concerned the need for observing the distinction between party and Government and of fulfilling the paramount task of maintaining law and order.

V.21 Selective invocation of provisions of various laws relating to the Press have been cited by witnesses. Partisan and politically motivated invocation of the provisions of laws by governments of different political complexions hardly promotes respect for the rule of law. Fair and evenhanded implementation of laws is essential for the independence of newspapers.

V.22 The Press should be able to resist not only external pressure but also inducements which would undermine its independence from within. Journalists should be on guard against the temptation to enjoy favours, whether from Government authorities, employers, advertisers or others.

CHAPTER VI

RIGHT TO PRIVACY

VI.30 The Indian Penal Code (Amendment) Bill, 1978, which incorporated the recommendations of the Law Commission in respect of invasions of privacy and which lapsed with the dissolution of the last Lok Sabha, may be reintroduced in Parliament as early as possible.

VI.38 Legislation incorporating a general right to privacy may not be advisable.

VI.41 The Press Council could appropriately be entrusted with the task of taking cognizance of complaints of unfair publication relating to matters concerning privacy. We suggest that in Section 13(2)(c) of the Press Council Act, 1978, the phrase "including respect for privacy" may be added between "public taste" and "and foster".

VI.42 Sensitive private facts relating to the health, private behaviour, home life or personal or family relationships should not be published except when it is in public interest to do so if the publication of these facts is likely to cause distress, annoyance or embarrassment to the person or persons concerned. Disclosure of remote criminal proceedings should be avoided.

Appropriation of the name identity, reputation or likeness of an individual for commercial or political purposes or for advancement of one's career or advancement in public life should be treated as objectionable. The facets of 'public interest' dealt with in the exceptions to section 499 IPC (defamation) should be utilised in deciding whether the publication is in public interest or not.

A matter may be said to relate to public interest if it belongs to one of the following categories:

(a) conduct of a public servant in the discharge of his public functions, or his character in-so-far as his character appears in that conduct, and no further;
(b) conduct of any person touching any public question, or his character insofar as his character appears in that conduct, and no further;
(c) any performance which its author has submitted to the judgment of the public, or the character of the author of the performance insofar as his character appears in such performance, and no further;
(d) matters arising out of any authority conferred by law or contract on one person to pass, in good faith, any censure on the conduct of another person, in matters to which such lawful authority relates;
(e) matter concerning any accusation made against any person to a person who has lawful authority over the person, with respect to the subject-matter of the accusation;
(f) matter concerning other matters which have been already dealt with–
    (i) before a court in judicial proceedings not held *in camera*, or
    (ii) before Parliament or Legislature in proceedings not held *in camera*, or
    (iii) before a public body or public servant in any proceedings not held in private; and
(g) Other matters not enumerated above, where it is for the public good that the information (though non-defamatory) may be published. This would include matters whose publication is necessary by way of a reflection on character or caution.

Apart from the plea of public interest, the following may be deemed as valid defence against a complaint of invasion of privacy:

(i) consent to publication,
(ii) availability of published matter from public record open to public inspection,
(iii) innocent publication, i.e., publication where the publisher did not know or had no reason to believe that it would cause distress, annoyance or embarrassment to particular

individuals;

(iv) matters published under legal authority to which a claim of privilege, as understood in the law of defamation, applies; and

(v) publication which is for the protection of the publisher himself.

VI.43 The Law Commission has recommended legislation intended to make a beginning with those invasions which amount to eaves-dropping and unauthorised publication of photographs. We endorse its recommendation that the Indian Penal Code be amended to include "offence against privacy".

VI.44 We are of the view that the Press should not be unduly inhibited in performing its important function of giving news in the public interest as distinct from news that may pander to prurient or morbid curiosity. But a correct balance has to be struck between the citizen's claim to privacy and the public's right to information.

CHAPTER VII

FREEDOM AND RESPONSIBILITY : ROLE OF THE PRESS COUNCIL

VII.1 The Press Council has functioned for 15 years. Within the limits set by the legislation its has done useful work and we recommend that the institution should continue.

VII.23 and 25 The Press Council has suggested to the Government that the 1978 Act be amended to empower it to recommend to the Central or State Governments, public sector undertakings, etc., stoppage of issue of advertisements, or disallowing any provision for growth in circulation in the matter of allocation of newsprint or suspension of concessional rates of postage, for a specified period, in the case of newspapers which are censured thrice. In the case of journalists and editors who are held by the Council thrice to have violated the accepted the principles of journalistic ethics, the Council desires to have the power to deny facilities of accreditation for a specified period. The Council has urged that it should be made obligatory on the part of the concerned authorities to carry out its directions in this behalf. We recommend that the Press Council be given the powers sought by it with the modification that a newspaper would invite sanction if it comes to the adverse notice of the Council thrice, whether by way of disapproval, warning, admonition or censure. Once these powers are given, it becomes essential to expressly provide in the Act that the Chairman of the Press Council should have a judicial background and should preferably be a retired judge of the Supreme Court. Sarvashri Girilal Jain, S.K. Mukherjea and H.K. Paranjape do not agree that the Press Council should be given penal powers.

VII.26 We are of the view that Section 15(4) of the Press Council Act, 1978, which empowers the Press Council to "make such observations, as it may think fit, in any of its decisions or reports, respecting the conduct of any authority including Government" is an adequate. We recommend that such observations should, as early as possible, be placed before both Houses of Parliament or the State Legislature as the case may be.

VII.32 We are of the view that it would not be desirable to draw up a code of ethics for newspapers. Such a code could be built up case by case over a period of time.

VII.35 The Press Council has suggested that it should be consulted on all proposed legislation concerning the Press. We endorse this suggestion.

VII.36 We recommend that the Research Section of the Council should be strengthened so that it can take up further studies on problems relating to the Press on a continuing basis.

VII.38 We are of the view that the Press Council's approach to complaints involving allegations of foreign money in the Indian Press. . . . should not be technical but substantive.

VII.39 In order to curb the influence of foreign money on the Press, we recommend the following five steps and the enactment of any necessary changes in laws for the purpose:

(i) There should be a specific legal provision under which no newspaper undertaking should have any foreign ownership either in the form of shares or in the form of loans;

(ii) Advertisement as well as printing contracts from foreign sources should be on terms no different from those applicable to similar work done for others;

(iii) Advertisement rates must be published each year, and on every revision, and there should be no discrimination in their application to foreign advertisers;

(iv) Once a year every newspaper should publish its profit and loss account, with separate information about foreign and Indian sources; and

(v) Every newspaper undertaking must submit with its annual account the following information to the Press Council:

  (a) Details of revenue obtained from advertisements and printing contracts in respect of foreign sources country-wise, including advertisements or printing contracts received through an Indian agency; and

  (b) names of the top 100 shareholders with their nationality and address and the number and proportion of shares held.

VII.41 and 42 The subject of training in journalism has not been included among the function of the Press Council listed in the Press Council Act 1978. We consider it desirable that the 1978 Act be amended so as to entrust the Press Council with the function of keeping under continuous review the adequacy and quality of journalism training facilities in the country, particularly in Indian languages, and suggestion improvements.

VII.44 We recommend that the Press Council should enter into arrangements with selected University departments of journalism, Indian Institute of Mass Communication, Press Institute of India and any other suitable organisations that can be relied on to take up the work of monitoring the performance of newspapers in respect of important issues from time to time in a given language or languages. We recommend that adequate funds should be made available to the Press Council to organise the monitoring of Press performance.

VII.48 It is desirable for the Press Council to secure information each year on the membership, finances and activities of the various associations that are notified for invitation to forward panels of names for the constitution of the Press Council.

VII.49 We recommend a suitable amendment in the Press Council Act so as to provide for the retirement of members by rotation in the interest of continuity.

VII.53 We welcome the efforts being made by the Press Council to become financially self-reliant. The Press Council's resources will be further augmented if the Government acts on the recommendations we make, in the Chapter on "Official Agencies and the Press", for the levy of a cess on newsprint consumption and a tax on newspaper advertisements, the yield from both to be earmarked in appropriate proportions for the Press Council and for the proposed Newspaper Development Commission.

CHAPTER VIII

OFFICIAL AGENCIES AND THE PRESS

(i) *Press Registrar*

VIII.4 In cases where claims of circulation certified by Chartered Accountants are found to be inflated, the Press Registrar should systematically apprise the Institute of Chartered Accountants of the situation. Disciplinary action should be taken, where it is justified, against Chartered Accountants who give false certificates of newspaper circulation.

VIII.5 The Press Registrar should pay greater attention to verification of the regularity of publication of newspapers. A newspaper which does not come out regularly cannot be regarded as a genuine newspaper.

VIII.7 It will be useful to set up an Advisory Committee of experts to assist the Press Registrar in the discharge of his non-statutory functions.

VIII.9 It is necessary to weed out from the Press Registrar's register non-existent publications and publications which are not brought out in conformity with the Press and Registration of Books Act. It is also necessary to obviate complaints of delay in disposing of inquiries relating to clearance of titles from intending printers/publishers and in issuing certificates of registration. There is need therefore to strengthen the organisation of the Press Registrar. We recommend the sanction of an adequate number of regional officers who should be conversant with the languages of the region to which they are posted.

VIII.10 The Annual Reports of the Press Registrar should contain data on some important aspects of the Press, for example the average page level of individual publications. He should keep himself informed of all significant developments in the field of newspaper publication including developments in printing technology. It will be useful for him to have a statistical and economic cell. He should also have information on the profile of readership of newspapers. The Press Registrar should take steps to speed up the printing of his annual reports.

(iii) *Communications*

VIII.17 Transmission of Press telegrams should be given the highest possible priority.

VIII.20 The Government should sympathetically consider the demand for lowering the postal tariff for newspapers.

VIII.22 For change in the posting date, the power to waive the condition of three days' notice should be delegated further down to as lower a level – Post Masters or Sub-Post Masters – as possible.

VIII.24 The Railway authorities should take special steps to see that the departmental instructions giving the highest priority to transportation of newspapers are observed.

VIII.25 A few contractors have a monopoly in vending newspapers at railway stations. We are of the view that as far as possible, this monopoly should be broken and competition encouraged. There should be at least two competing book-stalls at big railway stations.

(iv) *Accreditation of Correspondents*

VIII.34 Representation of all recognised organisations on the Accreditation Committee should be on a uniform scale. There is also need to review the representative character of different organisations from time to time so that the Committee enjoys the confidence of the profession. This review can appropriately be done by the Press Council.

VIII.38-39 Accreditation should be retained as a facilitating measure; it should not mean that the door is not open to genuine journalists other than accredited correspondents. We are of the view that the editor of a paper should get accreditation if he seeks it. Accreditation in the case of editors should ordinarily be limited to dailies and news agencies.

VIII.41 In Delhi as well as in State and Union Territory headquarters, Information Department offices are generally located in secretariat buildings, entry to which is regulated. There is need for free access to such offices.

(v) *Housing and Travel Facilities for Journalists*

VIII.49 We recommend that no further housing facility should be provided to journalists and that the existing allotments of government accommodation in the national capital and the States should be charged for at non-subsidised rates and phased out as the present occupants leave. Shri R.K. Ganesh and Girilal Jain do not agree with this recommendation.

(vi) *Newspaper Finance: Loans and Development Assistance*

VIII.61 We are of the view that there is no justification for excluding newspaper establishments from assistance for acquiring printing machinery through the National Small Industries Corporation.

VIII.64 Indian and Eastern Newspapers Society (IENS) pointed out that because of the long credit period (generally of 75 days) that is available for advertisements released through the accredited advertising agencies, the working capital requirements of newspapers are larger than those of most other industries. IENS wanted the large margin requirements or this type of cash credit from the banks to be reduced substantially. It also wanted the Bill Market Scheme of the Reserve Bank of India to be made applicable in the case of the sale of advertisements space by newspapers. IENS wanted commercial banks to give working capital to the industry against that large inventory of raw materials maintained by it. We recommend that these suggestions may be considered with sympathy.

VIII.65 Those small and medium newspapers which come within the definition of small scale industry should be treated as such and enabled to get loans at the rate of interest applicable to small scale units.

VIII.73 In the prevailing atmosphere of animosity between political parties and the tendency to exercise executive discretion for the advantage of the party for the time being in power, a system of direct financial subsidy to individual newspapers would be liable to be misused.

VIII.74 We see no need for a separate financial corporation for small and medium newspapers. There should be a priority status to small and medium newspaper undertakings for credit from the nationalised banks, State Finance Corporations and institutions for the promotion of small-scale industries, subject to the conditions as regards creditworthiness, security, etc.

Newspaper Development Commission

VIII.75 to 79 There is need for a body which will promote the development of the Press as a whole, as distinct from individual newspapers. The promotional effort we envisage will be in directions which will facilitate the growth in particular of Indian-language newspapers of whatever circulation category, and of local interest and other publications of small and medium size in terms of circulations. We recommend the establishment, for the purpose, of a Newspaper Development Commission which will offer its assistance on a generalised, non-discriminatory and non-discretionary basis. The objects which we envisage for the Commission are:

(i) To promote R&D in the newspaper industry, particularly research in and development of teleprinters in Indian Languages and of composing and printing technologies suitable for small and medium newspapers;

(ii) To promote the development of Indian language news agencies and to oversee the financial health of news agencies in respect of their domestic operations and the rates of subscription available to them from newspapers and Government subscribers such as AIR & Doordarshan;

(iii) To provide development assistance to the Press, especially to small and medium newspapers, through such means as the provision of subsidised teleprinter services on a non-discriminatory basis;

(iv) To arrange supply to newsprint to newspapers, other than those belonging to newspaper chains, in interior or remote areas at prices comparable to those prevailing at port-towns;

(v) To assist the emergence and growth of daily newspapers in remote and interior areas by subsidising the extension of the news agencies' teleprinter links;

(vi) To assist in obtaining for newspapers and news agencies reasonable tariffs for internal and external communication;

(vii) To appraise proposals for the publication of daily newspapers by the Government in areas without a daily Press, and, if the Commission approves the proposal, to advise on the kind of newspaper that should be brought out;

(viii) To liaise with various Government Departments concerned with the needs of the newspaper industry;

(ix) To promote and coordinate training in journalism (including of *'katibs'* for Urdu papers) in case the Press Council does not assume this function as recommended by us in Chapter VII;

(x) To provide financial assistance through grants to institutions engaged in R & D in newspaper publishing;

(xi) To commission studies relevant to the promotion of the above objects; and

(xii) To undertake such other functions as the Commission considers to be appropriate in pursuance of the above objectives.

Dr. H. K. Paranjape is not in favour of item (xii).

Composition

(1) The Commission should be headed by a full-time Chairman. He should be a person with experience of finance, industry, development administration or newspaper management and generally well versed in public life but not connected with any newspaper undertaking at the time of appointment.

(2) Two whole-time members (Managing Directors): one of them should be an expert in economics, finance and accounts; and the other an expert in journalism in particular and mass communication in general.

(3) Three representatives from newspaper organisation like IENS, ILNA and AISMNA.

(4) Three representatives of Working Journalists, provided that at least two of them shall be persons with wide professional background in Indian language journalism.

(5) Chairman of the Press Council or his nominee.

(6) Chairman of the Indian Institute of Mass Communication Society or his nominee.

(7) One representative each from the Ministries of Information & Broadcasting, Finance and Industry.

Membership of the Commission should be rotational, with one-third of the Members retiring every year or every two years.

Funding

In addition to an initial grant by the Government, the Commission should be funded through a small cess on all newsprint consumption by newspapers (including newspapers whose average page level is 12 pages or less); and a tax on the advertisement revenue of newspapers with suitable exemption limit. For earmarking income from a tax on advertisement revenue for the Commission, an amendment of the Constitution will be needed, Sub-clause (f) of Clause (1) of Article 269 (namely, "tax on the sale or purchase of newspapers and on advertisements published therein") will have to be deleted and suitable amendment made to ensure that the advertisement revenue is given to the Newspaper Development Commission. By this the States will not lose anything that they presently enjoy, since this taxation power had not been exercised by the Government of India over the last three decades.

The Newspaper Development Commission may set up Advisory Councils for each language. There can be more than one body for languages such as Hindi, English and Urdu which are multi-State languages. The Advisory Councils should consist on journalists and persons eminent in the literary and cultural fields.

The Advisory Councils set up by the Newspaper Development Commission could be consulted by financial institutions on the quality of a newspaper seeking credit.

VIII.84-85 The whole purpose of allotting land to newspaper undertakings at concessional rates would be defeated if the income derived from land and buildings built on them is not utilised for development of the newspaper or newspapers concerned. The Central Government in the Union Territories and the State Governments should go into this matter and take appropriate action wherever it is found that the lease agreements have been violated. Dr. Paranjape is of the view that the Press Commission need not concern itself with punishment for violation of the terms of agreements, which is a normal duty of the authorities.

VIII.86 In view of the possibility of discrimination in the allotment of Government land directly to newspapers at concessional rates, we recommend that in future all such allotments should be done through the Newspaper Development Commission, which should also monitor their utilisation for approved purposes.

(viii) *Advertising from Public Funds*

VIII.109-110 We broadly agree that advertisement should be considered as a means of communication and should be directed to newspapers according to the audience intended to be reached. We are of the view that advertisement should not be used as a means of financial support, especially in the context of our recommendation for setting up a Newspaper Development Commission.

VIII.111 Both the Central and State Governments should announce their advertising policy each year and adhere to it. Copies of the advertising policy should be placed on the Table of Parliament and the State Legislatures.

VIII.112-115 and 116 We recommend that DAVP be split and its function of handling Government advertisements entrusted to an autonomous corporation in the public sector. There should be similar autonomous bodies in the States. There should be no secrecy about the rates offered to different newspapers and the value of the advertisements placed with them. We recommend that the Central and the State Governments should lay on the Table of Parliament/State Legislatures each year a list of newspapers in which their advertisements, as well as those of public sector undertakings and other public bodies under them, were placed and the value of advertisements placed in each paper along with its circulation figure.

VIII.118 Rates for Government advertisements should be fixed on a realistic and fair basis.

VIII.119 Before the proposed autonomous corporation to handle Government advertisements comes into being, there should be an expert committee to advice DAVP on advertisement rates.

VIII.120 Public sector undertakings should not be able to take advantage of the DAVP rates for Government advertisements which are lower than the Commercial rates of newspapers in a number of cases.

VIII.122 Only such daily newspapers which subscribe to a wire service or have some other properly organised news service should be entitled to receive Government advertisements and those of public sector undertakings. The papers should also have a regularity of at least 90 per cent.

VIII.123 A democratic Government cannot lay down arbitrary or capricious standards in the matter of selection of newspapers for issue of its advertisements. The object sought to be achieved through the advertisement should be the main guiding principle in the matter of selection of the media.

VIII.124-125 We are of the view that the grounds for denial of advertisements to newspapers should have a reasonable nexus with the interest sought to be protected under Article 9(2) or the provisions of any law, e.g., the Penal Code or violation of the unwritten code of journalistic ethics. We do not think it is necessary to provide for an appellate body to consider complaints regarding denial of Government advertisements by an autonomous corporation. An aggrieved newspaper can always approach the Press Council or a court. We are also of the view that municipalities and other elected local bodies should be left free to make their own arrangements for issue of advertisements. Dr. Paranjape is, however, of the view that there is need for an appellate body to go in disputes between Government advertisers and newspapers as court proceedings can be time consuming and wasteful. Such a body, he thinks, can be set up either by the Press Council or the proposed Newspaper Development Commission.

VIII.128-129 In the context of the need to conserve imported newsprint, it is important that those who apply public funds to advertising should observe the greatest restraint and limit it to essential announcements. While it is perfectly legitimate for a Government to publicise its achievements in such fields as agriculture or health or industries, it should be possible to do so through the news columns of newspapers. Paid advertisements to ascribe all the credit for such achievements to the political personalities for the time being in power.

VIII.130 The findings of recent research highlight the importance of the rural audience and the growing rural market. This does not appear to have been sufficiently realised by advertisers and advertising agencies, whether in the public sector or the private.

(ix) *News services provided by the Government*

VIII.139 In order to improve the utilisation of the slow-speed bulletins, the languages in which the bulletins are broadcast and their timing and frequency need to be examined, in respect of each region and in relation to the constraints on total broadcasting time. Moreover, it should be ensured that the bulletins do not sound merely like government news and publicity.

VIII.145 It is better for a newspaper to receive all of a news agency's copy (free of cost if the Government is willing to pay for the service, or at a concessional rate subsidised by the Government) and make its own selection of news items, rather than for an official to make the selection on behalf of newspapers.

(x) *Publications and Press Relations*

VIII.154-155 We would urge all departments of the Central and State Governments which bring out periodicals to review the essentiality of the journals from time to time and to continue only those which are essential and preferably also command reasonable sale among the general public. Government periodicals are funded by public money. They should avoid giving the impression of being mouth-pieces of the party and the persons who are in power for the time being. Another reason for the limited reach of Government periodicals is the inadequate sales organisation for Government publications. This needs strengthening.

VIII.162 We are of the view that the Government should not take over newspapers even if they are faced with closure because of financial or other difficulties, although there may be no constitutional bar to such take-over.

VIII.167 to 169 We are in favour of daily newspapers being left in the private sector. However, in certain circumstances like those in Andaman and Nicobar Islands, where there is no daily Press, the proposed Newspaper Development Commission should be consulted and its approval obtained for a proposed Government daily newspaper as well as the pattern of its contents. If the circulation of a Government daily crosses the limit prescribed for the purpose, it should be brought within the purview of the Trust formula proposed in Chapter X. Shri K. R. Ganesh, however, does not share the view that the publication of daily newspapers by Government should be limited to exceptional places and circumstances. In his view, the totality of the need of communication in a country where the masses of the people to be informed, educated and mobilised for participation in the process of development, is so large that the medium of the daily Press cannot be left entirely to the private sector. The Government should be free to start daily newspapers in such languages and at such centres as may be found necessary to provide a supplement and/or corrective to the daily newspapers brought out by private publishers.

VIII.175 In the Press releases issued by the Central and State Governments, one-sided presentation of achievements alone, ignoring the problems and failures that the Press and the public are aware of, does not make for credibility.

VIII.176 There should be thorough reorganisation of the Press Information Bureau. It should be a news service functioning day and night, with its activities streamlined in such a way that district newspapers and the Indian language Press get its news releases promptly. To ensure that PIB is responsive to the needs of those sections of the Press which need its services most, we recommend the formation of an Advisory Committee comprising the users of PIB services.

VIII.178 The Principal Information Officer and other functionaries in the Press Information Bureau should be fully involved in the decision-making discussions in various ministries so that they can explain the decisions to the Press and public in an effective manner.

VIII.179 We welcome the guidelines issued by the Ministry of Information and Broadcasting to its Media Units during July 1980 stressing the importance of the official media remaining "credible as well as interesting to all sections of the society" and on news and views being disseminated in a fair, objective and balanced manner giving contrasting points of view and problems and issues being "covered from the public point of view without any hesitation in bringing out healthy criticism".

(xi) *Information Administration*

VIII.180 The Commission considers it desirable that the editorial staff of a newspaper should be insulated from undue or improper interference by the proprietors in their day-to-day work so long as they function within the parameters of the newspaper's policy. The same criteria should apply to journalism in the public sector.

VIII.182 Direct recruitment at senior level too is desirable in a professional service like the Central Information Service.

VIII.187 Journalistic aptitude and experience should be required or tested for direct recruitment at every level of the Central Information Service. Proficiency in Indian languages should also be ascertained before recruitment.

VIII.189 The Information set-up in the States should be headed by professionals and regular cadres constituted.

VIII.190-191 Professional autonomy is essential in the public sector of journalism as in the private. To permit this, it is essential that Ministers and senior civil servants should exercise self-restraint, intervening only to give policy guidelines and to correct any deviations therefrom. Information official should realise that Professional autonomy is something to be exercised by them.

VIII.194 On the lines of the Railway Ministry, there should be an information Board comprising senior professional heads of the media units to tender policy advice to the Minister. With the secretariat of the Ministry attending only to financial and administrative matters, not policy planning.

VIII.195-196 The Press Information Bureau, Publications Division and other units in the Information Wing of the Ministry should be headed by persons of acknowledged professional status drawn from newspapers and news agencies or the fields of advertising and public relations. The appointment of Principal Information Officer should be on a contract basis, terminable when there is a change of Government.

VIII.197 The Information officials in the Press Information Bureau or editors and business managers in the Publications Division can retain and improve their professional skills only if there is opportunity for movement in and out of the private and public sectors of newspapers and book publishing. We, therefore recommend that newspapers should let the Press Information Bureau have the services of their Assistant Editors/Special Correspondents on loan for a period of three to four year, and take suitable persons from the Central Information Service to work in the newspapers for similar periods, in the field as correspondents or at the desk as chief sub-editors/news editors.

VIII.198 The scales of remuneration in the Central Information Service should be improved and brought to a level comparable to those which now obtain in newspapers of repute.

CHAPTER IX

THE PRESS AS AN INDUSTRY

IX.87 The Central and State Governments as well as private advertisers and advertising agencies should make efforts to reach the rural audience more extensively, depending upon the nature of the product or the service advertised.

IX.88 The Press Registrar should collect information on the ownership structure of advertising agencies and their performance including the value of advertising handled on behalf of different clients and release of advertisements to different newspapers.

IX.90 Self-laudatory statements and photographs, whether put out by governments or by enterprises in the private and public sector or by other institutions, serve neither the advertisers' interest not the public interest.

IX.91 Any paid information published in a newspaper should be clearly identified as such. The Press Council should go into cases where newspapers do not observe this principle.

IX.98 While the MRTP Commission should look after the question of unfair trade practices, it is for the Press Council to oversee the observance of the ethics of advertising by the Press.

139 Cinema and sex magazines should not be allotted newsprint. The Press Registrar should determine whether a publication is a sex magazine or not. S/Shri Girilal Jain, Rajendra Mathur, H. K. Paranjape and S. K. Mukherjea have reservations about the recommendation.

IX.140 to 142 New publications are at present allowed an initial quota of newsprint for the first four months of their publications on the basis of their average circulation up to a maximum of 10,000 copies of eight standard pages in the case of dailies and 16 standard pages in the case of periodicals. We would like this system of allocation of newsprint to new newspapers to continue. However, if a new newspaper wants to start with a circulation higher than 10,000 copies, it should be permitted to do so provided the newspaper is in a position to furnish satisfactory evidence or its capacity in this behalf to the Press Registrar. Dr. H. K. Paranjape does not approve of the present system of newsprint import and allocation.

IX.143 There should be some mechanism to weed out spurious publications which do not come out regularly. We are of the view that for the purpose of allocation of newsprint, the requirement of regularity should be increased from the present 50 to 90 per cent in the case of dailies and two-thirds in the case of weeklies and other periodicals. However, allowance should be made for failure to publish on account of strikes/lock-outs, prolonged power cuts or other circumstances beyond the control of the publisher.

IX.154-157 Cutting down newsprint imports would not be proper as it is not a large drain on foreign exchange resources – an estimated 1.3 per cent of the value of total imports in 1980-81. We recommend that as far as possible a liberal allocation of foreign exchange should be made for newsprint imports to meet the demand of a readership that is growing steadily on account of the increase in population, literacy and purchasing power. Some ways have to be devised to discourage the use of newsprint for publication of image building and other wasteful advertisements. Classified advertisements relating to employment, matrimony, housing and the like serve a useful function, but a considerable part of display advertising is prodigal and has to be curtailed. Keeping the above considerations in mind, we recommend that newspapers should be allowed newsprint free of import/excise duty up to the level of 12 pages. Above that level, as long as the newsprint availability position continues to be difficult, there should be a progressively increasing rate of duty so that the tendency to increase the number of pages to accommodate more and more advertisements with a view to earning higher profits is rendered uneconomical. Government should work out the rates of import duty above the page level of 12 pages from time to time in accordance with the prevailing circumstances. S/Shri Girilal Jain, Rajendra Mathur, S. K. Mukherjea and H. K. Paranjape do not agree with this recommendation.

IX.166-167 In view of the dissatisfaction expressed by newspapers of all categories with STC's role, were commend that newspapers of all circulation categories should come together to form a co-operative to handle newsprint imports. Alternatively, while STC continues to negotiate with foreign suppliers on the prices and quantities to be purchased, newspapers may be allowed to make arrangements for shipping the newsprint. The proposed Newspaper Development Commission should subsidise small and medium newspapers for any escalation of shipping and handling charges under such an arrangement. If a small paper wants to use the agency of a big paper for the import of newsprint, it should be allowed to do so.

IX.172 There should be a differential in wastage margin for newsprint supplied to newspapers based on the distance of the newspaper press from port towns and newsprint factories.

IX.173 Standardisation of printing machinery and newsprint may help in reducing wastage. We would like the Indian Standards Institution to consider laying down standard for printing machinery and newsprint.

IX.194 While updating the teleprinter technology, the needs of various Indian languages should be kept in mind. Government should pay particular attention to this aspect as there is generally a resistance in bureaucratic circles to technological innovations.

IX.201 Litho printing machines are the only viable proposition for small and medium category Urdu newspapers, who cannot afford to acquire offset machines. But litho machines are not manufactured anywhere in the world now and the facilities for keep of the existing machines are not adequate. We recommend that the Government should take measures to meet the requirements of Urdu newspapers.

IX.202 Government should take steps to provide facilities to train

Katibs.

IX.209 It is for each newspaper to decide which technology would suit its requirements best. In certain circumstances, the latest technology may be the most appropriate technology. Newspapers, particularly those which want to grow, should have an open mind and a progressive outlook while selecting the proper technology.

IX.224 The proposed Newspaper Development Commission should pay special attention to the development of printing and other technologies suitable for the Indian Press, especially Indian language and small and medium newspapers. While importing technology from abroad, an attempt should be made to get only the latest and the best.

IX.225 The new electronic technology appears to have a clear advantage so far as composition in Indian scripts is concerned. With photo composition, matter can be composed and printed in Indian scripts without tampering with their aesthetics and integrity. But while adopting it, its physical requirements such as temperature control and assured power supply, etc., and the possible impact on employment opportunities should be kept in mind and provided for.

IX.227 To meet the requirements of small and medium newspapers, Government should sympathetically consider the import of rebuilt or reconditioned flat-bed and other machines which are available abroad at a price much lower than that of the indigenously manufactured machines. This may be subject to a suitable limit as regards the price. The Newspaper Development Commission, which we are proposing, should go into the question of import of reconditioned printing machines in detail.

IX.244 The proposed Newspaper Development Commission should help in providing common distribution arrangements for newspapers, especially those published in hilly and remote areas, which find it difficult to distribute their copies.

CHAPTER X

THE PRESS AS A PUBLIC UTILITY

1. *Ownership Patterns*

X.4 At present separate statistics on the circulation of daily newspapers owned by different categoris of owners are not being compiled by the Press Registrar; they are combined with the circulation of publications of various other periodicities. Hence forth, he should present circulation figures separately in respect of daily newspapers, news magazines and periodicals under different categories of ownership.

X.8 The requirement of publication of particulars of ownership annually under Section 20-A of the Press and Registration of Books Act needs to be modified to require every newspaper to give the names of the top 100 shareholders as well as the nationality, extent of shareholding and the main occupation of each such person. The names of the persons constituting the board of directors along with other directorships held by them should also be printed. This will enable readers to know the identity of persons controlling a newspaper.

X.12 and 13 On the bias of the data given in the Indian Institute of Public Administration study on *Ownership and Control Structure of the Indian Press*, rejoinders received from newspaper undertaking, and information obtained from the Department of Company Affairs of the Ministry of Law, Justice and Company Affairs and Registrars of Companies, we have put the top 54 dailies (multiple editions of a daily newspaper published from different centres taken as one newspaper) listed in *the Press in India* 1980 in the following categories:

Category	No.	Circulation	Per cent of the total circulation
1. Newspapers owned or controlled by companies or undertakings or businessmen with interest in other businesses or industries	27	54,05,711	40.87
2. Newspapers owned or controlled by companies or families or individuals or groups of individuals with primary interest in newspaper business	20	24,86,969	18.80
3. Newspapers owned or controlled by individuals or groups of individuals representing a variety of interests	1	3,08,833	2.33
4. Newspapers owned or controlled by Trusts or educational organisations with primary interest in newspaper business	1	1,56,689	1.18
5. Newspapers owned or controlled by Trusts or educational, cultural or religious organisations as a means to achieve their wider objectives	5	3,33,515	2.52
Total:	54	86,91,717	65.70

In deciding whether a newspaper in owned or controlled by companies or undertakings or businessmen with interests in other businesses or industries, we have taken into account the extent of ownership or the extent of control held by them and we have put in this category those newspapers in which 50 per cent or more of the ownership rights or control is held by companies or undertakings or businessmen with interests in other businesses or industries. While determining the extent of control, we have relied on *prima facie* evidence; for, we could not undertake a detailed study of the working of every newspaper undertaking in the country. Thus, if a newspaper company has five directors of whom three have directorships of other companies engaged in other businesses, we have put in the category (1) mentioned above.

X.14 and 15 We did not make an extensive study of the ownership patterns and linkages of periodicals because many of them deal with matters other than news and current affairs and the ownership linkages are not as crucial in their case an in the case of daily newspapers. Twenty-three of the top 50 periodicals, which are either owned by publishers of the top 54 dailies or about which we could get information from the IIPA study or other sources, fall in two categories

Category	No.	Circulation	Per cent of the total circulation of periodicals
(i) Periodicals owned or controlled by companies or undertakings or businessmen with interests in other businesses or industries	13	23,56,149	7.09
(ii) Periodicals owned or controlled by companies or families or individuals or groups of individuals with primary interest in newspaper business	10	17,32,718	5.22
Total:	23	40,88,867	12.31

X.16 It appears to us that a very significant part of the Press in the country in general, and a major portion of the all important daily Press in particular, is controlled by persons having strong links with other businesses or industries.

4. *MRTP Act and the Press*

X.31 There is no justification for exempting the newspaper industry from the provisions of the MRTP Act.

X.32 For determining 'dominance' or 'monopoly', the effective market of a newspaper should be considered; it may be the whole of India in the case of some newspapers and periodicals, and a State or a region in the case of others. As recommended by the Sachar Committee, the existing criterion of one-third should be reduced to one fourth share of the market for determining dominance. It should be left to the MRTP Commission to decide the matter in accordance with the facts of each case. We are of the view that no case relating to a newspaper should be decided under the MRTP Act without a public enquiry by the MRTP Commission. This would ensure that different aspects of the question of a situation of monopoly and concentration receive fair attention by an independent quasi-judicial body. The MRTP Commission should have the authority to act *suo moto* if allegations of monopolistic practices of a newspaper undertaking come to its notice.

5. *Delinking and Diffusion of Ownership and Control*

X.34 Freedom of the Press is not merely a professional right that inheres in journalists. It is essentially the reader's right to know. As William Ernest Hocking put it, in *Freedom of the Press* (1947), "The phrase freedom of the Press" must now cover two sets of rights and not one only. With the rights of editors and publishers to express themselves there must be associated a right of the public to be served with a substantial and honest basis of fact for its judgments of public affairs. Of these two, it is the latter which today tends to take precedence in importance; in Robert Leigh's pertinent phrase, freedom of the Press 'has changed its point of focus from the editor to the citizen". The Press is a public utility discharging the basic social function of informing, educating and entertaining the public. For the public interest in this vital area to be properly served, the presentation of news and views in the Press should be fair, accurate, objective, balanced and truthful.

X.36 In our view, the underlying principle that governs, or should govern, the Press is that the gathering and selling of news and views is essentially a public trust. It is based upon a tacit contract with the public that the news shall be true to the best of the knowledge and belief of those who offer it for sale, and that their comment upon it shall be sincere according to their lights. The same kind of trust is implied in the relationship between a doctor and his patients, though medical men work under the discipline of a professional code and are obliged to hold medical degrees, whereas journalism is a 'free' profession subject only to the external restrictions which the law of the land may place upon it. But the dishonest doctor can harm, at worst, only a few dozen, or a few score patients, while a dishonest journalist may poison the minds of hundreds of thousands or millions of his fellow men. A journalist who sells, or is a party to selling, news that he knows to be false or only partly true, or who trims opinions so as to make them palatable, is more guilty than a tradesman who gives short weight or a manufacturer who offers adulterated goods. The spreading of false statements is more harmful than the sale of material wares under false pretences. The journalist who betrays his trust is more blameworthy than a dishonest tradesman. Journalism, as the basis of the 'newspaper industry' holds a special position because its raw material is really the public mind and it trades chiefly in moral values. In a sense the trusteeship or moral responsibility of the Press is akin to that of ministers of religion, statesmen and leaders of public thought. In another sense it is subject to industrial and mercantile conditions that do not affect these other trustees in the same degree.

X.37 When newspapers are controlled by other big business they become vehicles of expression of the ideology of their owners and the selection, presentation and display of news in such newspapers would be dictated by that ideology. The newspaper industry in their hands becomes involuntarily the cultural arm of other businesses and industries and takes a vested interest in maintaining the existing socio-economic system. The newspapers controlled by them may be selective in their presentation of news and views in return for benefits conferred in respect of their other business interests. . . . Odd exceptions apart, commercial newspapers do not normally find a word to say in sympathy with the legitimate demands of the working class. They become naturally antagonistic to the implementation of certain key Directive Principles contained in Part IV of the Constitution. Legislative measures intended to ensure that the ownership and control of the material resources of the community are so distributed as best to subserve the common good, or, that the operation of the economic system does not result in concentration of wealth and means of production to the common detriment (Article 39 of the Constitution) run counter to their business and other economic interests. If all major newspapers come to represent a similar if not the same view-point as is not unlikely when all of them belong to large private business enterprises a view-point which is against the interests of big business may not receive a fair deal in their columns. . . . It is enough for our purpose to say that legislative measures needed for achieving the goals of our State run counter to the vested interests of the owners of those big newspapers who have large interests in other businesses.

X.39. It is precisely because the businessman owning or controlling big newspapers have not acted on the advice of the First Press Commission of creating trusts for their management that we are obliged to seriously consider the question once again and seek other remedies.

X.46 Today the Press is a big centre of power. No wonder Kipling wrote:

> "Remember the battle and stand aside
> While Thrones and Powers confess
> That King over all the children of pride
> It the Press – the Press – the Press",

The power associated with control of means of production in the past has now been, to a great extent, transferred to those who control the mass media as it can no longer be sustained otherwise. Those who control the means of production try to control the media not only for profit but much more so far perpetuation of power associated with their possession of means of production. . . . No one ought to exercise power in a democratic polity without responsibility. When a person's private interest conflicts with his duty to the public, there is every justification in a democracy for insisting that the exercise of power connected with his public duty be segregated from his private interest.

X.47 As we have stated elsewhere in the report, an informed citizenry is a fundamental postulate of democracy. The Press is the most important instrument in our country for educating the citizens in matters of public importance so that they may form an independent judgment to play their role as the ultimate governors of the country. It can hardly be disputed that the ownership structure of newspaper establishments determine the character and style of news report and news display as also the editorial viewpoint and other comments on the events of the day. What gets self-censored and gets blacked out might be as significant as what gets reported. News and views take their colour from the attitudes and postures of management and such attitudes and postures are dictated by considerations of the primary interest of the newspaper owners. The Press cannot be truly free if the communication industry is the channel through which opinions and values of its capitalist owners are disseminated for, in such a situation genuine freedom would exist only for those who control the Press.

X.49 The Joint Stock Company is the predominant type of ownership of newspapers in our country. It means generally the dominance of a few shareholders. The pattern of editorial working follows the pattern of ownership. When an industrialist owns a paper, it is subsidiary to some other industrial, business or commercial interest. Justice Frankfurter said in this context that freedom of the Press can be achieved by freeing the Press from the clutches of Press barons. If freedom of expression has to play its basic role in our democratic polity, it must be freed from the steamrolling of the commercial process so that it may mean maximum amount of freedom of expression for the maximum number of people.

X.52 We think that in the interest of the public it is necessary to insulate the Press from the dominating influence of other business interests. We propose the enactment of a law in the interest of the general public making it mandatory for persons carrying on the business of publishing a newspaper to sever their connections with other businesses to the extent indicated hereinafter by us. In this context we are using the expression 'person' in its legal sense so as to bring with in its ambit individuals, companies, trusts, etc. The central idea underlying the legislation would be that a person carrying on the business of publishing a newspaper should not have, directly or indirectly, an interest, in excess of the 'prescribed interest', in any other business, or begin a position of being controlled, directly or indirectly, by any other person or person having an interest, in excess of the prescribed interest in any other business. The expression 'business' should be defined to mean anything which occupies the time, attention and labour of a person for the purpose of profit but not any activity in the nature of exercise of a profession.

X.53 We are conscious that it would be impracticable to make the proposed legislation applicable to all persons carrying on the business of publishing a newspaper at one stroke. We are of the view that, in the first instance, it should be enforced in the case of all persons who are in a position of controlling the publication of one or more daily newspapers with the same or different titles, in one or more languages, the circulation of which, taken singly or cumulatively, exceeds one lakh copies per day. We do not think such a classification would be hit by Article 14. In *Gujarat* v. *Ambica Mills Ltd.,* it was held that the legislature cannot be required to impose upon administrative agencies tasks which cannot be carried out on a large scale at a single stroke. If the law presumably hits the evil where it is most felt, it is not to be overthrown because there are other instances, to which it might have been applied. There is doctrinaire requirement that the legislation should be couched in all embracing terms. The piecemeal approach to a general problem permitted by under inclusive classifications is justified because legislative dealing with such problems is usually an experimental matter.

X.54 We think the legislature is competent to enact the proposed law under Article 19 of the Constitution.

X.56 The detailed scheme of the proposed legislation has to be worked out by competent draftsmen. We are indicating here only the broad outlines of the same. There are two aspects of the proposed legislation. Firstly, the person carrying on the business of publishing a newspaper should not have, directly or indirectly, an interest, in excess of the prescribed interest, in any other business. Secondly, the person carrying on the business of publishing a newspaper should not be in a position of being controlled, directly or indirectly, by any other person having an interest, in excess of the prescribed interest, in any other business. The expression 'prescribed interest', will have to be defined in this context. We think the aggregate interest of the person carrying on the business of publishing a newspaper in any other business or businesses should not exceed ten per cent of the total interest involved in the publication of the newspaper. For example, in the case of a company publishing a newspaper, its aggregate interest in other businesses should not exceed ten per cent of its subscribed share capital. On the other hand, persons having interests in any other business or businesses should not, taken together, be allowed to have more than ten per cent interest in the business of publishing a newspaper. For example, in the case of a company publishing a newspaper, not more than ten per cent of its subscribed share capital should be allowed to be held by persons having interests in other businesses. These considerations will have to be kept in mind while defining 'prescribed interest' in relation to the two categories of persons involved, viz., persons carrying on the business of publishing a newspaper and persons having interest in other businesses, and, the manner of computing the 'prescribed interest' in the case of different categories of 'persons' will have to be precisely laid down. While computing 'prescribed interest' it would be necessary to equate loan interest (excluding loans from public lending institutions such as banks) with share holding or other interests.

X.57 The proposed legislation will also have to work out a concept of 'control' by persons having interest in business other than that of the newspaper concerned.

X.58 Our inquiry in regard to ownership of newspapers has revealed that most of the newspaper companies bringing our large circulation newspapers are clustered within the umbra or, at any rate, within the penumbra of giant industrial and business houses. The leading newspaper company, Bennett Coleman, has the House of Sahu Jain as its 71.15 per cent shareholder and Bennett Coleman has in turn cross holdings in companies of Sahu Jain House. The Goenkas who control the Express Group of newspapers and the Sahu Jains who control the Bennett Coleman & Co. are related by marriage. The newspapers brought out by them command a lion's share of elite readership in the country. The newspaper companies in turn have huge investments in concerns other than publication such as banking, jute, sugar, Ayurvedic medicines, automobile parts, electronics, plantation, steel rolling, groundnut oil mills, paper mills, textiles, agro-industrial units, etc. There is therefore need to safeguard against control of newspapers by other commercial interests through their associates. The proposed legislation should bai such an eventuality also by defining the term 'associate' much more comprehensively than in Section 6 of the Companies Act. If should not be necessary that the associate must be doing any business as he may be a dummy or a man of straw also lends his name out of obligation to the person doing business.

X.59 To enable persons engaged in or connected with publication of existing daily newspapers who come within the purview of the proposed legislation to divest their interest in other businesses, a reasonable time-limit may be prescribed by the law for the purpose. If the shares of a newspaper company are not readily purchased by eligible persons from the open market, such shares should be acquired and held by an autonomous body or agency to be specified by the legislation till they are purchased by eligible persons. The proposed legislation should provide machinery for computing the sale price of the shares to be divested.

X.60 The proposed law should provide for filing of a declaration, once in six months, by every person coming within its ambit, stating that the newspaper is not being published in contravention of the provisions of the proposed legislation. The appropriate authority before which the declaration may be filed would be the Magistrate authenticating the declaration of the newspaper under Section 5 of the Press and Registration of Books Act. On receipt of a complaint that the declaration filed by the newspaper undertaking is false, the MRTP Commission or such other independent or autonomous authority should have the power to enquire into the matter and enter a finding on the complaint. If the declaration is found to be false, the Magistrate acting under the PRB Act should have the power under Section 8B thereof to cancel the declaration of the newspaper filed under Section 5 of that Act. Accordingly, Section 8B of the PRB Act should be amended to include breach of the proposed legislation as a ground for cancelling the declaration. This penalty would be in addition to the penalty attracted by a false declaration under Section 176 of the IPC.

X.61 We are conscious that the newspaper which will come within the ambit of the proposed legislation are all quality newspapers rendering good service to the community. As the First Press Commission said, just as the public have a vital interest in the purity of their water supply, so they have an equally vital interest in the accurate and fair presentation of news and views. The profit motive does not serve the interest of the public in the area of supply of information which should be regarded as the most important public utility in a democratic society.

X.62 S/Shri Girilal Jain, Rajendra Mathur, H. K. Paranjape and S.K. Mukherjea do not subscribe to the views expounded and recommendations made in this section.

6. *Price-page Schedule and News-to-advertisement Ratio*

X.64 A paper with a large circulation, because of its lower cost of production per copy, enjoys certain advantages over other papers with smaller circulation. Similarly, a paper with large capital resources is free from certain handicaps which affect a paper with limited resources. A paper of long standing which has been able to build up a large and stable volume of advertisement revenue is in a very advantageous position as compared to others who have just entered the field. It is true that such economic advantages and handicaps exist in a number of industries but their presence in the newspaper industry is not conducive to the even and healthy development of the Press.

X.65 Newspapers serve as media for the free exchange of information and of ideas. The proper functioning of democracy requires that every individual should have equal opportunity, insofar as this can be achieved, to put forward his opinions. The freedom of the Press rests on the assumption that widest possible dissemination of information from diverse and antagonistic sources is essential to the welfare of the public. It is, therefore, necessary to reduce the differences due to economic advantages or other causes. Newcomers should be enabled to start publication with a fair chance of achieving success. Fixing a minimum price at which newspapers of a particular size could be sold, is the most effective measure to bring about an atmosphere of fair competition.

X.66 Advertisements occupy a substantial proportion of space in newspapers. It is imperative to ensure that the reader gets an adequate proportion of news and views and that advertisements are not reduced in effectiveness because there are too many of them. It is the reader who pays the net cost of the paper, partly as its price and partly through the advertised goods that he purchases.

X.77 As the Enquiry Committee on Small Newspapers observed, whereas the selling price of an industrial product is always above its cost of production, that of a daily newspaper is much below its cost of production and, how much below it is in a given case, is determined by the volume of advertisements carried by it. As already pointed out, the re-sale value of old newspapers in our country is very high and is an important consideration that weights with an average reader in making his choice of a newspaper. In view of this a newspaper giving more pages for the same price commands a larger circulation which also enables it to get more advertisements which in turn puts it in a position to be able to further reduce its selling price. In most other industries, in spite of the existence of a few big units, a new entrepreneur can enter the field because the big units cannot reduce the sale price of the product below its cost of production. As seen above, this is not true of the newspaper industry. There are other handicaps too! Apart from the physical limitations on the market of a daily newspaper, a stale issue cannot be sold as newspaper. A new entrant's survival itself may be rendered difficult if the established units in the field raise the number of pages offered by them for the same selling price as that of the new entrant. For the freedom of the Press to be effective, the present degree of dependence of newspapers on advertisements has to be lessened and the importance of circulation as a principal source of revenue must be enhanced.

X.78 Looking to the prevailing condition of the Press today, we are convinced that the prescription of a price-page schedule with a news-to-advertisement ratio is absolutely essential for promoting fair competition among the existing units and for providing a fair chance of success to newcomers in the interest of diversification of the sources of dissemination of information so as to provide for expression of a broad spectrum of views. While arriving at this view we have not been obivious of the fact that those papers which are today attracting a disproportionately large amount of advertisement revenue are utilizing it to a certain extent for improving their quality and subsidising the selling price for the benefit of the readers. We suggest that an expert committee be set up to work out a price-page schedule after taking into account the present-day economics of publishing a newspaper. As regards the proportions of news and advertisement in a paper, we recognise that the advertisement rates charged by newspapers vary very widely. In view of the need to help the small and medium newspapers overcome the disadvantage of lower advertisement rates and smaller number of pages we recommend that the news-to-advertisement ratio should be fixed at 60 : 40 for big, 50 : 50 for medium and 40 : 60 for small newspapers.

X.91 The Constitution confers several fundamental rights upon the citizen under Article 19. Article 19(1)(a) speaks of the fundamental rights of freedom of speech and expression. A person carrying on the business of publishing a newspaper, no doubt, exercises this freedom of expression. At the same time he is also engaged in a business activity for the carrying on of which he can also claim the right to form associations, the right to enter into partnership with others in carrying on his business, the right to move freely throughout the territory of India and the right to reside and settle in any part of the territory of India. Thus, if a publisher of a newspaper claims several fundamental rights under Article 19 in respect of his business, he cannot claim exception from the restrictions to which each of those rights is subject. The fact that the publisher carries on a business would attract the restrictions envisaged in Articles 19(4), 19(5) and 19(6).

X.92 Therefore, when the Constitution confers on a citizen several fundamental rights, the power to make laws which impose restrictions in public interest appropriate to each fundamental rights will be attracted. And, if the true nature and character of the law made in the exercise of that power is that it imposes reasonable restrictions on the right to carry on a business, then it is not invalidated if it affects incidentally matters which are outside this authorised field. Any other construction would lead to absurd results and would nullify the expressed powers conferred by the Constitution on the legislatures. If a publisher of a newspaper claims six fundamental rights, it is only proper that he should be subject to all the restrictions which are appropriate to the fundamental rights claimed.

X.93 It would seem than the *Sakal Newspapers* this aspect of the matter was incorrectly decided.

X.99 There is no warrant for the assumption that any law or executive action authorised by law which increases the price of a newspaper, or which diminishes the circulation would necessarily violate the freedom under Article 19(1)(a). It may be noticed that the restrictions which can be put on the fundamental rights under Articles 19(2) to 19(6) do not refer to tax at all. But a tax is a restriction on business. A tax on the sale of newspapers might diminish the circulation of the newspaper by increasing the cost to the purchasers. So also a tax on advertisements published in the newspaper might diminish the revenue from advertisements by which the cost of the newspaper might go up. Consequently, such a tax, being a restriction, will affect the freedom of the Press. For this reason it cannot be held that a restriction by the imposition of tax on the sale of newspaper or on advertisements published therein is a law in respect of the freedom of the Press; such a law is, in pith and substance, a revenue law which imposes reasonable restriction on the business of publishing newspapers.

X.100 As regards regulation of advertisement space in newspapers, we are of the view that a mere fall in circulation on account of a law regulating the business or commercial aspect of speech would not be hit by Article 19(1)(a). There is no question of a law regulating the extent of advertisements in a newspaper violating the freedom under Article 19(1)(a).

X.101 The decision of the Supreme Court in the *Sakal Newspapers* case merits a review. Laws for the welfare of labour, laws restraining monopoly and laws imposing a tax on the sale or purchase of newspapers or on advertisements published therein cannot be declared void merely because they would, to some extent, regulate the freedom of speech and of the Press.

X.102 Even if an amendment of the Constitution is required to give affect to our proposals regarding price-page schedule and news-to-advertisement ratio, we are of the view that such an amendment will not destroy or damage the basic structure of the Constitution. No doubt, Article 19(1)(a) has been held to be a basic structure of the Constitution; but a law prescribing a price page schedule on news-to-advertisement ratio is not a measure which will destroy or damage that freedom; on the contrary, its object being promotion of competition and prevention of monopoly, the law will advance freedom of speech and expression.

S/Shri Girilal Jain, Rajendra Mathur, S. K. Mukherjea and H. K. Paranjape are opposed to the prescription of price-page schedule and news-to-advertisement ratio.

7. *Internal Relations and Right of Reply*

X.104 In the case of a large newspaper operating in modern conditions, the right of the owner to have his point of view expressed through the newspaper should not extend beyond laying down the policy of the newspaper and the appointment of an editor of his choice. The editor chosen ought to be a man of known ability and integrity and should have sufficient authority to conduct the newspaper in public interest while following the policy laid down by the owner.

X.105 Journalistic freedom is the heart of freedom of the Press. The journalist should have an atmosphere of freedom. But the unity of purpose of the newspaper can be ensured only by the concentration of ultimate responsibility in one particular person and by the development of a spirit of co-operative enterprise whereby everyone realised that he is working towards a common goal.

X.106 The editing of big newspapers cannot be done or supervised by one person. Proper distribution of responsibility if inescapable. The adequacy of the editor can be sustained only by proper delegation of authority, viable distribution of work and by the habit of the widest possible consultation. It is only the cooperative endeavour of the entire editorial staff that can make for standards in a newspaper. However, the ultimate responsibility in the production of a newspaper should vest in the editor.

X.113 and 114 To provide an effective safeguard against proprietorial or managerial interference in editorial independence, there should be legislation for interposition of a board of trustees between the management of a large daily newspaper and its editor. The legislation should be applicable in the first instance only to daily newspapers with a circulation of over one lakh copies. The policy of every such newspaper should be clearly laid down in writing. The function of the boards of trustees would be to ensure that full effect is given to the policy of the newspaper and to act as umpire in disputes between the editor and the management of the newspaper. The trustees should be public men of unquestionable integrity and of eminence in the field of journalism, law, science, medicine, education or such other learned profession. They should be appointed by the managements of the newspapers themselves in consultation with and with the approval of the Chairman of the Press Council and the Chief Justice of the High Court or the Chief Justice of India, as the case may be, depending upon the area of circulation of the newspaper concerned. In the event of a difference of opinion between the Chairman of the Press Council and the Chief Justice on the choice of the members of the board of trustees submitted to them by the management of a newspaper, the view of the Chief Justice should prevail. Every board of trustees should consist of three members and they should be subject to rotational retirement every year or once in two years in the interest of continuity. S/Shri Girilal Jain, Rajendra Mathur, H. K. Paranjape and S. K Mukherjea are, however, not in favour of the recommendation.

X.115 The editor of a newspaper should ordinarily be appointed for a reasonably long term of say five years, unless he happens to be approaching the age of superannuation.

X.117 If individual newspapers experiment with internal ombudsmen, they might be able to improve their relationship with the readers and show acceptance and understanding of their responsibilities.

X.119 and 120 It is, no doubt, desirable to provide for a right of reply, as in our country, it is very difficult and cumbersome at present to pursue a case of defamation. The purpose of providing a right of reply is that the public should not be misled. Non-publication of a reply may be indicative of malice on the part of the newspaper and the plaintiff can attribute it in defamation proceedings while its publication will be a mitigating factor in the matter of awarding damages for defamation.

X.120 and 121 It is not appropriate to lay down that the reply should get the same prominence or display, or the same amount of space as the original report. It should best be left to the good sense and discretion of the editor as it depends, among other things, on the news fall at a given time. For the present, a right of reply should be recognised by convention as a part of professional ethics and complaints alleging denial of right of reply should be looked into by the Press Council, as it is already doing. Dr. H.K. Paranjape is, however against authorising the Press Council to look into such complaints in view of the recommendation made in Chapter VII for giving the Council penal powers.

CHAPTER XI

NEWS FLOW : INTERNAL AND INTERNATIONAL

XI.9 and 10 There is a definite role for small agencies in providing news of local interest and significance, as well as for agencies offering news andcommentsin different perspectives. We would like tosee the emergenceof more agencies specialising in photographs, cartography and other visuals.

XI.11 There is scope for the pooling and country-wide dissemination of the more significant stories of success and failure in rural development – in economic terms as well as of social change – selected from the coverage done by local news agencies in different parts of the country. Any news agency, wire or non-wire, which comes forward to undertake such pooling and dissemination and demonstrates its organisational and professional competence to do so would deserve financial support from the Newspaper Development Commission.

XI.12 and 15 A good news agency set-up should be capable of ensuring a continuous flow of information from and to the people. This social responsibility has to be recognised as part of the concept of freedom of the Press. News agency reporting should be linked to a greater extent with the life and problems of the rural people, the news agencies have to explore hitherto untapped areas of news to give news reporting a new purpose and utility.

XI.29 We consider that big newspapers are in a position to pay much more as subscription to the wire agencies.

XI.35 and 37 A rational and equitable basis for working out AIR's payment to the news agencies is essential. In the event of a dispute raised by a news agency or agencies or by AIR/Doordarshan regarding the rates of subscription, it will be appropriate to refer the dispute to the MRTP Commission. The sound approach would be to determine the payment on the basis of the total revenue derived by AIR from licence fees and commercial advertising, the amount of broadcasting time applied to news bulletins and the extent of contribution made by the news agencies to the news broadcasts. The same approach should be applied also in the case of Doordarshan.

XI.38 Any formula that is worked out to determine AIR and Doordarshan's payment to news agencies should take into account the fact that the broadcast media have a large stake even as newspapers do, in the growth of the news agencies.

XI.39 The growth component proposed by us in the rates to be paid by the Press and the broadcast media is on the basis of the technology of news transmission presently employed by the news agencies. This is distinct from the *development* resistance to news agencies that has been envisaged by us as one of the functions of the proposed Newspaper Development Commission.

XI.42 The new technology of facsimile transmission has great possibilities but large scale adoption of it by Indian news agencies will have to wait till telecommunication facilities are further improved and the production of equipment becomes cheaper. The facsimile trans-receiver machines developed in India, can, however, be of use even now for the transmission of photographs, maps, charts and other material not requiring high-speed transmission, by agencies dealing in visuals.

XI.45 and 50 Ideally an Indian language news agency – or a federative system which brings several regional language agencies together – should develop through the pooling of resources by newspapers published in Indian languages. A cooperative enterprise launched by publishers of Indian language newspapers in the manner in which PTI and UNI were formed, but with more broad-based participation, would be commendable on several counts. If, however, neither the existing agencies nor the Indian-language newspapers come up with a satisfactory scheme for the provision of an efficient news service in Indian languages, we recommend that a statutory corporation should be set up. Sarvashri Girilal Jain, S. K. Mukherjea and H. K. Paranjape are opposed to the idea of a statutory corporation.

XI.47 So far as news services in English are concerned we recommend that the present position in which PTI and UNI offer competitive services be left undisturbed.

XI.48 It is necessary that the claims made by the different wire agencies regarding wordage put out per day, number of subscribers, etc., should be assessed objectively on the basis of uniform criteria.

This can be done for the present by the Present Council and more appropriately by the Newspaper Development Commission, when it comes into being.

XI.49 All the news agencies should strive to provide better service to newspapers through wider rural coverage and a broader range of themes. In order to discharge the hitherto neglected functions the agencies will have to introduce new services. Some of these might require subsidy. We are of the view that such a assistance should be sought by the news agencies from the Newspaper Development Commission and not directly from the Government. All subsidies should be temporary and should be gradually withdrawn.

XI.57 The News agencies should make a special effort to improve the spread of their shareholding.

XI.58 The Central and State Governments should in fixing the rates of advertisements fix two rates; one for daily newspapers which do not subscribe to any wire agency, and a higher rate for dailies which subscribe to a wire agency.

XI.59 To provide for public accountability and to ensure the representation of medium and small newspapers, we recommend that in addition to the directors elected by the shareholders, the board of directors of each wire agency should have:

(i) A director jointly nominated by the Speaker, Lok Sabha and the Chairman, Rajya Sabha (who need not necessarily be a Member of Parliament).
(ii) A director nominated by the Chairman, Press Council (who need not necessarily be a Member of the Press Council).
(iii) Two directors representing the small and medium newspapers respectively, by co-option is such directors do not happen to have been elected.

XI.60 When the Newspaper Development Commission, is set up, it should also have a nominee on the board of directors of each of the wire agencies.

XI.61 Shareholding newspapers should nominate only journalists as their representative on a news agency board.

XI.62 UNI and Samachar Bharati should adopt a limitation on voting rights broadly on the PTI pattern.

XI.67 The cost of maintaining Indian correspondents abroad, of their travel within the country and regions assigned to them and the cost of transmission are so high that no Indian news agency can finance its foreign operations from its own revenues. Assistance from the Government on substantial scale is therefore inescapable. Given the constraints of the country's resources of foreign exchange, it is evident that it will not be possible for the Government to assist more than one agency to expand the number of bureaux abroad for the collection and dissemination of news.

XI.70 The Commission is of the view that it will be rational and expedient to assist PTI to improve its international operations both for collection of foreign news and the dissemination of Indian news abroad. However, it is not our intention that any other agency should be prevented or discouraged from news collection and dissemination abroad. We recommend that assistance be extended for operations abroad by UNI or other news agencies also in respect of selected neighbouring and other countries, news from which is of great interest to Indian readers.

XI.71 We welcome the recognition by the Government of the inescapable need to meet part of the cost of maintaining news agency correspondents abroad. We recommend that this policy be continued and further liberalised so as to fill up the yawning gaps in the coverage of Africa and Latin America and large parts of Asia.

XI.72 The External Affairs Ministry spends a substantial sum on preparing an sending news bulletins for the benefit of Indian Missions abroad. PTI felt that the bulletins could be prepared within the parameters of policy and transmitted fast and more economically by the agency. We think the suggestion is worth consideration.

XI.73 We recommend that the Government might take a comprehensive look at the structure of Overseas Communication Service rates. The Newspaper Development Commission may keep a constant watch on the situation and may suggest lowering of rates unilaterally by the Overseas Communication Service in appropriate cases in the interest of the development of international services of Indian news agencies.

XI.74 While providing assistance on international coverage, the Government should ensure that the news agency sends out correspondents who know the languages of the respective countries to which they are posted.

XI.88 The Commission broadly agrees with the recommendations of the Conferences of Communication specialist and Administrators from South Asian Countries organised in September 1980 by the

Indian Institute of Mass Communication in New Delhi, which endorsed the basic approach of the MacBride Commission's Report.

XI.90 We recommend that India should continue to play an active part in drawing up and implementing programmes from year to year under the international programme for Development of Communication.

XI.91 We welcome India's participation in the non-aligned news pool and recommend that the Indian news agency handling the work of the Pool should not merely be a passive recipient of material sent by other participating news agencies but should actively seek news and background information on tasks faced by India in common with other developing countries.

XI.92 We recommend that the editorial staff of Indian newspapers should be on the look for and utilise to a greater extent useful information pertaining to Third World Countries.

X.193 We recommend that adequate resources be made available to the Indian Institute of Mass Communication for the continuance and expansion of the training of news agency journalists from various countries of Asia, Africa and Latin America.

CHAPTER XII

TRAINING AND RESEARCH

XII.23 Because of the unique nature of the Press, we recommend, on the one hand, that journalism training should be expanded and improved and, on the other that journalism should continue to require no prior licence for entry.

XII.26 Journalism training is a proper concern of the Press Council and we have recommended suitable amendment of the Press Council Act in Chapter VII.

XII.27 In the qualification prescribed by U.G.C. for recruitment as Lecturer in Journalism, work experience in a newspaper or other communication agency should be made an essential requirement. As regards posts of Readers and Professors, there ought to be a balance between academic qualifications and experience. There are subjects that ought to form part of journalism education and for teaching which an M. Phil. or Doctorate can appropriately be insisted on, with the teacher not necessarily being part of the journalism faculty. The imparting of the practical skills of journalism, however, requires experience of many years at responsible level in newspapers or news agencies of repute. Such experience, together with a good academic background should be deemed to be more than equivalent to M. Phil or Doctorate.

XII.29 University departments of journalism should utilise teachers in other departments such as, Sociology, Economics, Politics and Linguistics. The full-time faculty strength should be supplemented, for teaching of sub-editing and reporting, by drawing on the services of retired editors and senior practising journalists to conduct units of courses on a part-time basis or as Visiting Professors.

XII.30 In view of the considerable growth in the language Press which is to be expected in the coming decades, the need to train manpower for Indian language newspapers has particularly to be borne in mind. Exceptions apart, practical training in journalism should be imparted in an Indian language besides English.

XII.31 It is pointless for each university to institute a journalism course. But there should be at least one university or professional training facility of high standard in every major linguistic region.

XII.32 We recommend the establishment of a National Council for Journalism Training, preferably to be sponsored by the Press Council of India. It should comprise not only journalism teachers but also newspaper publishers, editors and distinguished men of letters. Such a Council could institute fellowships, for training and research and awards for meritorious performance in journalism. In time, it can begin to supervise and certify journalism training. The certifying body need not be statutory.

XII.32 Journalism training institutes should pay particular attention to the imparting of reporting skills. The emphasis should be as much on problem identification and analysis as on interesting description.

XII.35 Training institutions, organisations of publishers and editors and the Press Council should encourage preparation of text-books in the nature of model work books which will serve as practical guides in trainee journalists, specially in Indian languages.

XII.36 There is need to encourage specialisation in reporting on developments in such areas as science and technology economic affairs and social change.

XII.37 We suggest that the institution of correspondence courses for training district and block-level part-time reporters. Peripatetic training teams and training personnel on a part-time basis should supplement more formal, full-time training.

XII.38 We recommend the holding of workshops for exchange or experience among teachers and practitioners of journalism, specially in the Indian languages.

XII.39 Admission to all journalism courses should be after aptitude tests.

XII.40 Ways should be found to attract trained women journalists in large numbers to the Press, particularly Indian language newspapers, by providing facilities such as transport to their homes after late duty or night shifts.

XII.41 Training should comprehend not only the skills but also the values of journalism. It should be part of training to make the would be journalist realise that he can contribute to the economic and social betterment of the under-privileged.

XII.42 Trainees should be made aware that they are going to play a very responsible role as 'gatekeepers' of news:

XII.58 The research in connection with the Satellite Instructional Television Experiment brought out the limitations of centralised communication and the need, if communication is to be effective, for decentralised preparation of messages addressed to specific rural communities in the dialects which they actually speak. The findings are of relevance to the growth of the Indian language Press.

XII.60 to 62 The findings of the audience research conducted by All-India Radio and Doordarshan are generally not available to researchers and the public. We are of the view that it will be in the public interest to know how much listening there is to the various programmes addressed to different sections of the urban and rural population. In the absence of such information there has been little realisation of the need to organise community listening/viewing facilities for social education programmes. One limitation of the Audience Research of All-India Radio is that it confines itself almost entirely to members of families owning radio or television sets, whereas the majority of listeners and viewers are non-owners. Another limitation of audience research is that it does not generally take into account the audience below the age of fifteen. There appears to be need to make the audience research of AIR/Doordarshan more broad-based so as to cover non-owning listners/viewers as well as the adolescent audience. We are of the view that the research design and findings should be made accessible to qualified researchers for the mutual benefit of AIR/Doordarshan (who ought to have critical appraisal of their research methodology) and to the academic community of communication scholars (through access to data on the reach and impact of the electronic media).

XII.64 The I.I.M.C. should publish the findings of its communication research as a matter of course.

XII.69 Communication research can become socially relevant and useful only to the extent that it frees itself from its commercial moorings and becomes an instrument for promoting non-formal or social education.

XII.70 It is desirable that institutions engaged in communication research should keep each other informed of their present and proposed studies.

XII.71 When an apex body for journalism training emerges, as recommended in XII 32, it will be fitting for it to concern itself with the promotion and coordination of communication research, with particular reference to newspapers. Such a National Council for Journalism Training and Communication Research might be sponsored jointly by organisations of newspaper publishers and editors, the Press Council and the proposed Newspaper Development Commission with support from AIR/Doordarshan.

AN AREA OF DIFFERENCE

(i) Joint minute of dissent by Justice Sisir Kumar Mukherjea, Shri Rajendra Mathur, Shri Girilal Jain and Prof. H.K. Paranjape.

PART I

When the First Press Commission finalised its report in July 1954, India was still a land of heart's desire struggling to be born. Men and women of vision regarded her a tabula rasa, a clean slate on which they could inscribe their own ideals. The country was an isle full of noises, sounds and sweet airs and its leaders were Ariels. The thrill of beginning a new experiment was in the air, and in their innocence, they believed that they would soon be fashioning a new society which would be a model for the rest of the world. The country owes a lot to that generation because without their vision, courage and even innocence, India as we know it today would not have existed.

2. For many of the distinguished members of the First Press

Commission* refashioning the Press was part of the larger enterprise of refashioning society. When the First Press Commission came to the end of its labours, the Avadi Session of the Indian National Congress, which adopted, too hesitantly for some, a "socialistic pattern of society" as the nation's goal was still some months away. The middle class intelligentsia were waiting to watch, and to participate in, the working out of an alchemy which would fuse together the concepts of democracy and socialism in a gigantic crucible. And the Press was to be one component of the alchemy.

3. Twenty-eight years later, we, the dissenting members of the Second Press Commission, cannot pretend that 1982 is 1954, and that we have learnt nothing from the souring of dreams. Ours may not be a generation distinguished for vision or idealism, but it surely has more experience, and a greater awareness of pitfalls. We cannot pretend that the grand experimental envisioned in 1954 is still on and that the restructuring of the ownership of the Press is still a part of the grand design of restructuring the society and its property-relationships. In fact, the catchword which were with us even ten years ago are now being given up, and there is little desire to tinker with the geometry of the stage in order to improve the drama. We thus find ourselves unable to share the ease with which the majority of our colleagues have reiterated (Chapter X) some of the postulates and recommendations of the First Press Commission in regard to delinking and diffusion of ownership and control, a statutory news to advertisement ratio, and compulsory price-page schedule.

4. When the First Press Commission was appointed in 1952, there was not a single daily in the country with a circulation of one lakh. The *Times of India* printed 94,748 copies, the *Statesman* 65,032, the *Hindu* 69,748 and the *Hindustan Times*, a meagre 48,141. These were our four major newspapers from the four metropolitan centres. The position of Indian language dailies was even worse. *Swadesamitran* with 39,509 copies was regarded as a successful daily; so were *Sakal* (27,262), *Mathrubhumi* (25,736), and *Andhra Patrika* (23,086). There were no worthwhile dailies in several states and languages. The capacity of newspapers, therefore, to influence public opinion for good or ill was strictly limited.

5. And yet the First Press Commission remarked with some

Note: * The members of the First Press Commission were: Justice A.S. Rajadhyaksha, Dr. C.P. Ramaswami Aiyar, Acharya Narendra Dev, Dr. Zakir Hussain, Dr. V.K.R.V. Rao, and Sarvashri P.H. Patwardhan, T.N. Singh, Jaipal Singh, A.D. Mani, A.R. Bhat, and M. Chalapathi Rau.

concern: Out of a total of 330 dailies, five owners control 29 papers, and 31.2 per cent of circulation, while 15 owners control 54 newspapers and 50.1 per cent of the circulation. There can, therefore, be no denying the fact that there already exists in the Indian newspaper industry a considerable degree of concentration. We feel that there is a danger that this tendency might further develop in the future. We are of the opinion that it would not be desirable in the interest of freedom of choice that this tendency should be accentuated". (Para 818). The Commission was even concerned that the Telugu daily *Andhra Patrika*, selling a pitiful 23,086 copies, accounted for more than 50 per cent of the circulation in its language area.

6. When the First Commission was deliberating, the influence of Britain of the thirties was too much with us. Its members, like many other Indian intellectuals, transposed the British Left's perceptions to a very different Indian reality. They did not talk of the ills which beset the Indian Press then, but of the ills which might beset it decades later. With a diffusion rate of only seven copies of daily newspapers per 1,000 of the population, the primary concern of the First Press Commission ought to have been the growth and expansion of newspapers in India rather than the distortions that might be created by the ownership structure.

7. Even now, twenty-eight years later, we do not have many mass-circulation dailies or weeklies in the country. In 1886, the Paris-based *Le Petit Journal* sold more than a million copies per issue. In 1900, the *Daily Mail*, London, crossed the seven figure mark. In 1979, the Japanese *Yomiuri Shimbun* sold over 13 million copies per day in a nation of just over 110 million. In Britain, with a population of about 55 million the *Sun* sells four million copies a day. We can cite many such instances; but these should suffice. In India in 1981, with a population of 68 crores, and 24 crores people at least nominally literate, there is not a single newspaper daily, weekly or of any other periodicity, chain or non-chain, linked with monopolies or totally non-linked, single or multi-edition – which has yet crossed the seven figure barrier. With the increase in the cost of newsprint and other inputs, it seems unlikely that that million mark would be crossed in the near future even by any multi-State newspaper. And even if a paper like the *Indian Express*, published from ten centres, were to cross it, it should not be a cause for concern; for France and England are comparable not with India, but only with some of the Indian States.

8. In the case of the Indian languages, there is no daily selling more

than five lakh of copes, although the *Malayala Manorama* and the *Ananda Bazar Patrika* may soon make it; and there is only one Tamil periodical, *Kumudam*, which has crossed the half-million mark. In many of the Hindi-speaking States, a circulation of 50,000 copies was something to crow about even ten years ago. State level weeklies have not yet come into existence in Hindi. India is thus nowhere near the point at which the countries of Western Europe stood even at the beginning of this century. Their problems, are, therefore, not our problems.

9. The majority view, it appears to us, is a nostalgic throwback to the days when metropolitan English language newspapers were dubbed contemptuously as the "Jute Press" by the neo-Brahmin politician, the I.C.S. bureaucrat an the academic of Oxbridge vintage who looked down on the businessman and the industrialist who had taken over some of the British-owned newspapers. The monopoly of the mass circulation newspapers, the concentrations of ownership, the capacity to pollute the inky Ganga of the print-media at its source – all these eventualities which the First Press Commission apprehended have not materialised; but our colleagues appear to think they have.

10. What are the arguments which the majority members of our Commission have advanced in support of their recommendation, for delinking from other businesses, as an experimental first instalment, thirty-two daily newspapers each selling over a lakh of copies and for diffusion of their ownership and control?

11. One strand of argument runs thus: "The power, associated with control of means of production in the past has now been, to a great extent, transferred to those who control the mass media as it can no longer be sustained otherwise. Those who control the means of production try to control the media not only for profit but much more so for perpetuation of power associated with their possession of means of production". (Chapter X, Para 46)

12. And again: "When newspapers are controlled by other big businesses they become vehicles of expression of the ideology of their owners and the selection, presentation and display of news in such newspapers would be dictated by that ideology. The newspaper industry in their hands becomes involuntarily the cultural arm of other businesses and industries. They become naturally antagonistic to the implementation of certain key Directive Principles contained in Part IV of the Constitution. It is enough for our purpose to say that legislative measures needed for achieving the goals of our State run counter to the

vested interest of the owners of those big newspapers who have huge interests in other businesses." (Para 37)

13. Delinking and diffusion, the interposition of trustees between the management and the editor, the price-page schedule, the fixing of a news-to-advertisement ratio, the imposition of a penal import duty on daily newspapers whose average page level exceeds 12 per day, all these are measures recommended by the majority to insulate the newspaper-office from the winds of production-relations which are blowing outside, so that the Press does not become a spokesman of the propertied classes, which they contend have always opposed measures designed to ensure social justice and to reduce disparities of income and property.

14. According to the school of thought whose arguments have found favour here, all institutions are inevitably moulded by the pattern of production-relations obtaining in a given society. The institutions may be social (family, marriage, caste), political (parties, elections, government, judiciary), academic (universities, seats of learning), or even aesthetic (folk arts, poetry and traditions), but they cannot avoid the tell-tale fingerprints of the economic processes which have shaped them. Thus according to this logic, insulation of the Press from production-relations as recommended by the majority should be a chimera, just as bourgeois democracy should be a chimera for them, because the Press is only the super-structure, the apex-manifestation of a whole range of economic processes which it has no power to control or regulate. But it seems that according to the majority, the twentieth century is not like the nineteenth, and that the Press is now not the super-structure, but a part of the foundational-structure of capitalism, so that without the active support of a monopoly-dominated Press, production-relations as they obtain today would suffer a grievous collapse.

15. This faith in the power of the Press is touching, but we believe that it is misplaced. We are living under the aegis of a mixed, plural system which has its own virtues and vices. The Press too is a part of that rich plurality. Pressmen cannot be turned into charming goldfishes swimming effortlessly in an artificially lit aquarium, protected from the eddies and whirls of their natural habitat. Is it feasible or desirable to put the Press under a glass-domed oxygen tent of its own, so that pure minds may breathe pure oxygen, and survive under a round-the-clock vigil?

16. Another strand of thought which runs through this portion of

the Report (Chapter X, Section 5) is again riddled with contradictions. The majority members are dissatisfied not merely with the fact that the newspapers are linked to their owners but also with the fact that they are linked to their readers. On the one hand, they have a great revulsion against the sinful notion of profits on the other, they are scared of what might happen to newspapers if they come under the debasing influence of their readers. They want the newspapers to be delinked even from the temptations of circulation, because for the sake of circulations they might ponder to the leering, lascivious devil that is there in all of us.

17. The majority says: "But news when printed and published has to be sold. The newspaper-buying public may not like unpleasant news or distasteful opinions. The production of newspapers . . . depends upon public favour. But how far are they entitled to court public favour in their efforts to earn more profits? To what extent do they betray their trust if they trim their news or their opinion to suit the public taste?"

18. Quoting Professor O.R. McGregor of the British Royal Commission on the Press, the majority state: "A newspaper cannot, therefore, raise its standard far above that of the public, and may anticipate profits from lowering its standard in order to gain an advantage over a competitor."

19. "A successful newspaper", they complain. "tailors its contents to the demand of mass circulation with a mixture of news, features, serial stories and pictures, all kept brief, designed for casual reading, slanted to entertainment value and intended to attract as broad a cross section of the potential public as possible." (Para 48)

20. The complaint, in substance, is that a newspaper is a newspaper, and not a research journal or a sociological tract. The complaint is that newspapers present news and views in a readable form. The complaint is that they care for the readers.

21. We are of the opinion that this is another case of the British perception of British reality being transposed to the Indian scene. "Popular" and "quality" dailies (as they are known in England) do not yet coexist in India, because most of our dailies are "quality" ones, or are at any rate trying to emulate the virtues of the quality newspapers. Few of them are "popular", or trying to imitate the vices of popular British newspapers. Therefore, these fears are vicarious.

22. The majority state: "If the *raison d'etre* of mass media is not to maximise discussion but to maximise profit by resort to sensationalism and extravagance, or to indulge in biased presentation and display of

news and opinion with a view to boosting some personalities or carrying on propaganda against others, its performance will hardly comport with its social responsibility." And through their recommendations they expect to change this *raison d'etre*.

23. But are these the major blemishes of the major newspapers of India? Although in other Chapters of the Commission's Report, tribute has been paid to the soberness, responsibility and sense of social commitment of the Indian Press, although it has been acknowledged that the "popular" Press of the West thriving on stories of sex and crime has no counterpart yet in India, in this portion of the Report the majority seem to believe that sensationalism and depravity are the major blemishes of the leading dailies of the country, which require instant rectification.

24. The class-character of the owners is not the only factor which worries the majority; the class-character of readership is also galling to them. Newspapers are oriented towards the urban elite, they grumble, (Para 37) and lament that the rural masses, and the poorer sections of society, are neither covered properly, nor do they have as adequate a choice of newspapers as the richer city folks have.

25. In Chapter III (Role of the Press) the Commission has taken note of the fact that in spite of their urban middle class backgrounds, our journalists have an adequate sense of guilt, and that they go out of their way to highlight the problems of the oft-forgetten poor. But how is the press to blame if its readership is predominantly urban? Surely it is not as if there is a ready market for, another genre of rural newspapers in the countryside, which the Press in India has failed to serve? In producing a newspaper, how can anyone address non-readers? One can at the most make the readers aware of what the non-readers are missing.

26. In Chapter III, the Commission has visualised a three-tier development of the Indian Press consisting of papers having multi-State circulations, those having State-level impact, and those catering to clusters of districts. The district Press in India has not yet come of age, and the Commission has suggested various measures, including the setting up of a Newspaper Development Commission to assist its growth. But the nature and role of the three tiers is different, and a paper with multi-State circulation cannot be expected to play the role of a district paper, or *vice versa*.

27. There are other objections too. The majority want (Para 50) to delink the Press from the boorish semi-literate businessman who wants

to earn profits on what should be a public utility, who has no aptitude or training for the learned profession of running a newspaper, who is not steeped in the ethos of journalism and would not fight for its causes, who cannot converse wit an editor on the same intellectual wave-length, and cannot indeed brook the idea of an independent-minded editor. This approach as we have said, is unrealistic.

28. "Persons who control the newspaper world ought to have an intellectual and educational background", the majority state. This time they have a quarrel not with the tastes of the readers, or the property background of the owners, but with the ethos of the proprietors. "A person who has taken special interest in the newspaper business itself is likely to have a greater understanding and competence in such matters. He is also more likely to fight for the principles for which he developed the newspaper. This is less likely to be the case with a businessman for whom the newspaper is one among many businesses or is an instrument to help his other business interests."

29. The idea here is that an owner should be ready to incur losses and even to preside over the liquidation of his business for the sake of the high ideals of journalism. But is it seriously believed that legislation can create such owner-martyrs? There would always be owners who are bold and idealistic as well as owners who are timid and security-conscious.

30. The majority seem to think that mercantile winds are blowing over the Press more furiously than they do elsewhere. They say: "In a sense the trusteeship or moral responsibility of the Press is a kin to that ministers of religion, statesmen and leaders of public thought. In another sense it is subject to industrial and mercantile conditions that do not affect these other trustees in the same degree."

31. It is true that the democratic managers of our political system are trustees unaffected by industrial and mercantile conditions? All the ills to which the press is allegedly heir have a more virulent counterpart in the political system. Not all our politicians are delinked from money-bags, nor are they delinked from votes, because of which they have to pander to the aspirations as well as to the bigotry and parochial interests of the electorate. All voters are not equal; there is a vote-tilting elite whose influence on the system is far greater than its numerical strength. If newspapers are vendors of news, politicians have to trade off assurances, and rose-tinted horizons, which may turn out to the phoney. Of course, this parallel does not absolve the Press;

but parallel has been drawn only to point out that there are no panaceas.

32. And the majority, if they could have their way would have the newspapers delinked also from advertisements, because of which the papers are sold below cost, and for the sake of which they have to strive for a higher circulation. A higher circulation depends, according to the majority, not on the quality or the coverage of a newspaper but on its sensationalism. Since advertisers look out for a readership with high purchasing power, the 32 top dailies are forever on the look-out for an urban readership and perhaps wilfully shutting out the rural subscribers.

33. Editors, according to the majority, are caught in a pincer. On the one hand they have to play the tune which their masters want them to play; on the other, they have also to provide what the readers demand. Thus they have to part company with their conscience and conviction in the service of the two masters. The editor's mind, according to this view, is a hollow hulk from inside, of which noises emerge purely as a result of the interplay of the conflicting pressures of the owners and the readership.

34. The ultimate quarrel of the romantic revolutionary who wants to restructure human society is perhaps with the fact that society is human, and that human beings are so classed and intractable, so unable to transcend their human condition. The ultimate quarrel of the majority-members who want to restructure our most responsible and quality-conscious dailies seems to be with those very elements which place some of them qualitatively in the top class. They want them to be free by transcending every earthly necessity. The papers are enjoined to transcend the property interests and the cultural backgrounds of the owners, the depraved inclinations of their readers, the necessity of a certain optimum proportion of advertisements and so on. Their vision of a restructured press could find embodiment only if the Press became a disembodied spirit, and severed all connections with the blood-vessels of the dark, messy womb of society within which it is growing and finding sustenance. Is it feasible? Can the Press grow like a bambino who is in the womb, and yet not a part of it?

35. The majority want the Press to be turned into a monastic order, with strict rules relating to celibacy, pollution, purity, penances, fasts, and so on. They want the profession to be handed over to a collegium of angels, so that newspapers are run by an ethical-intellectual aristocracy the like of which is to be found only in Plato's Republic.

We have nothing but respect for this ardent vision, but we see no way of bringing it down upon this planet.

36. As we said, delinking would not exorcise the pall of curses which according to the majority hangs over the newspapers, the thirty-two big dailies, or the other 17,000 most of them poorly run. It would not turn this industry into a vocation, or give it a set of Hippocratic oaths. After newspapers are delinked from other interests, they shall still be run by owners, whoever they may be. Their ideological alignments will not necessarily be different from those of today's owners. The production-relations of our society shall not leave them untouched. Even monastic Buddhism, let it be remembered, could not be delinked from the prosperity of trading Vaishya castes, whose emergence made it possible for this non-conformist religion to prosper. The concern of non-linked owners with profitability is likely to be more absolute and obsessive because, being non-linked, they would have no other financial resources to cushion their losses, whether the non-linked owners would have any greater flair for or commitment to the profession of journalism is doubtful. In thousands of small and medium newspapers, we have non-linked owners; but is it seriously contended that their professional norms or ethical standards are higher than those of the linked ones? Are they better qualified to run their papers than those whose circulations have crossed one lakh?

37. If the big dailies are delinked, and their owners have no other business or industrial interests, how is it likely to curb the alleged tendency of the newspapers to sensationalise, and to pander to the baser instincts of the readers for the sake of circulation and advertisement? How is it likely to ensure that newspapers would no longer address themselves to an urban elite, that all of a sudden, their contents would undergo a seachange so that a vast new readership waiting in the countryside would begin buying them by the million? Are the papers which are non-linked performing any such function? Is it not obvious that this problem has nothing to do with ownership links? The fact of the matter is that papers are not being read in the villages because of illiteracy, lack of purchasing power and lack of communications. It may be true that not many owners and journalists with their upper or middle class backgrounds know what changes in content would make their papers appealing, useful, and instructive to a rural readership, but that is no the major hurdle, for if there were a potential market, papers which requisite contents would come up in no time.

38. The problem of the weak editor who is dominated by an overbearing owner is not solved by delinking; nor the alleged tendency of the editor to pass off a fake and adulterated opinion as his own (Paras 35-36) under the twin influences of what the readers demand and what the owner wants to supply. In fact apart from a few hundred newspapers who run their concerns according to some norms, weakly or strongly adhered to, quite a large part of the newspaper business follows no norms, and the institution of the editor, as distinct from proprietor, does not even exist in may among them.

39. As a matter of principle, and as part of an overall policy against concentration of economic power, it might be desirable to delink the Press from other industries. However, there is no specific evidence before us that industries with such links are exercising appreciable influence on the news and views which appear in such newspapers. We also find that no overall policy of curbing the growth and breaking up existing concentrations is being followed in the country, and any policy which affects only the newspaper industry may cause more harm than good. Moreover, it must be recognised that there is no virtue in delinking for its own sake. Delinking, if it is to be fruitful, must promote the growth of newspapers on right lines and not result in their emasculation and eventual closure. It is significant that no credible answer to the question how a newspaper could be properly run after it is delinked could be provided by any one who appeared before the Commission or submitted a memorandum. There have been some proposals which, on the face of it, appear to be impracticable. An alternative, like the running of a newspaper by an employees' cooperative has been tried and has failed. In such a situation, unless we can suggest a workable substitute, we consider it highly undesirable to adopt a doctrinnaire attitude and to recommend delinking. It might starve a quality paper of necessary finances and spell its ruin. On an anxious consideration and having due regard to the absence of a feasible alternative, we are unable to recommend delinking merely as an article of a faith.

40. To conclude, we are of the opinion that newspapers are neither all virtuous nor vicious. They are a mixed lot, but their plurality, we believe, should not be done away with though massive State interference, because the remedy would be worse than the disease. That, of course, does not mean that we are smugly content with things as they are. That is why we have whole-heartedly endorsed or made significant recommendations in this Report which we believe would

change the journalistic scene in India. Even in regards to delinking and the price-page scheduled, we are recommendation elsewhere what we consider to be worthwhile alternatives.

41. We believe that it would be tragic beyond words if, in trying to turn the Press into a public utility, its viability as an industry were to be destroyed. Press as commerce and Press as a mission may seem to be too contradictory to reconcile on a purely abstract plane, but in real life such contradictions are resolved in a working synthesis.

PART II

THE ECONOMIC ASPECTS

The National Monopoly Houses

To begin with, the Commission decided to establish the facts – which of the newspaper undertakings were owned or controlled by a large industrial or business groups. The IIPA was engaged to undertake a study on this subject. On receiving the study, we found that, while it provided certain valuable material, it failed to arrive at clear and indisputable conclusions.

2. The study uses a category called "national monopoly houses", but does not define it. It does not say what tests have been applied to include a particular newspaper undertaking in this category. The Commission found it difficult to pursue this matter further and therefore decided not to rely on this concept. In fact, it has been stated in the relevant Appendix that "it is not possible to come to a definite finding on the question whether the Benett Coleman and Company (publishers of the *Times of India* group of publications) is a constituent of the Sahu Jain House". Similarly the Commission's office in its appraisal of the IIPA study comes to the conclusion that "it is not possible to confirm the IIPA report finding that the *Statesman* Ltd., is an enterprise 'under joint ownership and control of a group of private industrial houses'." About the *Indian Express* group, it is clearly stated that "it is not possible to confirm the study finding that the Express Newspapers belong to a National Monopoly House".*

---

* Appendix X. 4.

Why a New Category?

3. That is presumably why the report has evolved and used a different categorisation. The two most important categories under its scheme are: "(1) Newspapers owned or controlled by companies or undertakings or businessmen with interests in other businesses or industries"; and, "(2) Newspapers owned or controlled by companies or families or individual or groups of individuals with primary interest in newspaper business".* The approach is to include in category (1) all newspapers in which 50 per cent or more of the ownership or control is held by companies or businessmen with interests in other businesses or industries. We find that this categorisation is based on nebulous concepts.

4. As for ownership, it is hardly possible for newspapers to be owned and run by individuals, companies or trusts with *no* other business interests. The report itself further admits that, while determining the extent of control, "we have relied on *prima facie* evidence; for we could not undertake a detailed study of the working of every newspaper undertaking in the country."

5. The basis of this categorisation apart, surprisingly a group like the *Indian Express* has been included in category (1). Even the Monopolies Inquiry Commission had stated that the Express Group Chairman, Shri Ram Nath Goenka's "industrial interests (outside the Press) do not appear to be large." It is true that this finding was made in 1965; around 1969-70 Shri Goenka was involved in large-scale purchases of shares of the Indian Iron and Steel Co., and a company called Express Traders was set up, one of whose activities was to carry on the purchase and sale of shares on the stock exchange on behalf of the newspaper companies. But IISCO has since been nationalised and with that Shri Goenka's association with the steel industry has ceased.

6. Similarly his association with the jute industry also ceased as a result of the nationalisation of the National Company. Outside the newspaper world he is known to have acquired interests only in companies engaged in the real estate business. The main assets of those companies are the building which are used mainly to house the offices, etc., of his newspapers and also for letting out. It is true that the *Indian Express* Group of companies did not respond to the request of information from the reconstituted Commission on some of these matters. But that cannot invalidate Shri Goenka's evidence before the Commission in which he explicitly stated that "most of the buildings

come within the purview of the newspaper company. The Express building also belongs to the newspaper. Every penny earned by the Company has been ploughed back to the Company itself". He also pointed out that for quite a long period now he was not a director of any company outside the *Indian Express* Group.*

7. For the purpose of the categorisation made in the report, only newspaper companies in which either 50 per cent or more of the shares are held by persons with their main interests in other industries or businesses, or in which more than 50 per cent of the directors held directorship of other companies or businesses unconnected with newspaper publishing and allied fields are included. This latter categorisation is also difficult to understand. It is well known that a large number of individuals are appointed on boards of directors mainly for the purpose of obtaining the benefit of their knowledge and experience. Many of them do not necessarily have much control by way of share ownership in the undertaking in which they are directors. Some companies do not even require qualification shares to be held by their Directors. Benett Coleman is one such company. Therefore, to take note of the other directorships held by directors of a given undertaking, and on that basis to say that a substantial control over the newspaper company is exercised by persons with interests outside the newspaper business, is again to take an unrealistic view of the manner in which businesses are organised and directors are appointed.

8. In the case of *The Statesman*, the report** proceeds on the ground that three of the five directors have interests outside the newspaper industry. But it is well known that Shri J.C. Shah, a retired Chief Justice of India has only a nominal shareholding in the *Statesman* Limited. By calling he is not a businessman and, whatever other directorships he holds, as for example in the Bombay Gas Company, he does by virtue of his knowledge and experience. In fact, Shri C.R. Irani is known to control *The Statesman* and his own interests are confined to the newspaper world.

9. It is, however, not difficult to understand why the report seeks to build up this category by using criteria which are neither meaningful in terms of the actual working of business concerns nor very logical and

---

* Also see Shri Goenka's interview in the *Sunday* magazine 7-13 March, 1982, pp. 19-22, "Every pie that I earned went into this expansion (of the Express)."

** Appendix X.7.

clear. For it is obvious that our colleagues have done so in order to find support for their recommendation in favour of delinking the ownership and control of newspaper undertakings from other businesses.

Are Commercial Considerations Irrelevant?

10. We have no quarrel with the general propositions which are laid down in the report regarding the necessity to ensure "the fullness and unbent integrity of news and comment on news."* We wish some notice of the State monopoly in India in the field of broadcasting had been taken in this context. But nothing has been said on the implications for the Press of State monopoly in broadcasting.

11. We are principally concerned with the assumption that in order to ensure that newspapers are properly conducted, it is necessary to delink them from other businesses. The majority quote with evident approval the phrase "the jute Press". This is highly unfair to the Indian Press. It is also factually inappropriate. The jute industry is in the doldrums and this declining industry cannot be said to exercise much control over any important newspaper concern. They use unfortunate phrases such as "professional mercenarism". But they do not give serious consideration to the fact that the Press has to be run as an industry, a business, and only its successful conduct as a business can enable it to satisfy the interest of its readers and of society. The report shows a peculiar hostility to business considerations. "Although the first duty of a newspaper must remain the supply of reliable and comprehensive news and honest editorial comment, it is obvious that, after all, the business is concerned directly with the value of its advertising and the cost of its newsprint."** If these are to be ignored, how is the Press to operate? By relying on subsidies from Government, or by becoming sick? The report merely shows disregard for economic considerations without any understanding of the nexus between the freedom of the Press and its commercial soundness.

12. The country accepts a pattern of mixed economy in which large inequalities of incomes and consumption continue, and consumerism is not only permitted but encouraged. It is then realistic to expect that newspapers should not use advertisements from such producers as a major source of revenue. Is not the Government itself permitting the

---

* See Chapter X, Para 34.

** Chapter X, Para 48.

broadcasting media under its direct control of obtain revenue from advertising in the same manner? Moreover, how can delinking of the ownership and control of newspaper business from other types of business bring about a change in the attitude to and role of advertising in the newspaper industry, unless it is to be assumed that the delinked papers can ignore commercial considerations?

Alleged Impact of Links

13. It has been alleged in the report that newspapers controlled by other big businesses become vehicles of expression of the ideology of their owners, and the selection, of news in such newspapers is dictated by that ideology. The report cites no evidence to support this contention. Nowhere does it show that the choice of news for prominent display differs significantly in newspapers which are differently owned.

14. In support of their charge of prejudice on the part of major newspapers in favour of "vested interest", the majority have said that they have opposed policies and legislations that went against the interests of private big business such as the Companies Act, the MRTP Act and nationalisation proposals. The least they could have done was to show that all leading newspapers had taken the same line on these and similar issues and that those newspapers which are not linked with other businesses (e.g., *The Hindu*, the *Ananda Bazar Patrika* or *Sakal*) took a different line. In the absence of evidence to that effect it is a mere conjecture to suggest, as the report does, that, "legislative measures needed for achieving the goals of our State run counter to the vested interests of the owners of these big newspapers who have large interests in other businesses."

15. A reference is made in the report to the Vivian Bose Commission (1962) which inquired into the Administration of Dalmia-Jain Companies and pointed out some of the malpractices indulged in by the businessmen then controlling the affairs of Bennett, Coleman and Co. The implications of this have not been spelt out. Does it imply that businessmen should not control newspaper undertakings? By this logic, no major industry should be left in the hands of private entrepreneurs. Moreover, is it suggested that such malpractices and manipulations are to be found only in large business organisations, and not in medium and small business organisations? Above all, is it not common knowledge that Government companies

and departments are not immune from similar practices?

16. It has also been pointed out in the report that it was stated in the evidence before the Commission that attempts were made to suppress the circulation of news reports about these matters not only by the newspapers belonging to this Company but by newspapers generally.* From the data on which the majority relies, it is apparent that the *Statesman* gave an adequate coverage to the report. The *Hindu* carried a story based on the PTI version. This can be characterised as inadequate. But, on the basis of this instance which too have not been fully investigated as indicated by the fact that the story in only two newspapers has been cited, what conclusions can be drawn? Surely the recommendation for delinking cannot be based on so slender a basis.

17. A further point made in this context is that "particular individuals or groups could manage through various devices like inter-corporate investments, etc., to exercise a degree of control, grossly disproportionate to their own financial contribution or stake in the newspaper organisations". The data given in the Palekar Award Report of the slender capital base of a company like Bennett Coleman is cited in this connection.** But that inference regarding delinking can be drawn from this? This can happen in any well-established or financially well-managed concern, delinked or otherwise. And is this to be deplored?

18. Mention has been made in the report of a Bill that had been prepared in 1971 to bring about a change in the ownership of newspaper companies. Comments also appeared in newspapers about serious thought being given by the Government in 1974 to this question, and even the preparation of the draft of a Bill in this regard. Apparently, after deliberation, the authorities came to the conclusion either that the move was not feasible or that it was not desirable.

Linked Units – Nebulous Concept

19. As explained earlier, the concept – "newspaper owned or controlled by companies or businessmen with interest in other industries", is both nebulous and of doubtful utility. A much better way of approaching the problem would be to use the approach taken by the

---

* Chapter X, Para 41.

** *Ibid.*

Monopolies Inquiry Commission whereby the substance of control was sought to be examined.* Where data showed that a particular business was substantially or effectively controlled by a particular business group taking into account various data, such as shareholding – with various interlocking and other methods of control through shareholdings, inter-locking directorships, etc., these were treated as belonging to the same business group. This of course would have been a formidable task for a Press Commission.

20. The other and more practical approach for our Commission would have been to take the criteria laid down in the MRTP Act, viz., either the undertakings whose own assets together with the assets of interconnected undertakings are not less than 20 crores of rupees in value or a dominant undertaking where the assets together with the assets of inter-connected undertakings are not less than one crore of rupees in value. Bennett, Coleman and Co. Ltd. which controls the *Times of India* group of newspapers, and the *Indian Express* group are already registered under Section 20 of the MRTP Act, so also the *Eastern Economist* of the Birla group and Associated Publishers (publishers of the defunct *Main* of Madras) of the Amalgamation group.

21. If the majority had decided merely to confine their efforts to show that the *Hindustan Times* is controlled by the Birla groups, the *Anand Bazar Patrika* by the Sarkar family and the *Hindu* by the Kasturi family, there would have been no real difficulty. The difficulty arises because of the desire to establish something for which there is no clear evidence. For example, the majority wants to prove not only that the *Indian Express* Group of newspapers is controlled by Shri Ram Nath Goenka but that Shri Goenka and his family are substantially interested in other lines of business. They want to do this because their recommendation regarding delinking would lose much of its relevance at least for some of the protagonists of this idea if the *Indian Express* and the *Statesman* are excluded.

22. Some information about the *Indian Express* Group of companies has already been given above. *The Statesman* Limited is the other case of the same kind. Except for two corporate shareholders holding 12.56 per cent and 7.48 per cent of share capital, there are no other companies among the top 10 shareholders. Andrew Yule and

* See Annexure A to Appendix X.4.

Company Limited, holding 12.56 per cent, is now a Government of India enterprise. Thus, Guest Keen William Limited with 7.48 per cent shares, is the only private undertaking which is a top shareholder. The other top shareholders are combinations of individuals. The report claims that these "include a number of people connected or associated with big business undertakings".* This is a strange statement as there is no way in which it can be verified. Some of the individuals are lawyers, one is an educationist, one a medical practitioner and one a chartered accountant. They may also be associated professionally or in other ways with some business concerns. But it is highly in appropriate on that ground to say that this proves that the statesman limited is controlled by individuals who are otherwise interested in other industries and business. The report refers to an allegation that shares of the *Statesman* held by a number of individuals are held in *benami* names.** The circumstances during the Emergency in which corporate shareholders of the *Statesman* felt obliged to transfer these shares have been mentioned in the Appendix. Shri C. R. Irani, in his evidence before the Commission, also referred to this matter and contended that the corporate shareholders transferred their shares in order to avoid pressure from the Government.

23. As regards the board of directors, it is said that three of them. Shri J. C. Shah, Shri Birendra Mukherjee and Shri C. C. Choksi held other directorships. As the report puts it, "three have links with big business undertakings including some companies registered under the MRTP Act." But this cannot be taken to be a proof that the company is under the control of individuals with main interests in other industries or business activities. The data given in the Appendices show that the shares held by these individuals are quite a small proportion of the total shareholding. It is thus obvious that their "control" arises more from the confidence reposed in them by the majority of shareholders. It will thus be seen that the inclusion of the *Statesman* in this category is also more due to the pre-conceived notions of the majority of our colleagues than to an investigation made on the basis of any proper analysis.

24. A further example can be given. It relates to the Thanthi

---

* Appendix X. 7.

** *Ibid.*

Group.* The data available with the Commission only suggests that Shri B. S. Adityan who appears to be the major trustee of the Trust which controls the newspaper – "also holds directorships" in a number of other companies. No proof has been produced to show that he has a controlling interest in any of these companies or that he is substantially interested in these industries.

25. *The three examples show that our colleagues are ready to categorise newspapers undertakings on the basis of slender data.*

No Scrutiny of Product Monopoly

26. It would have been quite meaningful if the Commission had attempted to locate instances of product monopoly in the case of newspapers in a proper sense of the term. The Commission has adopted a definition of "dominance"** which we accept. But no attempt has been made to collect data which would suggest whether by that criterion any newspapers are dominant in their respective areas of circulation. The result is that at the end of the Commission's labours we are not better off in understanding the extent to which there is monopoly in the newspaper industry in any scientific sense of the term.

27. The Commission has provided data about the circulation of two dailies with the highest circulation in each state in 1979 (Appendix IX.9). But as admitted in the report***, there is no real competition among newspapers which come out in different languages. And if we take the newspapers in the particular language, it will be found that there are only a few situations of either dominant or monopolistic undertakings in the sense in which the MRTP Act uses these terms given if we make the wholly unrealistics assumption that the whole state constitutes an effective market for a newspaper. *Malayalam Manorama* in Kerala, *North East Mirror* is Shillong, *Samaj* in Orissa, *Punjab Kesari* in Punjab, *Tribune* in Chandigarh and *Nav Hind Times* in Goa have a circulation exceeding one third. Of these, all except *Malayala Manorama, Punjab Kesari* and *Tribune*, are dominant in states where the overall circulation of newspapers is pitfully small. Similarly, situations of "monopolistic" undertakings are also to be found mostly only in small States or States in which the total circulation of newspapers is very small.

28. If we examine the data given in Appendix X.10 about the circulation of the top two dailies in each language over the whole

* Appendix X 7.

** Chapter X, Para 32.

*** *Ibid.*

country, we find that the only cases of dominant units are those of *Dainik Asom* in Assamese, *Ananda Bazar Patrika* and *Jugantar* in Bengali, *Praja Vani* in Kannada, *Malayala Manorama* in Malayalam, *Samaj* in Oriya, *Hindustan* in Sindhi and *Eenadu* in Telugu. Even if we assume that the whole area of a language is to be treated as an effective market, quite an unrealistic assumption, this shows that what are popularly called monopoly papers are not dominant in the proper sense of the term.

29. Thus, the *Indian Express* with its 10 editions and the *Times of India* with its three editions together account for only 37 per cent of the total national circulation of the English language dailies. The really significant cases of monopolistic situations are those of *Ananda Bazar Patrika* in Bengali, *Praja Vani* in Kannada, *Malayala Manorama* in Malayalam and *Eenadu* in Telugu.

30. In any case, the majority does not claim that there is a dangerous monopoly situation in the newspaper industry; or that the existence or even the expansion of chain newspapers in the relevant areas would create such a situation. No celar case for any urgent action in this respect has, therefore, been established in the report. Of course, we agree with the majority view that there is no reason to exempt the newspaper industry from the MRTP Act.

Use of the MRTP Act

31. Our differences with coleagues in this regard arise from the further recommendations made by them relating to what they all delinking and diffusion of ownership and control. In this context, the initial point which we would like to put forward is that, while we entirely agree with the basic approach laid down in the Directive Principle (Article 39 of the Constitution) that the operation of the economic system should not result in the concentration of wealth and means of production to the common detriment, and therefore with the basic approach underlying the MRTP Act, we do not think that it is either appropriate or necessary to go further and single out the newspaper industry for discriminatory treatment in this matter.

32. The question about the growth of concentration of economic power of some of the large private business groups has been in the public eye for at least 20 years now, and the matter has received much public attention. The extent of such concentration was highlighted in the Report of the Monopolies Inquiry Commission in 1965. The

manner in which instrumentalities under the control of Government operate to help sustain and increase such concentration were brought out and remedies suggested in the Report of the Industrial Licensing Policy Inquiry Committee (1969). When the MRTP Act was passed in 1969 and the MRTP Commission set up in 1970, it was expected that rapid steps would be taken to examine to what extent some of the existing concentrations are against the public interest and, where this was found to be so, measures would be taken to bring about de-concentration. There was a provision for such action under Section 27 of the MRTP Act.

33. What has happened in the period of over a decade is well known. Little action has been taken to bring about any de-concentration, the only case regarding which a reference was made under section a reference which was made during the internal emergency period in 1976 when the *Indian Express* group of newspapers had become anathema to those in the ruling circle of Government. That this was a political action pure and simple was underlined by two further developments. When as a result of certain negotiations between the Government of India and the *Indian Express* Group, the Board of Directors of the *Indian Express* Group was reconstituted and Shri Ram Nath Goenka agreed to have a Government nominee as Chairman, the Government nominated Shri K.K. Birla as Chairman. Shri K.K. Birla was not only a prominant industrialist and one of the main persons controlling the large industrial house known by thier family name, but was also already Chairman of another major newspaper company, the *Hindustan Times* Limited. In spite of this, the Government thought it fit to nominate him as Chairman of the *Indian Express* Group. The reference under Section 27 of the MRTP Act was withdrawn in 1977 when a new Government came into power.

34. Whatever that might be, it can be clearly seen that the Government has hardly shown any interest in using the MRTP Act, and especially Chapter III of the Act, for bringing about any de-concentration of economic power in respect of large business groups. Not even one case has been examined with a view to ascertaining whether the existing concentration is harmful to public interest. Moreover, in the latest Industrial Policy Statement of August 1980, various concessions to large business groups have been announced. In March 1982 itself, the Prime Minister has clarified that Core Sector industries would be open for entry by Large Industrial Houses. In such a situation, would it not be invidious to single out the

newspaper industry as one where some special and early steps for bringing about delinking and deconcentration should be taken?

35. A major objection to the newspaper industry being singled out for separate and special treatment in this matter is that there is enough evidence to suggest that there has been an increasing tendency on the part of the Government to create difficulties especially in the way of those newspapers which show an independent outlook. The larger newspaper undertakings are in a better position to maintain their independence than the smaller ones, though there have been excellent examples of some small newspapers who have shown courage to brave the wrath of the authorities. It would, therefore, be risky to arm the Government with further powers in relation to newspaper undertakings.

Use of Press Units as Adjuncts

36. The report speaks of a tendency among those who control newspaper undertakings to use these as adjuncts of other types of business. They have pointed out that the profits of a newspaper undertaking may be used for the benefit of other business. The only example cited in support of this is that of the *Indian Express* whose management used the funds of the newspaper companies to buy shares of IISCO. The explanation given by the management is that this was an attempt to invest the newspaper funds in a 'blue chip' for the benefit of the newspapers. We cannot pursue — the Commission has not pursued — this enquiry further. The data are inconclusive. Moreover, this argument can also cut the other way. For, there are instances of owners having used their profits in other industries to finance newspapers. As it happens, not many newspapers in the country make substantial profits, and their position is likely to deteriorate further as a result of rising costs.

37. The report also cites the example of Bennet, Coleman and Co. It has made a provision in its Memorandum of Association to carry on other business activities such as (1) rural development; (2) chemicals, cement, synthetic fibre and yarn and jute industries; (3) manufacture of items using jute, bamboo, grass, sugarcane, hessian, gunnies, asbestos, waste paper, etc.; (4) processing of agricultural produce and making of oil etc., from the same; and (5) manufacture of paper. The Company has also decided to add shipping and electronics to its business activities and the necessary application for amendment of the

Memorandum of Association has already been made. While we agree that such diversification may be undesirable and should be discouraged, it is apparent that such additions to the Memorandum of Association cannot have been made without the approval of the Government, and we understand that the Government has given such approval in this case.*

38. Moreover, a company registered under the MRTP Act – as this company is – cannot take up new activities without the Government's permission under that Act. But, as pointed out earlier, it is not at all certain what use Government will make of these powers. The inter-connections between this newspaper undertaking and other undertakings can also be scrutinised and an enquiry ordered under Section 27 of the MRTP Act if this it found necessary. But Government has not used these powers. We see no point in arming Government with more powers. It would have been a different matter if the majority had recommended that an independent body like the MRTP Commission should be authorised to scrutinise all such matters. They have made no such recommendation. They have only proposed that any action under the MRTP Act in respect of a newspaper undertaking should be taken after consultation with the Commission so as to ensure a public hearing of the matter. We support this recommendation.

Indifference to Labour

39. It has been stated in the report that "odd exceptions apart, commercial newspapers do not normally find a word to say in sympathy with the legitimate demands of the working class".** It is true that most large newspapers are not too pro-labour : the trade union side of industrial disputes and problems of rural labour often do not receive their sympathetic attention. But to some extent this is in keeping with the overall professional in adequacies that we find in the newspaper industry. It has little to do with the ownership structure, because it is not as if delinked papers or smaller papers – except those run by political parties of the left or by committed individuals – act differently. Similar is the case in a number of other fields. There are

---

* Letter from the Company Affairs Department to the Press Commission (No. CLB/WR/Bench/Gen/82, dated 16-2-1982).

** Chapter X, Para 37.

large geographical areas in the world, including many Third World countries, to which little attention is paid even in our major newspapers. The same holds for science and technology and many basic social and economic problems facing the country. But these inadequacies are not likely to be removed by delinking. In fact investigative journalism which has unearthed the oppression of bonded labour, agricultural labour and *Harijans* as well as many other oppressed sections has been more vigorously pursued in what have been considered by the majority in the Commission as 'linked' papers as much if not more than the unlinked ones.

40. Where taste for information on literature and the arts is lacking, the taste has to be created. Reports and features on these subjects have to be obtained, written up in a manner where they will be appreciated by new classes of readers and the general level of readership raised. Financially strong papers can do this more easily. Thus what is required is an improvement in the financial strength of newspapers and also better training facilities for journalists and greater competition among newspapers. We support such measures. That is why we have been so enthusiastic about the unanimous recommendations of the Commission for the setting up of a new organisation – the Newspaper Development Commission – for this purpose and would like the Government to give it the highest priority.

Dislike of Good Editors

41. The Report also states that "newspaper proprietors today dislike editors and editorial writers of strong personality. They prefer that their own personalities should be served by expert scribes, who can be trusted to advocate whatever view the proprietor may wish to proclaim. In the old days many proprietors cared . . . for the freedom of the Press".* Leaving aside this constant harking back to the old days when proprietors – and everyone else – are supposed to have been must better, one may well ask what proof there is that newspaper proprietors dislike editors and editorial writers of strong personality? None of the editors who are Members of the Commission have had such experience. There would obviously be some proprietors who prefer to have only submissive persons working with them as editors; but there

* Chapter X, Para 48.

would be others who are different. Unless the proprietors are not interested in, making their newspaper ventures a success, they would obviously not like to have editors or editorial writers who make no impact on the public mind because in such an event their papers would have less credibility and this cannot but affect the circulation of the paper. At the same time, there are personalities in all walks of life, whether it is newspapers, other business or politics, who are so egotistical that they would expect nothing but subordination and sycophancy from their employees or followers. It is, however, usually understood that such an approach is self-defeating, short-sighted and does not help long-term success whether of the business venture or of the political organisation.

42. It would indeed be a short-sighted and stupid business magnate who will appoint a sycophant or a stooge as an editor of his newspaper, because that way lies the road to ruin of the newspaper, as a business. In fact, such cases may be found more frequently, not among large newspaper enterprises where proprietors cannot but be more careful with the very large investments which are involved, but in small enterprises where the proprietors themselves are rather inadequate in their education and business undertaking. Among the newspapers which have suffered as a result of interference by management, one finds examples not of those belonging to large newspaper organisations, but of small ones.*

43. The report says: "Persons who control the newspaper world ought to have an intellectual and educational background". A persons who has taken special interest in the newspaper business itself is likely to have greater understanding and competence in such matters."** While this statement is unexceptionable, does it imply that all those who control a newspaper undertaking should be either journalists or those who are communications specialists? If so, it will require a change in the whole set up of ownership and control not only in the private sector but also the public sector; for it will pertain to the qualifications of owners as well as Ministers. By this logic, many of our top people in various fields should not hold the positions they do. There is here a confusion between true ability and aptitude on the one

* For example, see the record in this respect of the Associated Journals Limited — special report in *India Today*, February 15, 1982. This is not a business enterprise, but one run by a trust under political control.

** Chapter X, Para 50.

hand and formal education on the other.

44. The report makes the point that a proprietor "who has taken special interest in the newspaper business itself is likely to have greater understanding and competence in such matters. He is also more likely to fight for the principles for which the developed the newspaper". This proposition ignores the possibility that such a person is likely to interfere far more with the edition if the editor is different from the proprietor. Evidence before the Commission confirms our impression in this regard.

The French Ordinance

45. In support of the proposed measure, to delink newspaper business from other business activities, the report cites* an Ordinance issued in France in 1944. The emphasis of the French Ordinance, which was issued on the second day after the Liberation of Paris is August 1944, is on ensuring that everything important about the ownership and financing of a newspaper should be open to public scrutiny. It prohibits the flow of foreign money in any form in a newspaper undertaking. It also attempts to ensure that different newspapers do not get linked under a common direction. But it is well known that no administrative regulations or procedures for follow up of this last provision have been prepared and hardly any action taken against the concentration of ownership in the newspaper world. Increasing costs, intensive competition from radio and TV and other economic compulsions appear to have persuaded the French Authorities to put the Ordinance in cold storage. This history emphasises what our colleagues in the majority would like to ignore; the compulsions of the economic logic of a mixed economy and modern technology under which the Press has to function.

The Proposal for Delinking

46. An equally curious feature of the report is that the proposal of delinking is to apply to newspapers with circulations of one lakh and above. As mentioned above, there is not the slightest proof – if there is any proof, it is to the contrary – that these newspapers are either

---

* Chapter X, Para 51.

professionally or otherwise not serving the reader and the country in a reasonable manner. It is true that the majority approach is that one must make a beginning somewhere; but then why make a beginning with that section of the Press which is, by and large, serving the country better than the other sections? Why disturb them and take the risk that the reading public and the country will be illserved for quite some time to come as a result of the possible disturbance to the smooth functioning of these newspapers?

47. We are also unable to agree with the impractical proposals the report has put forward in this regard. Delinking* is expected to take the form of "a law in the interest of the general public making it mandatory for persons carrying on the business of publishing a newspaper to sever their connections with other business". Such a person, in the sense of an undertaking, "should not have directly or indirectly an interest in excess of the prescribed limit, in any other business. . . " In this context, "business" is supposed to mean "anything which occupies the time, attention and labour of a person for the purpose of profit". This last part of the definition is likely to lead to anomalies similar to those which attempt to distinguish between amateurs and professionals in the field of sports. It will merely mean, that those who describe themselves honestly as businessmen will have to be replaced – and can easily be replaced under the proposed measure – by those who describe themselves as practising other professions.

48. It has been proposed that "the person carrying on the business of publishing a newspaper should not have, *directly or indirectly*, an interest, in excess of the prescribed interest, in any other business. Secondly, the person carrying on the business of publishing a newspaper should not be in a position of being controlled, *directly or indirectly*, by any other person having an interest in excess of the prescribed interest."** The 'prescribed interest' is defined as interest exceeding ten per cent of the total interest involved in the publication of the newspaper. While there would be no difficulty in limiting the interest of the newspaper undertaking itself in other business activities to 10 per cent or less of the value of the assets of the undertaking, what would be difficult is to limit the interest of other persons who directly *or indirectly* control the newspaper. If it is the Chairman or the Managing Director whose interest is sought to be limited, that would

* See Chapter X, Paras 52-53.

** Chapter X, Para 56 (emphasis added).

pose no difficulty. But if this is to be applied to all directors, the implication would be that no director with any other business interest or holding directorships anywhere else can be a director of a newspaper company. This approach will do no good to a newspaper company.

49. A question arises whether this restriction is to apply even to shareholders. The report speaks of *direct or indirect* control. If this is to mean that the shares of newspaper companies are only or mainly to be owned by those who have no other business interests (including shareholding), they can then circulate only among persons who do not normally buy shares. This would confine the shareholding to a very limited group of persons. As it is, the shares of newspaper companies cannot be attractive because often there are no profits or very small ones. This restriction will make the shares even less attractive.

50. There are two other aspects of the proposals which need to be noted: One is that if the shares are sufficiently widely distributed among the public, even a 10 per cent shareholding can ensure control. It will also not be difficult if those in charge of the under taking reorganise their shareholdings in such a manner as to satisfy the requirements of law and still maintain their control. In this context, a statement made by the Chairman of Hindustan Times Limited* on the proposal regarding the divestment of shares is relevant. He had pointed out then that this could be done without affecting the editorial policy and in effect the control of the paper.

51. The majority recognises such possibilities and points our that various steps will have to be taken to work out a concept of control which will make such manipulations difficult. They have mentioned various possibilities of chain shareholding, *benami* holdings, etc., and suggested that special measures will have to be taken to prevent such practices. Among other aspects, they state,** "A concept of shareholding interest will have to be developed to work out the controlling interest of such a person over the newspaper company. While tracing the controlling interest from one company to another certain mathematical rationale could be employed. . . . " To take all types of director indirect beneficial interests, "it may be necessary to lay down that a person who is beneficially entitled to any shares shall be deemed (but not to the exclusion of any other person) to be in a

---

* See Annexure 1, Vol. VIII of the Report.

** Chapter X, Para 57.

position to exercise control of the voting rights in respect of those shares. . . . The concept of control which we contemplate is one which includes control as a result of or by means of agreements, *benami* transactions, trusts, arrangements, understandings and practices whether or not having legal or equitable force and whether or not based on legal or equitable rights".

52. We have serious doubts whether the Commission is competent to go into these wider questions relating to the Companies Act and the MRTP Act. In any case, the Commission has not given adequate thought to these matters in its deliberations and we feel concerned at the manner in which the report includes recommendations which have not been properly discussed and examined.

53. The cavalier approach in the report is also well-illustrated by the statement about the family relationship between the "Goenkas who control the Express Group of Newspapers" and the "Sahu Jains who control the Bennett Coleman and Co.'* It is mentioned that this is based on the fact that the daughter of Shri Shriyans Prasad Jain was married to the late Shri B. D. Goenka, son of Shri Ram Nath Goenka. But no mention is made of the fact that Shri Shriyans Prasad Jain or his daughter have no control over Bennett Coleman and Co. On the basis of such slender evidence, a horrifying picture of monopoly is attempted to be built up. "The newspapers brought out by them (i.e., the marriage-related Jains and Goenkas) command a lion's share of elite readership in the country". And the industries in which Bennett Coleman hold share (the Express Group has no such major industrial shareholdings now) are mentioned to show the extent of the aggregate empire ! The whole approach is unreal and based on a misconception.

Dangers Involved in the Proposal

54. The report also makes a proposal that every newspaper undertaking should file a declaration once every six months that the newspapers is not being published in contravention of the provisions of the proposed legislation. We wonder how any newspaper undertaking will be able to ensure that it has full information about the shareholdings of all its shareholders; how it will be able to make sure that it has information about *benami* shareholdings or various other

* Chapter X, Para 58.

indirect ways of holding and controlling shares. We are afraid that our colleagues have not really given enough thought to the practicability of the proposals they are making. In fact, some of them insist that practicability is not what they need to bother about, "Leave all that to Government", is their approach. Our fear is that such proposals can be used by those in positions of political and administrative power, to threaten newspaper undertakings so as to force them to fall in line with their wishes.

55. Our fears are justified by the approach taken in the report that on receipt of a complaint that the declaration by the newspaper undertaking is false, the MRTP Commission "or such other independent authority should have the power to inquire into the matter and render a finding on the complaint. If the declaration is found to be false, the magistrate concerned under the PRB Act should have the power . . . *to cancel the declaration of the newspaper*". Putting forward inpracticable conditions to be fulfilled by newspaper undertakings, and then threatening them with inquiries which can lead to threats of closure is the surest way of arming executive authorities with powers which can be abused.

56. Our colleagues in majority say in the report that they are "conscious that the newspapers which will come within the ambit of the proposed legislation are quality newspapers rendering good service to the community".* Yet in the interest of "accurate and fair presentation of news and views", they have recommended delinking. But, as we have pointed out, they have not adduced any evidence to show that the existing structure of ownership of major newspapers is leading to a distortion and unfair presentation of news and views. They quote the McGregor Commission's statement that "the Press should neither be subject to State control not left entirely to the unregulated forces of the market", but fail to draw the correct conclusion and make recommendations which may easily lead to State control of the Press.

57. This is amply proved by their proposal that persons who come within the purview of the proposed legislation will have to divest their interests, "If the shares of a newspaper company are not readily purchased by eligible persons from the open market, such shares could be acquired and held by an autonomous body or agency to be specified by the legislation till they are purchased by eligible persons."** A way

---

* Chapter X, Para 61.

** Chapter X, Para 59.

is thus to be opened for the backdoor nationalisation of substantial equity interests in important newspaper undertakings. The natural result – if not necessarily the intention – of the recommendations of our majority colleagues is thus amply clear.

No Strait/Jacket Solution

58. This does not mean that everything is fine in the world of newspaper ownership and control. In fact, there is evidence that control of newspapers by businessmen with other business interests exposes them to the risk of pressure from governments and ministers. It has thus been alleged that the Government tried in 1975-76 to put pressure on business concerns who were shareholders in the Statesman Ltd. to either sell their shares to nominees of the then Government, or at least hand over proxies to Government nominees so as to enable it to change the management and with it the editorial policy.

59. But our view is that there is no one and common solution which can be prescribed for all situations. To some extent, newspaper organisations themselves may carry out improvements, in form or in practice, or both, under pressure of public opinion. Witness the measure of independence editors in the Bennett Coleman and Co. group enjoy as shown by the evidence before the Commission.

60. *The Statesman* decided long ago that not more than 13 per cent of its shares should be held by any one business unit or group. When corporate shareholders found themselves under pressure, they took care to pass on their shares to individuals who in their view, would respect the traditions and autonomy of the newspaper. The correspondence between Shri K.K. Birla and Shri B.G. Verghese brings it out that the proprietors of *The Hindustan Times* were agreeable at one stage to the creation of a trust to take over certain aspects of management. Similarly, Shri Ram Nath Goenka in his evidence before the Commission stated that it will be his endeavour to create some sort of an organisation of a trust which will keep this paper alive after his death.

61. Certain changes will come about voluntarily as public opinion develops to demand and support such changes. Meanwhile it is necessary to remember that the newspaper industry is a sensitive one, and any outside interference with it should follow if at all, only after a most detailed and careful scrutiny, in each individual case, and the intervention should be the minimum necessary. A

bull-in-the-Chinashop approach will destroy such good institution as exist, without putting anything better in their place.

Proposed Board of Trustees

62. The report has also gone into the question of editorial independence. It has cited two example of conflicts between the management and the editor. Both these relate to important English-language dailies, viz., the *Hindustan Times* and the *Statesman*. We have no comments to offer on those two cases not do we disagree with the conclusions in the report that it will be useful to have an overall editorial policy laid down by the proprietors, and the editor left free so long as he functions within that framework. Where there is a distinct demarcation between the editorial and the managerial departments, as happens to be the case in large newspapers we also agree that the editor or the chief editor as the case may be, should have the authority and responsibility in respect of recruitment training, posting and promotions of the journalistic staff assigning work to them and supervising it. Obviously it would also be a good management practice not the editor is appointed for a reasonably long-term five years or more so that he can carry on his work with a long term perspective. All this is common ground between the majority and ourselves.

63. But we are unable to agree that difficulties regarding editorial independence arise only or mainly in newspapers with large circulation and that, therefore, steps be compulsorily taken regarding them.* As we mentioned earlier, no proof of any kind is available to show that these papers are not doing their job properly or that their editors are suffering by way of interference or bad treatment by their managements. No study is available to enable us to make a comparative statement regarding the position of editors in large, medium and small papers. But many of those acquainted with the journalistic world would vouch for the proposition that the position of editorial and journalistic staff is far worse in many of the medium and small papers than in the larger ones.

64. The report recalls the recommendations of the First Press Commission that the management of newspapers should be transferred to public trusts without making any changes in the ownership of the paper. "If this suggestion had been acted upon by the owners of big newspapers", the majority report state, "perhaps we may have had no

occasion to think of delinking ownership and control of newspapers from other business interests. It is precisely because the businessmen owning or controlling big newspapers have not acted on the advice of the first Press Commission of creating trusts for their management that we are obliged to seriously consider the question once again and seek other remedies."**

65. While making this statement, our majority colleagues have overlooked the fact that the owners in no industry or business of any magnitude in the country have practised such self-denial. Even the government authorities have refused to part with control over the broadcasting media to public corporations.

66. The report not only proposes the delinking of all large newspaper undertakings from other businesses by legislation but also the creation by law of controlling-cum-advising agencies for them.*** These authorities are to consist of three members subject to rotational retirement. The members – public men of eminence – are to be appointed by the managements of the respective newspaper undertakings, "in consultation with and with the approval of the Chairman of the Press Council and the Chief Justice of the High Court or the Chief Justice of India as the case may be depending upon the area of circulation of the newspaper concerned".

Editorial Independence

67. We regard it highly invidious that all such measures should apply only to newspapers which by all accounts are reasonably well managed and conducted, and that small and medium newspapers should be left alone, even though many of them may be far from being professionally well conducted and the treatment of editors and journalists may be far from satisfactory. We think that it is only appropriate that, in the interest of the proper conduct of all categories of newspapers, some effort should be made to ensure that a degree of protection is provided to editors and journalists from capricious interference and treatment. We, therefore, think that, except in the case of newspapers whose circulation does not exceed 25,000 per issue (which may have to be excluded on practical grounds), all newspaper

* Chapter X, Para 39.

** Chapter X, Para 113.

*** Chapter X, Para 113.

undertakings should be obliged to have a system by which the appointments, promotions, dismissals and disciplinary action regarding all editorial and journalistic staff should be subject to special scrutiny by a group of persons who are not involved in the ownership and management of the newspaper and who can be expected to have both an appreciation of the public responsibilities of the newspaper and a status which will ensure that their advice will be acceptable to the managerial and propretorial as well as the editorial and journalistic sides of the undertaking.

68. We, therefore, recommend that in all newspaper undertakings which are organised in the form of joint stock companies, one-third of the directors should be persons of eminence with experience in journalism, literature, administration, economics, law, science or other such professional fields. They should be selected by way of co-option by the Boards of Directors but should have a tenure of not less than three years each with a provision for rotational retirement. In the case of newspaper undertakings whether owned by trusts, or by individuals and partnerships, we recommend that an advisory board consisting of three members with backgrounds as indicated above should be constituted with a similar tenure and provision for retirement. The terms and conditions to be offered should be such as would enable capable persons to give the necessary time for accepting such responsibilities.

69. We further recommend that in all cases of appointments, promotions, dismissals or other disciplinary action relating to editorial and journalistic staff, the views of the special directors mentioned earlier, or of the advisory board as the case may be, must be ascertained by the managements of the newspaper undertakings and, in case there is a persistent difference of opinion between the management and these, the matter should go to arbitration.

70. We believe that it would be wrong to impose external control on news paper undertakings because their owners and managers must remain responsible for their financial soundness and viability. We cannot, therefore, endorse the recommendation in the report regarding the appointment of trustees being subject to the approval of outside authorities such as the Chairman of the Press Council or the Chief Justice. We also feel reinforced in our view by the fact that it would be impossible for the Chairman of the Press Council, however eminent and well-in-formed, to know about suitable persons in different parts of the country to work on the controlling boards of a large number of

newspapers published in different languages. We would not like the Chief Justice either of the High Courts or of the Supreme Court to be involved in such work for two reasons. One: They will have no machinery through which they can obtain confidential information about the names suggested and they themselves will normally not be knowledgeable enough about persons who would be suitable for such work so as to suggest alternative names. Two: It may well be that differences arise and prove difficult to resolve and lead to legal disputes. Finally, we think it only proper that the owners and the managers, just as they would be entitled to lay down the policy of the newspaper should also be entitled to appoint the eminent persons whose advice they would like to seek. The ownership and management cannot be divorced from the technical operation of what in the last resort is a business undertaking. Protection should be provided only against temporary aberrations and capricious behaviour. Our recommendation would take care of this.

Groups and Chains Not to be Deplored

71. There has been a persistent tendency in discussion relation to the Press industry not only to decry the relationships between certain newspaper undertakings and other business undertakings through business links and common ownership or control but even to speak about newspaper groups, combines or chain, as if these were in all cases to be deplored.

In this context, it needs to be kept in view that there are major economies of scale in the Press industry as in many others, and these arise on the journalistic, printing as well as commercial sides. Thus a newspaper group can benefit from the services of its own correspondents in different parts of the country and abroad and be in a position to offer more original news than its competitors. It can afford the services of high calibre cartoonists and also pay better for contributed articles. A good printing press with various up-to-date technical facilities can be intensively used if a number of publications are sharing its use. The purchase of various materials like newsprint and ink, the distribution of newspapers including incentives for distributing personnel, a well-organised advertisement department with its own technology and modern commercial practice, all these offer major advantages of economies of scale. There is no reason why these should be decried. In fact, the existence of groups and chains would enable better and richer newspapers to be brought out at less cost than would normally be the case otherwise. Some of the economies would accrue to a number of newspapers published from one centre, and some to multiple editions of the same newspaper published from different centres. Both are of significant importance.

72. A well-organised newspaper group, financially sound and commercially successful, would be in a better position to try its hand at new and pioneering attempts. On the basis of the successful functioning of the paper at one centre, it can attempt to set up an edition in another centre and sustain itself through the initially difficult period. It may similarly sponsor a newspaper in an Indian language, or a periodical, general or specialised. In all such cases a large initial investment has to be made, and a waiting period in which losses are unavoidable has to be faced. Only a successful newspaper undertaking can face such a challenge. If new ventures in the newspaper world are to be attempted, new tastes have to be created and various experiments launched. This may be possible mainly if not only for groups or chains or at least for well-established newspaper organisations. For any individual to venture in this field on his own is difficult. This does not mean that, if anyone is prepared to make such an attempt, he should not be supported. We hope the Newspaper Development Commission and public sector financial institutions will take the maximum interest in any such worthwhile attempts. But it should not be forgotten that the best chances of more and better but different newspapers coming up is through some of the existing successful and venture some newspaper enterprises. It may sound ironical, but it would not be wrong to say that more competition among newspapers may be fostered through the venture some activities of the stronger newspaper groups – some times called monopolistic.

Other Measures of Curbing

73. In addition to delinking and the application of MRTP Act to the newspaper industry the majority have also stated that "other measures are necessary to ensure conditions of fair competition among newspapers".* They point out that papers with large circulation can have lower cost per copy and those with larger capital resources will

* Chapter X, Para 63.3.

have fewer handicaps. Their approach regarding such situations is expressed in the following words, "It is true that such economic advantages and handicaps exist in a number of industries but their presence in the newspaper industry is not conducive to the even and healthy development of the Press.

74. They justify curbs on economically better off newspapers on the ground that the "widest possible dissemination of information from diverse and antagonistic source is essential to the welfare of the public." They rightly state that "newcomers should be enabled to start publication with a fair chance of achieving success". But instead of relying on facilities such as those to be provided by the proposed Newspaper Development Commission or by public financial institutions, they regard it more appropriate to create difficulties in the successful functioning of the larger and better placed newspapers. They mainly rely on three measures for this purpose: (i) a limit on the number of pages to be permitted to a newspaper; (ii) a price page schedule; and (ii) a limit to the ratio of advertising space varying according to the circulation of the newspapers.

75. The main argument in favour of limiting the number of pages is that a large part of the newsprint has to be imported and that foreign exchange is very scarce. Therefore, they have suggested that newspaper should get newsprint on a free-of-tax or minimum-tax basis only to the extent of what is required to bring out a twelve-page paper. Extra pages should call for either steep taxation or obligation to use paper other than newsprint which, of course, would increase the cost of the newspaper.*

76. They have also argued that fair competition requires fixing of a minimum price a which the newspaper of a particular size should be sold. This they consider to be "the most effective measure to bring about an atmosphere of fair competition".**

The Price-page Schedule

77. A point in favour of the price page schedule can be that, in respect of newspapers which directly compete with each other, established newspapers with larger circulations may enjoy a special advantage compared to the not so established competitors with lower

---

* Chapter IX, Para 156.

** Chapter X, Para 65.

circulation. This may happen because the former will attract considerable advertisement, and on that basis, will be able to provide more pages and also more news. It is said that a price page schedule will obviate this disadvantage.

78. It should be remembered in this connection that, to the extent that the price page schedule makes no distinction between the space devoted to advertisement and the space devoted to reading matter, it really amounts to forcing a reader to pay more than he needs to pay. This is not only unfair to the reader, but it is also a step which is likely to adversely affect the good quality newspapers whom we should encourage. What needs to be discouraged is excessive advertisement and not more reading matter. Moreover, for reasons given later, classified advertisements should be encouraged. We find that in the case of quality newspapers, they take up a significant portion of space. That is why a price page schedule is not proper but positively harmful to a proper development and improvement of quality newspapers.

79. An alternative to the price page schedule suggested by some is a kind of rule by which the price of the newspaper should at least cover the material costs such as newsprint and ink. It has been pointed out that, if a newspaper follows a price policy which does not ensure this, it is subsidising not only its overhead costs from advertisement revenue, but it is even subsidising its basic material costs from that sources. In such a case, especially if its advertisement revenue is large because of its circulation and established reputation, it will make the position of an existing or potential competitor very difficult. This difficulty may become specially enhanced in times like the present when newsprint and other material costs are going up more rapidly than other costs. While a reader is certainly not attracted by the number of pages in relation to the price as the most important factor, it is not unlikely that if he finds that the price of a competing paper, much smaller in size, is actually higher a potential or even existing reader may be repelled unless the paper is of a special type or quality which appeals to certain readers. It is, therefore, claimed that, unless some such relationship between the price of the newspaper and its material costs of production is ensured, it may bring about a destruction of smaller competitors prevent the growth of potential competitors and thus create monopoly conditions.

80. It must be conceded that this a persuasive argument. Our answer, however, is that laying down any kind of general rule which should apply in all conditions to all newspapers is inappropriate. We do

not see much logic in insisting upon a fixed relationship between material costs and the price of the newspaper, while showing flexibility regarding other elements even of prime cost, such as printing, leave along the costs on journalistic and editorial staff. It is an accepted practice all the world over that these latter kind of costs are all met from advertisement revenue, and it is in this that the strength of the better quality newspaper often lies. If some newspaper wants to set out on a new course by not wanting to develop much of advertisement revenue or even by keeping advertisements of certain kinds out, it should ensure that it has a clientele which shares its approach to advertisement revenue and would therefore be ready to pay a higher price.

81. We would, however, not completely discountenance the possibility that the whole situation in respect of a certain market for newspapers may be such that, unless a minimum price in relation to material costs is insisted upon, existing competition may be eliminated and potential competition thwarted. Our support to the proposal that MRTP Act should apply to the newspaper industry, and that the circulation of newspapers in a particular area in a particular language should be taken as the basis for examining dominance or monopoly is specially meant to look after such possibilities. This would be an appropriate situation where action by the MRTP Commission would be justified and there are enough provisions even in the existing Act under which directions can be given which will ensure that the weaker competitors can be protected and helped to sustain themselves. We emphasise that we are not supporting the development of a monopoly Press where larger newspapers will have maximum freedom to destroy all the existing or potential competition. We however, do not favour a general and strait jacket solution because we are afraid that this will merely create difficulties for the existing good quality newspapers, only because they have large circulations, and at the same time not necessarily help the sustenance or coming into existence of similarly good quality but smaller circulation papers. We should also make it clear that we are not convinced that the small is always beautiful any more than the large and that all small newspapers deserve to be protected from competition.

Advertisement as a Source of Revenue

82. The majority also point out that the advertisement revenue is

shared very unequally among different types of newspapers, the large circulation English language dailies cornering the lion's share and the large circulation Indian language dailies another large chunk. Between them they account for almost 60 per cent of the total advertisement revenue earned by the Press.

83. They add that the percentage of space devoted to advertisement has been increasing in the last 20 years and that it is very high now, especially in the larger circulation papers which are also able to charge high advertisement rates. This in turn enables these papers to provide much more page-area to a newspaper buyer in terms of the price he pays.

84. While admitting that every newspaper has to rely on advertisement revenue for making both ends meet, the majority feel that "greater dependence on advertisement revenue exposes a newspaper to pressure from advertisers".* Further, "it would be unfair to the reading public if the newspapers devote a large proportion of space to advertisements".** for the freedom of the Press to be effective, the present degree of dependence of newspapers on advertisements has to be lessened and the importance of circulation as a principal source of revenue must be enhanced".@

News-to-Advertisement Ratio

85. Our colleagues, therefore, state their conviction that, in the prevailing conditions of the Press in India, "the prescription of a price-page schedule with a news-to-advertisement ratio is absolutely essential for promoting fair competition among the existing units and for providing a fair chance of success to new-comers in the interest of diversification of the sources of dissemination of information". They make this recommendation while acknowledging that "those papers which are today attracting a disproportionately large amount of advertisement revenue are utilising it to a certain extent for improving their quality and in subsidising the selling price for the benefit of the readers".

86. They are uncertain about the impact of the proposed measure on the economics of publishing newspapers and therefore suggest the

---

* *Ibid.* Para 67.

** *Ibid.* Para 74.

@ *Ibid.* Para 77.

setting up of an expert committee to work out a price-page schedule after examining the relevant facts; but they still make a firm recommendation that the news-to-advertisement ratio should be fixed "at 60 : 40 for big newspapers, 50 : 50 for medium and 40 : 60 for small newspapers". They have also supported, if necessary, a constitutional amendment to make such a restriction on newspapers legally feasible.

87. This approach is bound to hurt large circulation newspapers. Thus, according to the ORG survey, total advertisements take up 58 per cent of space in the 'Very Big' English newspapers, over 44 per cent in 'Big' ones and over 45 per cent in 'Medium' ones (See Table I). The advertisements take up over 45 per cent space in 'Very Big' Hindi newspapers, and over 47 per cent in 'Big' ones. The proportion in Bengali is over 49 per cent in 'Very Big' ones, in Gujarati it is about 45 per cent in 'Very Big' and about 44 per cent in 'Big' ones. Similar is the case in the Malayalam and Marathi. All these newspapers will suffer as a result of the proposed ratio restriction.

88. Whether other newspapers will benefit from such a restriction on the larger ones is doubtful. No data are given by the majority to support any such contention. They also accept that the economics of the newspaper industry needs a more detailed study than the Commission has been able to undertake, yet they have laid down news; advertisement ratio regard less of consequences.*

89. We are opposed to these recommendations, we do not believe that larger newspapers should be denied the advantages in terms of economies of scale and advertisement revenue which are bound to accrue to them. We do not share the assumption that, if advertisements are not permitted to be published in the large newspapers, these would automatically shift to others. We reject as untenable the position that dependence on advertisement revenue exposes a newspaper to pressures from advertisers. On the contrary, the large papers with varied and multiple sources of advertisement revenue are far less amenable to pressures from any particular advertiser, including the Government.

---

* While the Bhabatosh Dutta Committee on Newspaper Economics recommends a 50 : 50 ratio, our colleagues have proposed a 60 : 40 ratio for the larger papers. A substantial (five to four) minority in the Enquiry Committee on Small Newspapers (1965) had opposed the statutory ratio. For extracts from these reports, see Appendices 'A' and 'B' to our Minute.

Advertisement Revenue and Quality of Papers

90. The majority talk of the large circulation English dailies securing "a disproportionately" large chunk of advertisement revenue, without defining the term. The advertisement rates of a newspapers inevitably depend upon its circulation and the advertiser's calculation of the income class of its readership Neither consideration can be called unfair, unless advertisements are to be treated as favours which are conferred or withheld on other considerations. At the most one can say that some of the advertisers are not adequately conscious of the advertisement potential of some of the Indian language dailies and papers that circulate more in the rural areas. But this problem cannot be solved by placing curbs on advertisement in a rough and ready fashion. To say that it is unfair to the reading public if a large proportion of space in devoted to advertisement is to assume that the advertisements do not serve any worthwhile public purpose and also that the readers have no choice in respect of which newspapers to buy.

91. We contest all such assumptions. If the readers are unhappy over the space allottee to advertisement in a particular newspaper, they can shift to another. It is not as if all competing papers in a particular language or in a particular locality devote the same space to advertisement. Probably most newspapers would like to devote 50 or 60 per cent space to advertisement if they can obtain more revenue. But some of them cannot obtain so much from advertisement and therefore utilise less space for it. The reader has the option to choose such papers if he dislikes so much space devoted to advertisement. What happens is that the newspapers which give more advertisement, can also afford to have more pages. They also appear to be able to make their paper more interesting. This is how the economics* of the newspaper industry operates.

92. The attempt of most newspapers is to recover through the prices charged to readers the material costs as well as the printing costs for producing the newspaper. The advertisement revenue is mainly used for meeting other costs – news collection, editorial and other overheads. It is thus claimed that, with the rapidly increasing cost of materials, especially newsprint, more advertisement revenue is essential if the quality of the newspaper is to be maintained at a high

---

* For some general analysis of this aspect, see *Business World*, June 8-21, 1981, pages 26-39.

level or further improved.

93. As it is, newspapers have had to raise their prices in order to meet increasing costs. If advertisement space and revenue are curbed, they will have to raise their prices steeply. We have little doubt that, in the present situation, to insist on a larger proportion of revenue coming from circulation, will greatly reduce their circulation. Data given in Chapter II paras 89-90 show how the recent increases in newspapers prices have led to a fall in their circulation. This suggests that a point of high elasticity of demand has been reached in respect of at least major and high price newspapers. Any insistence on changes which will force further price increases may be the end of high-quality papers.

94. The majority also assume that the reader's choice of a newspaper is significantly governed by the number of pages it offers. They approvingly quote a passage from the Report of the Enquiry Committee on Small Newspapers and the conclusion reached by a columnist in a newspaper to this effect. We doubt that the reader is oblivious to the contents of newspapers and is only bothered about their relative weight! By this logic, only the Hindu should sell in Madras, the *Times of India* in Bombay and so on.

95. Frankly, we are surprised that our colleagues should have proposed news-to-advertisement ratios without any reference to the present-day economics of newspaper publishing. We have little doubt that its implementation will make it extremely difficult for the larger newspapers to survive. A price-page-schedule, in our opinion, will have a similar effect on their fortunes. It needs to be emphasised that, as the economy is at present organised, advertisement revenue cannot be treated as an evil source of finance. So long as we have a largely free enterprise and market oriented economy, advertisement will remain an integral part of the system.

96. The fact that All India Radio and Doordarshan are increasingly promoting paid advertisements is a clear indication that even Government financed media consider this source of revenue useful* and necessary. Experience in other democracies suggests that the broadcasting media, and especially T.V., increasingly take up a larger share of the total national outlay on advertising. India is not likely to be an exception. AIR has recently decided to throw open its normal radio channels – in addition to Vividh Bharati – to advertisements. This may considerably reduce advertisements available to all newspapers whatever their size.

97. That apart, it has been claimed – and rightly – that certain kinds of advertisements are of considerable interest and importance to readers. Classified advertisements – including those relating to employment opportunities available or wanted – are of great interest to many readers. So are marriage advertisements. Many newspapers treat them as social service and some even provide concessional rates for them. Similarly, advertisements relating to entertainment programmes available in the locality are wanted by readers in many cases almost as much as news. One cannot therefore say that space devoted to such advertisements is unfair to the readers.

98. Advertisements which are meant to persuade readers either to buy a particular product or service, or to create in their minds a favourable image of an individual, a product or an organisation, may be said to be less useful but by no means harmful. They appear in all worthwhile newspapers all over the world, even in market oriented Communist countries like Hungary and Yugoslavia.

99. One method of looking at the problem would be to examine the revenue-cost situation of different newspapers and ascertain what percentage of space devoted to advertisement and at what rates is necessary to ensure the economic viability of a newspaper. But even this kind of analysis would abound in difficulties. Not only would the costs vary from time to time with rapid changes in the prices of materials or wages, but they would also vary from one paper to another depending on how much it depends on news gathering, a competent editorial staff, and various other aspects such as features, cartoons, etc. The advertisement rate would be another important variable, depending on the circulation of the paper, and the income status of its readers. It is obvious, that this is a complex matter, and simplistic solutions and rigid formulae are likely not only to be ineffective but also harmful.

100. It is generally accepted that the quality of the Indian newspapers leaves much to be desired. This is especially so of the Indian language newspapers and newspapers which are published outside metropolitan areas. Many of these newspapers would like to

---

* A.I.R's revenue from advertisements has increased from Rs.296 lakhs in 1970-71 to Rs. 1140 lakhs in 1980-81 (11 months). (Chapter IX, para 45). The revenue of Doordarshan from Commercials has increased from Rs. 77 lakh in 1976-77 to Rs.6 crores in 1979-80 (*Ibid*; Para 50).

provide more and better material to readers provided they can afford the costs. But their this would mean that they would have to increase the number of pages from four, six or eight that many of them now provide to six, eight, ten or twelve. That would place an unbearable burden on their already weak finances.

101. Similarly, even the best known of our newspapers like *The Times of India*, The *Hindu*, The *Indian Express*, The *Statesman* or The *Hindustan Times* cannot be considered to be anywhere near the top class newspapers in developed countries either in the quantity of news that they provide or the quality of the information, feature articles and cartoons, etc., that they contain. If they have to improve, they will require more pages rather than less. Even at the present increased prices of newsprint, there is a large gap between the cost of putting an extra page and the revenue obtained from an extra page of advertising by some of the quality papers. It is this difference that enables a newspaper to spend more on improved service to its readers.

102. It has to be noted that even with as much as 51 per cent of the space devoted to display advertisements and six per cent to classified advertisements, the large circulation newspapers have recently been forced to raise their prices to high levels as result of the increase in the price of newsprint. There is no indication that there would be a let up in the future in the tendency for material prices as well as printing costs, etc to rise. Any curbs which would force these newspapers to reduce the advertisement space that they are allotting now to it will most likely lead to forcing them to reduce the quality of their service and into serious economic difficulties.

103. It is also important to note that not infrequently the benefit to the reader varies in proportion to the advertisement revenue of the newspaper.*

It has already been pointed out in the report that the return per paisa to a newspaper reader in terms of the page-area he gets is much higher of he buys a paper with larger circulation.** A quick study made by us (see Table 2) further shows that the news and editorial space per paisa

---

* It should also be noted that in the U.K., the national quality dailies earn far more from advertisement revenue as a proportion of total revenue than the popular and other dailies. This surely does not suggest that more advertisements revenue means a lower quality newspaper (Ref: Royal Commission on the Press: Final Report, July 1977, page 32).

** Chapter X, paras 74-75.

spent by the reader does not decline in the large circulation newspapers though they devote more space to advertisement.

The *Hindustan Times* in New Delhi gives 52 column centimetres news space per paisa against 80 column centimetres of advertisement space. As against this a very small paper, *Tej*, which gives only six column cms. of advertisement space per paisa also gives only 45 column cms. of news space per paisa. Other large papers like The *Statesman*, The *Times of India* and The *Indian Express* also provide larger news space per paisa even though their advertisement space is also larger. The only exceptional cases are those of *The National Herald* where the news space is 91 column cms. per paisa even though advertisement space is only 33 column cms. per paisa, *Qaumi Awaz* which gives 68 columns cms. per paisa of news space, even though the advertisement space per paisa is only six column cms., and *Patriot* which gives 82 column cms. per paise of news space as against 35 column cms. of advertisement space.

104. These last examples merely prove that the economics of different newspapers can be significantly different. From this limited study, it is not possible to say whether all these newspapers are operating on sound economic and financial basis.* What is indicated is basically that the reader is not being defrauded in terms of news and editorial space in the newspaper per paisa spent by him even if the advertisement space is also larger. In fact, he usually gets more news and editorial space per paisa spent by him in such larger advertisement space newspapers.

Pressure from Advertisers

105. Objection to advertisement is taken by various people on two other grounds. One is that greater dependence on advertisement revenue exposes a newspaper to pressure from advertisers. Assuming that same advertisers would try to put pressure on newspapers and this is as true of governmental and other public authorities as of private authorities – the extent to which the newspaper would succumb to such pressures would very much depend upon the degree to which a

* To what extent the *National Herald* and *Qaumi Awaz* satisfy such a criterion is doubtful, See *Sunday Weekly*, 7th February, 1982, p. 40, and also *India Today*, Feb. 15, 1982, pp. 52-54.

newspaper depends upon a particular advertiser for a significant part of its advertisement revenue. The likelihood of any large newspaper with many advertisements from a number of sources being pressurised is far less than that of a small paper whose sources of advertisement revenue are limited, and it therefore depends significantly upon a particular source.

106. Our analysis shows that the dependence on government sources of the smaller papers is far more than of the larger papers; and this is bound to open them to considerable pressures from government authorities.* Even local advertisers such as cinema owners may be able to pressurise small and local papers considerably. This cannot easily happen to the larger papers who can withstand the loss of these advertisement for long. In fact, the correspondence between Shri K. K. Birla and Shri B. G. Verghese brings out the point that not only the editor of the *Hindustan Times* took no notice of the pressure brought to bear on his paper by the Modis, a business group, regarding some news item of Court cases against them, but even the proprietors only suggested that the editor might take up such news in the right spirit and not possibly face allegations of carrying on the campaign, even the proprietors did not tell the editor to adjust news items so as not to annoy actual and potential advertisers.*

107. It should also not be overlooked that a newspaper cannot ignore the importance of its credibility among its actual and potential readers. Any impression that it is yielding to outside influence is likely to hurt it at its most sensitive point, viz., its circulation. As a recent study of the British media points out, "The board shape and nature of the press is ultimately determined by no one but its readers".**

Harmful Effects of Advertisement

108. Another point that is made is that advertisements are not only somewhat vulgar but that they also are economically harmful. The alleged harm arises on two counts. One, that a significant cost is incurred on advertisement and finally this is recovered from the consumer of the product. While this is true, all one can say is that since advertisement for consumer products is considered an appropriate

---

* See Tables 4 to 7 of this Minute.

** J. Whale: Politics of the Media, (Fontane 1977) p.85

method of persuading consumers in a given economy – and this is so in India – the press cannot be expected to forego this source of revenue. If consumerism is to be discouraged, this has to be done by a radically different approach to the organisation of the economy. The Press Commission is hardly the appropriate body to go into this larger question. As regards the advertisement of harmful products such as cigarettes or liquor, if the Government passes general legislation banning all advertisements of such products, through all the media that would apply to the Press also, and one cannot have any quarrel with it.

109. It may also be suggested that a number of advertisements are misleading. They put forward fake claims and misguide the public. There is no effective remedy for such advertisements in any media at present. The Sachar Committee has suggested that this be treated as an unfair trade practice and be dealt with under the MRTP Act. We agree.

110. The argument of economic waste may also be made regarding a number of display advertisements which have little to do with information to the consumer regarding the product; such advertisements may be more to create a favourable impression in the minds of the readers regarding the advertiser, whether it is a Government authority, a business group or a particular producer. Many people think that such advertisements should be stopped as it involves considerable waste of resources and also, as only large advertisers like governmental authorities and big business groups indulge in this type of advertisement on a large scale, the possibility of their trying to abuse such advertisement expenditure is greater.

111. Again, the matter does not lie within the purview of the Press Commission. If it is decided that advertising which has no direct bearing on the business of a company should be banned, this can be done by appropriate amendments in the company and taxation legislation. As regards Government authorities, there should be no difficulty in their accepting a self-denying ordinance not to indulge in this kind of self-advertisement through newspapers.

The Constitutional position

112. There are lions in the way of implementing the majority's recommendations in respect of price-page schedule and a statutory news-to-advertisement ratio. The majority have sought to overcome these difficulties by asserting that the Supreme Court decided the *Sakal Newspapers*' (3 SCR 1962) case incorrectly, and by subscribing to the

sole dissenting judgement in the *Bennett Coleman* case. Indeed the relevant section of Chapter X, entitled "Press as Public Utility", leans heavily on the theories propounded in the dissenting judgement of Mr. Justice K. K. Mathew.

113. The Supreme Court, in its judgement in the Sakal Case has held:

> "The right to propagate one's ideas is inherent in the conception of freedom of speech and expression. For the purpose of propagating his ideas every citizen has a right to publish them, to disseminate them and to circulate them. He is entitled to do so either by work of mouth or by writing. The right guaranteed thus extends subject to any law competent under Article 19(2), not merely to the matter which he is entitled to circulate, but also to the volume of circulation. It cannot be gainsaid that the impugned order seeks to place a restraint on the latter aspect of the right by prescribing a price-page schedule. We may add that the fixation of a minimum price for the number of pages which a newspaper is entitled to publish is obviously not for ensuring a reasonable price to the buyers of newspapers but for expressly cutting down the volume of circulation of some newspapers by making the price so unattractively high for a class of its readers as is likely to deter it from purchasing such newspapers.
>
> "The first decision of this Court in which this was recognised in *Romesh Thaper v. State of Madras*. There, this Court held that freedom of speech and expression includes freedom of propagation of ideas and that this freedom is ensured by the freedom of circulation. . .
>
> "Though the prices of newspapers appear to be on low side, it is a fact that even so, many people find it difficult to pay that small price. This is what has been pointed out by the Press Commission in paragraph 52 of its report. According to it, the most common reason for people in not purchasing newspapers is the cost of the newspaper and the inability of the household to spare the necessary amount. This conclusion is based upon the evidence of a very large number of individuals and representatives of Associations. We would, therefore, be justified in relying upon it and holding that raising the price of a newspaper even by a small amount such as one paisa. In order that its present size by maintained would adversely affect its circulation.

"We would consider this mater in another way also. The advertisement revenue of a newspaper is proportionate to its circulation. Thus the higher the circulation of a newspaper the larger would be its advertisement revenue. So if a newspaper with a high circulation were to raise its price its circulation would go down and this in turn would bring down also the advertisement revenue. That would force the newspaper either to close down or to raise its price. Raising the price further would affect the circulation still more and thus a vicious cycle would set in which would ultimately end in the closure of the newspaper. If, on the other hand, the space for advertisement is reduced, the earnings of a newspaper would go down and it would either have to run at a loss or close down or raise its price. . . . When a law is intended to bring about this result, there would be a direct interference with the right of freedom of speech and expression guaranteed under Article 19(1)(a). . . . The freedom of a newspaper to publish any number of pages or to circulate it to any number of persons is each an integral part of the freedom of speech and expression. A restraint placed upon either of them would be a direct infringement of the right of freedom of speech and expression. Perhaps an illustration would make the point clear. Let us suppose that the enactment had said that newspaper 'A' or newspaper 'B' (ignoring for the moment the objection to the illustration based upon Art. 14) shall not have more than a specified number of subscribers. Could such a law be valid in the face of the guarantee under Art. 19(1)(a)? The answer must unhesitatingly be no, because such a law would be recognised as directly impinging upon the freedom of expression which encompasses freedom of circulation and to restrain the citizen from propagating his views to any other beyond the limit or number prescribed by the statute. If this were so, the fact that the legislation achieves the same result by means of the schedule of rates makes no differences and the impact on the freedom would still be direct notwithstanding that it does not appear so on its face.

"It [Newspaper (Price and Page) Act 1960] seeks to achieve its object of enabling what are termed the smaller newspapers to secure larger circulation by provisions which without disguise are aimed at restricting the circulation of what are termed the larger papers with better financial strength. The impugned law far from being one which merely interferes with the right of freedom of speech incidentally, does so directly though it seeks to achieve the end by purporting to regulate the business aspect of a newspaper. Such a course is not permissible.

"Finally, it was said that one of its objects is to give some kind of protection to small or newly started newspapers and, therefore, the Act is good. Such an object may be desirable but for attaining it the State cannot make inroads on the right of other newspapers which Article 19(1)(a) guarantees to them. There may be other ways of helping them and it is for the State to search for them but the one they have chosen falls foul of the Constitution."

114. Most of these arguments have been endorsed by the Supreme Court in its majority judgment in the *Bennett Coleman* (2 SCR 1973) case and we would not wish to repeat them here. Suffice it to say that the Court has held, after quoting the *Sakal* case at length that newsprint control could not be turned into an instrument of newspaper control, and that it could not be used for promoting small newspapers, reducing alleged monopoly, making unequal newspapers equal by giving the weaker papers a fairer opportunity, and promoting a more competitive market-place of ideas.

115. But there is one more point. In his dissenting judgment in the *Bennett Coleman* case, Mr. Justice K.K. Mathew too did not seem to be saying that the Sakal case was wrongly decided. He wrote:

> "In Sakal Papers (P) Ltd. and other v. Union of India, this court was concerned with the validity of the Newspaper (Price and Page) Act, 1956, and Daily Newspaper (Price and Pages) Order, 1960. *The whole subject fell directly under Article. 19(1)(a)*. It was not a case where he infringement of the freedom of speech was indirect. The legislation in that case *directly* restricted circulation of newspapers. The *direct* effect of the legislation, in other words, *was to abridge the freedom of speech by curtailing circulation*. The learned judges, after referring to the Express Newspaper (12 SCR 1959) case said that the impugned law, far from being one which merely interfered with the right of freedom of speech incidentally, did so directly." (Emphasis ours)

116. In support of their recommendations regarding price-page schedule and a news-to-advertisement ratio, the majority members advance a theory which state that if the pith and substance of a

proposed piece of legislation is related to reasonable restrictions on the business of running a newspaper in the interest of general public permitted under Article 19(6) of the Constitution the mere fact that those restrictions leave an impact upon the right of freedom of speech conferred under Article 19(1)(a) is quite immaterial for adjudging the validity of the law. They state:

> "In such a case, the solution to be thought of is to decide what exactly is the pith and substance of the legislation. In other words, the appropriate mode for resolving the conflict is to look at true nature and character of the legislation and decide whether it is really a restriction upon the freedom to carry on the business or an indirect attempt to suppress the freedom of expression. The test is the pith and substance of the matter and not the indirect effect of the legislation."

117. The proposed legislation, then, is being supported under Article 19(6) and the majority seems to be concluding that it does not fall *directly* under Article 19(1)(a). Also the majority have advanced the theory that a abridgement of speech (meaning thereby the abridgement of volume of speech, or the abridgement of the size of newspapers, does not amount to an abridgement of the freedom of speech, which is related to content and not to volume. But this view runs contrary not only to the majority judgment in the *Sakal* and *Bennett Coleman* cases, but also to Mr. Justice Mathew's views on the *Sakal* case as stated in his dissenting judgment in the *Bennett Coleman* case. Leaving the legal controversy raised by the majority in the Report severly alone, it is pertinent to observe that under the law as it has been declared by the Supreme Court a price page schedule will be legally invalid under the Constitution. Moreover, in our opinion, it is not for the Press Commission to pronounce upon the correctness or otherwise of Supreme Court judgements, which is the law of the land.

Tax an Advertisement as a Disincentive

118. This is not to say that there is no case for some limit on the use of advertisement by newspapers. We agree that some curb on the use of a scarce resource like newsprint for advertisement would be appropriate. But, in keeping with our overall approach that no straitjacket solutions should be adopted, we would rather suggest a

more flexible way to discouraging excessive advertisements than what our colleagues have done. We shall not lay down a fixed proportion of space which should be used by a newspaper for advertisements. We would rather recommend an approach by which a disincentive in the form of a progressive tax on the use of newspaper space for advertisement is levied so that each newspaper will be able to complete the worth-whileness of devoting more space to advertisement in the light of the tax which will have to be paid.

119. We would place the exemption limit at 50 per cent of newspaper space exclusive of classified advertisements which, all agree, are of much service to the readers and to the community. They provide hard and useful information. We recommend a progressive tax on advertisements beyond 50 per cent of the total newspaper space, exclusive of classified advertisements, increasing the progression in such a manner that the marginal advertisement revenue becomes negative beyond 75 per cent. We think such a flexible approach of permitting the newspaper to experiment would be better than a fixed general prohibition. We also think that it is unfair to the reader to make a distinction in this respect between a small, medium and large paper. Our colleagues' suggestion of permitting as much as 60 per cent of space for advertisement by small papers while consceding only 40 per cent to a large papers does not commend itself to us. For administrative convenience, however, small papers with circulation below 25,000 should be exempted from the tax on advertisement. A possible schedule of such a tax is given below:

Per cent of space devoted to advertisements	Tax as per cent of advertisements revenue
Upto 50%	Nil
Between 50 and 60%	35%
Between 60 and 65%	55%
Between 65 and 70%	75%
Between 70 and 75%	100%
Between 75 and 80%	110%
Between 80 and 85%	200%
Above 90%	300%

120. In calculating the space devoted to advertisement, classified advertisements which satisfy prescribed criteria regarding the type

used, size and purpose should be exempted. It may be said that, at present classified advertisements are a major source of revenue only to be larger circulation papers and play only a minor role if any in providing revenues to the small and medium papers (see Tables 2 and 3). This is true. But we see no reason why regional language papers in not only cities but even in towns should not, with proper effort, be able to build up classified advertisements as an important source of revenue. The potential demand for such information as classified advertisements provide is bound to exist even in the other cities and towns. It only requires proper effort* to bring it out and develop this as an important source of revenue as well as community service.

121. The amount which a company can spend on advertisement is limited, and the economic returns to advertising expenditure decline after a certain stage. The proposal is, therefore, likely to bring about a change in the quantity and size of newspaper advertisement. The newspapers are bound to raise their advertisement rates, and especially make them stiff in respect of larger advertisements, covering quarter page, half page or full page. This may help to reduce the total space devoted to advertisement.

122. Another possible objection is that the tax would be complicated to administer in that a record of the distribution of space for each issue of a newspaper would have to be kept. This cannot be considered to be a serious objection. Far more complicated records are kept, presented and scrutinised in respect of various taxes.

123. The question of the use of foreign exchange required for the import of newsprint has often been raised in this connection. It is pointed out in the report that valuable foreign exchange is being spent and that a disproportionate proportion of a scarce commodity bought with the use of foreign exchange is used by a small number of papers. But in all such discussions, the fact is overlooked that those papers serve a very large number of readers; and that is why they take up such a large proportion of newsprint.

---

* This will be supported by the rapid increase in classified advertisements which some of the larger newspapers have been able to achieve in a short time. The Delhi edition of the *Times of India* is a good example. It appears that even in the U.K., not only the national quality papers, but also, the provincial papers, have been able to obtain a significant increase in classified advertisements. See Royal Commission on the Press, Final Report 1977, pp. 34, 40-41, Appendices, p. 134.

Why Not Free Import?

124. The import bill on account of newsprint, even though it has increased considerably in recent years, cannot still be considered to be a major drain on the country's foreign exchange resources. Even now it does not constitute more than two per cent of the total import bill of the country. When considering how much the country should spend on the import of newsprint, it needs to be kept in view that the newspapers are the major media through which the largest body of citizens is kept informed on public affairs. This communication of information from various angles is of great utility in any country. It is of special importance in a democracy where the common body of citizens is the final arbitor of events. We have to educate our masters and obviously the newspapers is the most important medium for imparting such education.

125. Broadcasting is developing rapidly in India and it is also playing a major role in the task of educating citizens. It needs, however, to be kept in mind that, with State ownership and management of broadcasting media, the latter cannot be the most effective media either for covering various kinds of news or for the presentation of alternative views including unorthodox ones and those critical of Government. The newspapers have therefore to be relied upon for fulfilling this role. The major handicap in the successful functioning of our democracy upto now has been the illiteracy of large numbers of our people. It is to be hoped that, with the emphasis on the spread of primary education as well as adult education, this difficulty will be increasingly overcomes. As this happens, it would be necessary for an increasingly larger number of people to read newspapers and the circulation of all newspapers especially in Indian languages will have to increase substantially.

126. All over the world, the experience has been that the spread of broadcasting, and especially of TV, reduces the urge to read newspapers. If the production of newspapers is made difficult through various handicaps and the prices of newspapers have to increase, the situation may aggravate. This would surely not help the healthy growth of our democracy. The question of the liberal import of newsprint has to be viewed in this context.

127. In this view, there is no reason why the newsprint import should not be put under Open General Licence. It appears unlikely that this would lead to a large increase in imports in the near future. It may

at best mean a slow but steady increase. In fact, the escalation in world prices of newsprint has already made the position of Indian newspapers difficult; they are afraid of facing an elastic readership demand, and they are unlikely to import much more and increase the number of pages, even if the import is freed of all restrictions.

128. Some schemes for newsprint production in the country are already licensed. To the extent that these materialise, the import bill will come down. This process could be further helped by clearly laying down that newsprint will not be used for publications other than newspapers.

129. A major advantage of this approach is that it will help eliminate the continuous wrangling between the Press and the Government. It will also discourage false claims in respect of circulation figures. To the best of our knowledge the Government has not used newsprint allocations to put pressure on newspapers. But a Government in future may, if it is so disposed. The possibility will be greatly reduced if newsprint is put on OGL. It would also eliminate the difficulties that many smaller papers to experience in ensuring that their quotas are properly decided.

130. Such a policy will also dispose of the problem of black-marketing of newsprint. It has often been alleged that not only a large number of small but also some medium and large newspapers indulge in this activity. In the absence of evidence, we cannot say how serious the problems has been. But the problem has existed and can be solved if our proposal is accepted.

Import duty not desirable

131. We should also mention in this context our total opposition to any import duty on newsprint. As already mentioned earlier, in a growing democracy like ours, the most effective medium for informing the common citizen about the developments in the country and abroad, and on the major issues about public policy as they involve his exercise of citizenship rights, is bound to be the daily newspaper. Anything that would impede or inhibit the production and its circulation among the largest possible body of citizens would be to create an obstacle in the way of this essential facility. We therefore think that the recent imposition by Government of an import duty on newsprint is an undesirable measure. In our situation, a duty on newsprint is a tax on knowledge and information and should invite criticism similar to a tax

on school books on other academic material. Surely the amount which the Government obtains from the proceeds of this import duty is nothing in comparison with the benefits that cheaper newspapers would confer on the education of our citizens. We would therefore, urge the Government to remove the import duty and take a firm decision not to impose it again. We are glad to note that this view of ours is shared by the present Minister of Information and Broadcasting.

132. It is possible that when newsprint begins to be produced in India on a larger scale than now, there may still continue to be a cost difference as well as a quality difference between the indigenous product and the imported product. In such a case, we would recommend the grant of subsidy by Government for encouraging the use of the indigenous product rather than an import duty to serve the same purpose. If the Government insists on raising the price of newsprint through taxation of one kind or the other, an inference may arise that the Government would prefer that the circulation of newspapers should be curbed and that the common body of citizens should not find it easy to have this facility at the cheapest possible price. Surely the Government will not like to give such an impression.

Remove Channelisation

133. That is also the reason why we also recommend that the channelisation of newsprint imports through the State Trading Corporation should be removed. If a co-operative of the users can be formed, so much the better. If that is, however, found difficult, each major user of newsprint should be permitted to have the facility of importing newsprint on his own or through the Sate Trading Corporation, whichever course he prefers. The S.T.C.'s claim that they have been able to attain major economies as a result of channelisation remains unproved. On the other hand, practically all major users expressed unhappiness about S.T.C.'s handling of imports, and especially the inefficiency regarding the schedule of supplies so that users are put to much hardship – either because they have too little in stock or too much. The users should, therefore, be freed from this compulsion. The State Trading Corporation should of course continue to import newsprint for the benefit of the small and medium users of newsprint. This will also provide a check on the import prices so as to prevent misuse of foreign exchange. The small and medium papers, as the majority also agrees, should be free to join up with a large importer

for meeting their import requirements it they consider that course to be better.

Liberal Policy re: Import of Machinery

134. We would also strongly urge a far more liberal policy regarding the import of printing machinery for the Press, Technology in this area is rapidly improving and the Indian newspaper industry, by and large, is lagging far behind others. With vast masses of our population still to be reached by newspapers, it is obviously necessary to encourage the rapid expansion of the Press by all possible means. The use of the best technology available in this area should, therefore, be facilitated.

135. With new methods of photo-composing and printing, a small scale unit may be able to bring out a local newspaper at a comparatively cheaper cost. Thus the growth of local newspapers may be facilitated by encouraging the use of new technology in this sphere.

136. Modern technology also enables a newspaper to bring out facsimile editions from a number of centres. The Hindu does. This can promote the development of truly national and all-State newspapers. We need the development not only of local papers which can cater to local needs but also All-India and all-State papers which will help the process of national integration. It is, therefore, necessary on both these counts that modern technology is encouraged in the printing industry.

137. We are not in a position to say to what extent we should aim at self-sufficiency in the short-term in printing machinery. We would, however, like to emphasise two points. First the proper development of the Indian Press requires it to be able to use the best technology available in the world without undue time gaps. Secondly, if imports are unavoidable in respect of certain types of machinery, we would recommend that such imports should be freely permitted to those who are interested in those types of machinery and no discrimination as among different newspapers should be practised.

A Liberal Economic Approach

138. To conclude this section, our approach, in contrast with that of our colleagues, to the main problems relating to the economic position as well as the monopoly aspect of the newspaper industry is that we would like to be very cautious in suggesting changes both because this

is a very sensitive industry and also because its independence and growth are vital for the functioning of our still young democratic system. We would not restrict a major source of revenue like advertising, and consider it improper to lay down rigid formulae. At the same time, we realise that it may be necessary to restrict the use of newsprint for an increasing proportion of space being devoted to advertisements. We, therefore, have suggested the imposition of a progressive tax on advertisement revenue, after exempting all classified advertisements, and display advertisements up to 50 per cent of the total newspaper space. We have also suggested that in respect of import of newsprint and machinery, a liberal policy should be adopted, keeping in view the vital importance of this industry and the necessity not to give cause for any suspicion of discrimination.

139. We do not support the proposals for fixing a maximum number of pages for a newspaper, a price page schedule or a news-to-advertisement ratio. We also would not recommend delinking of newspaper business from other types of business on the lines recommended by our colleagues. This does not mean that we do not want to ensure fair competition in the newspaper world. We think it necessary that a reasonable degree of competition in the newspaper industry be maintained. This is necessary both to ensure efficiency of the newspapers and a minimum of choice for the readers.

140. At the same time, we cannot ignore certain facts. The newspapers in India are still in the embryo as compared to these in the developed countries. They have a far smaller reach as yet as compared to what is necessary in a democracy. With all other media being operated as a government monopoly, the importance of ensuring that the Press develops on an efficient and economic footing cannot be over-emphasised. The economies of scale in modern printing as well as news collection and dissemination cannot be ignored if better newspapers are to be produced and made available to the readers at the lowest possible price. Not can the fact that large newspaper organisations are in a better position to withstand the pressures from advertisers as well as government authorities.*

141. In view of all this, we are convinced that at this stage all that is

---

* *cf.* "Only very rich, very powerful corporateinstitutions like (the Washington Post, the CBS and the *New York Times*) had the impact, the reach and above all the resources to challenge the President of the United States". David Halberstam; The Powers That Be (Dell, New York, 1979), p. 994.

necessary is to ensure that the MRTP Act is fully applied to the newspaper industry. We have already indicated that in defining the dominant or monopolistic character of a newspaper, its language and its circulation area should be taken into account. Wherever, such a situation is found to have arisen, the concerned newspaper undertakings will be necessarily registered under Section 20(b) of the MRTP Act unless it is already registered under Section 20(a) of the Act. In all such cases, their expansion, amalgamation with or takeover of other undertakings, or establishment of new undertakings by them would all be subject to approval under the Act. It would also be possible under Section 27 of the Act to have enquires made as to whether separation of the newspaper undertaking from other business undertakings interconnected with it would be in public interest.

142. It is true that the MRTP Act has many inadequacies. Some of these are attempted to be removed by the recommendations of the Sachar Committee. We hope that the Government is taking action to make the MRTP Act more effective in the light of that Report. It should also be possible to use the provisions regarding monopolistic and restrictive trade practices – as well as the new category of unfair trade practices – to safeguard the interests of readers and of smaller papers.

143. Our emphasis on the use of the MRTP Act may be criticised on the ground that we are putting too much faith in one instrument, an instrument, it may be said, which has up to now proved not to be very effective. Our answer is that the ineffectiveness of the MRTP Act and the MRTP Commission up to now has largely been due to the Government's ambivalence. Very little use has been made of the provisions in Chapters III and IV of the MRTP Act for ensuring effective competition, reducing undue concentration and preventing monopolistic practices. The fact that, even though the Sachar Committee reported on the MRTP Act in September 1978, the Government has not still taken any action to improve the MRTP Act so as to make it more effective is also a telling commentary on the main reason why the MRTP legislation has up to now been ineffective. It has also been adequately proved in practice that, where an autonomous body like the MRTP Commission is authorised to take *suo motu* action in the case of restrictive trade practices, much better results have been achieved. Therefore, it, as suggested by the Sachar Committees, the MRTP Commission is authorised to undertake *suo motu* action in respect of all trade practices, it should be possible for situations of

unfair competition and monopolistic practices to be properly enquired into and dealt with. It should also be possible for the Government, including the Press Registrar, to ensure that appropriate cases under Section 27 and other provisions of Chapter three of the MRTP Act are referred to the MRTP Commission. It is possible that the investigating machinery as well as the membership of the Commission may have to be expanded if such use is to be made of the MRTP Act. There is no reason why this should be difficult.

144. At the same time we would suggest two major modification in the application of the MRTP Act to the newspaper industry. First, the Press Registrar should be enabled to become a party to press cases coming up under the MRTP Act. With the increasing information that we hope will flow to this office, and with the higher status that we envisage for the Press Registrar, he should be in a position to render valuable assistance to the appropriate authorities in respect of enquiries under the MRTP Act.

145. Secondly, no final action under the MRTP Act should be taken unless the MRTP Commission has been brought into the picture, a public enquiry is held by it, and a report submitted to the Government. At the minimum, such procedure would ensure that there would be little suspicion that any discrimination is being practised by the Government against particular newspapers for extraneous considerations.

146. We, however, are firmly opposed to giving Government undue powers which may be used for threatening the newspapers which they do not like or which may be used as a kind of Damocles' sword to create nervousness among newspapers. Nor do we want to support any idea which is likely to create undue difficulties in the smooth functioning of the good quality newspapers. For a country of our magnitude, the newspaper industry is very much underdeveloped at present and its further growth, quantitatively and qualitatively, needs encouragement. We would not like to support any steps which, however laudable their objects might be, are likely to create obstacles in efficient functioning and further development of the good quality newspapers in the country. This in our view must be kept as the primary aim in the policy to be advocated by the Press Commission.

Arbitrary use of Controls

147. One reason why are very much against arming Government

with various controlling instruments in respect of the newspaper industry is that the possibility of their partisan and arbitrary use is must greater in this sensitive industry. In this context, we are concerned not only with the present Government but also with governments of the future. It has been observed, even in a country like the United States, that many ways are open to the executive wing of Government to create problems for the media. It is, therefore, found even there that the executives of the media normally tend not to do anything that might offend the Government.* This would be far more so in the Indian context. We would, therefore, suggest an approach where either there is no control or, where the control is unavoidable, it should be exercised through clearly laid down guidelines with a legal appeal permitted; or where the control would be exercised after a public inquiry conducted by an independent body like the MRTP Commission.

148. Our colleagues have recommended that the present practice of permitting newsprint to be used by all periodicals except specified categories should be modified so as to exclude cinema and sex magazines and further that the Press Registrar should determine whether a publication is a sex magazine or not.** The data given in Appendix X.25 shows that this is unlikely to make a significant dent on the use of newsprint in the country. But more than this, our objection is to permitting the Press Registrar, who would work as an officer subordinate to a Minister, to decide which publications are to be declared as belonging to these categories and, therefore, denied newsprint. We object to this kind of power in principle. As for cinema journals, while some of us may have no liking for them, we see no reason why we should object to those who are interested in such news and make those journals more expensive. This is taking too puritanical a view. Similarly, what is to be dubbed as a sex magazine is not easy to define. It is well known that even magazines attempting to propagate

* "The government was increasingly sensitive to the power of broadcasting, and this sensitivity was matched by a parallel awareness within the networks of just how many legal ways the Government had to lean on the networks. All this produced a desire among networks executives not to do anything that might offend either the government or the Madison Avenue." David Halberstam; The Powers that Be, Dell, New York, 1979, page 197.

** Ch. IX, Paras 138-139.

sex education, including education on family planning methods, have been objected to by many. We would not, therefore, like to give such powers to the Press Registrar. Of course, as far as the use of newsprint is concerned, we have recommended that free import should be permitted. If the use of such cheap raw material is to be denied to anyone, the proper approach would be to ban the use of newsprint for any periodical which is priced high, say, at Rs. 5 per issue or more. That may be a better way of denying a cheap raw material to those who can afford to pay more.

Right of Reply

149. One argument, which is crucial to the case of the majority members, is this: Freedom of expression does not mean that only those who own the forum and the platform have the freedom to say what they like, without let or hindrance; it also means that those who do not own the forum or platform shall also have the opportunity of having their say. Although the forum is privately owned, and has to earn a profit for its upkeep, it should be accessible to society including those who are hostile to the forum-owners.

150. It is a noble sentiment. But none of the several hundred witnesses the Commission has examined, none of the scores of memoranda we were presented with, has told us of those very worthwhile ideologies or seminal ideas which failed to emerge and gain public attention because newspapers refused to publish them. All newspapers worth their salt have a certain policy-emphasis in their editorial pages; but it cannot be said that even our major right of the centre dailies or weeklies have wilfully prevented the Naxalite or the CPI (Marxist), or the extreme rightist point of view from emerging in their papers. If this were not so, people would be knowing about such ideas only from certain obscure weeklies, or from underground literature. This is not so. Of course, a paper owned by big business would not be plugging the Marxist line day after day, but that is not what is expected of it. What is expected is that the present of such ideas should be reflected in its columns. What we should further seek to ensure is that there should be a plurality of forms, that people of as diverse persuasions and ideological beliefs as possible should be enabled to own forums if they so desire and that no new entrant should

suffer an insurmountable handicap. But no newspaper can be compelled to launch a campaign in favour of idea which it does not believe in, and which its readers may not be prepared to buy. An editor who is as neutral as a traffic policeman in regulating the flow of material which comes to him would be an imbecile. When the majority-members plead for a regime in which everything worth saying shall be entitled to be said by everybody in newspapers whose prices, pages, advertisement ratios, shall also be pre-determined, they are conjuring up a fantasy.

151. As for the right of reply which figures in the report*, our view is that most newspapers provide for its exercise on reasonable basis. In our view, such a right arises only in respect of references made to an individual or an organisation where the latter may feel it is factually inaccurate or is deliberately distorted. Individuals or groups who hold points of view other than those of the newspaper cannot demand the right of reply as a matter of right except to a limited extent in the reader's column. It may be useful for newspapers themselves to make adequate space available for readers' views in order to create a sense of participation. But again, we would like to leave such matters to the good sense of editors. We would not, therefore, support the proposal to enforce this right through the Press Council. It is not impossible that such a provision would become an open invitation to a large number of persons who are always eager to see themselves in print even though the editors of newspapers may find that what they write is not worth publishing. Moreover, in a competition for space, which is often scarce, even between scripts which deserve to be published, a discretion has to be exercised in preferring the one to the other, having regard to a multitude of circumstances peculiar to a particular newspaper at a particular point of time. The Press Council can hardly be expected to be equipped to decide the issue in such a situation. In our opinion, these matters should best be left to the judgement of the editor. Besides, we do not think the Press Council would be an appropriate body to be entrusted with such work, especially in view of the possibility that it may be flooded with such complaints.

---

* Ch. X, Para 118-121.

Summing Up

152. To put it in a nutshell, the aim of our recommendations is to ensure the qualitative and quantitative growth of the Press in India. We need more and better newspapers, especially in Indian languages, and catering to the needs of various hitherto neglected sections, such as those in the rural areas and among the poorer sections of our people. It is also necessary to ensure that a far larger number of citizens are reached by newspapers than happens to be the case now. This also means that the newspapers should be enabled to reduce their prices so as to make it possible for the largest possible number to buy them. Policies which go against these ends on grounds which are vague and in the nature of ideological prejudices not supported by reasons should be firmly resisted.

153. In our opinion the report has prescribed multiple penalties and deterrents. Steeply escalating import duties on newsprint consumed beyond a fixed page-level should be restrictive enough. Newspapers will increase their page levels to accommodate more advertisement only if they find the penal duties bearable. The duties would be an indirect tax on advertisement. Not content with this, the majority goes on to recommend an arbitrary news-to-advertisement ratio. There would then be two options: reducing editorial inputs which make for excellence or increasing the price. But not content with a news-to-advertisement ratio, the majority wants a price-page schedule which would compel newspapers to increase prices in proportion to their pages. An increase in price would be more of the same thing. It would reduce circulations, and hence advertisement rates and revenue. One wonders why a whole armoury of weapons, each of them deadly enough, is being recommended against the best of our newspapers. If all of them are triggered off together, our Press Commission may well come to be known as the Press Annihilation Commission.

154. With all our major papers condemned to be statutorily sick, who would want to own or launch newspapers, and work with zest for their development? And yet, not content with hobbling and hamstringing the economy of newspapers, our colleagues go on to enjoin (among other things) that no one having business interest elsewhere will have more than 10 per cent ownership in newspapers. An industry which will be turned sick is to be delinked from all resources of capital, with the consequence that no attempt at resuscitation will succeed. We cannot support such a prescription.

PART III

Government-Press Relations

A major lacuna in the report is that it does not provide a comprehensive overview of Government-Press relations as they have evolved since the First Press Commission reported in 1954.

2. This is not a matter of mere academic interest for us; we feel that the failure to analyse this relationship has vitiated the conclusions of the Commission. If this relationship is not analysed, it would not be possible to do justice to our terms of reference.

3. In the Report, there is no reference to the Internal Emergency (1975-77) and the trauma of censorship which the Press in India experienced for 21 months. There is a Section on Pre-censorship in the Commission's Report. The relations between the Government and the Press during the Emergency has a lesson to teach. The best use of history can be made not by forgetting what is distasteful but by learning the lessons which it has to teach.

4. Let us begin at the beginning. In the very nature of things, conflict between the Government and the Press may easily arise in any democracy and, within limits, there is nothing alarming in it. Mutual criticism is useful, healthy and beneficial to both the Press and the Government in the performance of their respective roles. Soon after Independence, a certain tension started emerging in the relationship between the Government and the Press in India. The attitude of some stalwarts who had often denounced the press-laws framed by the British as obnoxious underwent a change after 1947, and their enthusiasm for the Press wanted, because the parallax changed. It is significant that, soon after the enactment of our Constitution, the Home Minister, Shri C. Rajagopalachari, found it necessary to pilot the Press (Prevention of Objectionable Matters) Act, 1951 in Parliament. The usual noises about its being a black Act were then made, but in retrospect, no one would say that our founding fathers had authoritarian designs; even unconscious ones. However, the problems of administering a vast and complex country like India which had little experience of handling the apparatus of a nation-state had a sobering effect on them. Some schizophrenia was inherent in the situation; hence some of the members of the First Press Commission thought it fit to write a note of dissent about the desirability of the Press (Objectionable Matter) Act, and the first amendment to the

Constitution. The Act lapsed a few years later, and no attempt was made to legislate anything similar until 1976.

5. Relations between the Government and the Press were more or less smooth in the halcyon decade of the fifties. The leaders at the top were Olympians, and although they sometimes snubbed the Press with charming petulance, their credentials as liberal democrats were never in question. The Press adored them, as did the people. Once in a while the leaders would wonder if the Press in India was not taking the monopoly-road which it had taken in the West, or they would question what function a managing editor could have in a newspaper, or they would be irritated by the attempts of upstart tycoons to boost their own image and project their own egregious views through the columns of their newspapers. What have these people done to enjoy such a high profile except owning newspapers, they would sometimes ask. Circulations were low, and much significant activity took place without newspapers carrying to scrutinise it. Things happened without being chronicled. A few of the weeklies specialised in scandal busting, and were read avidly. Even if they presented our politicians as gnomes, they performed a useful function, because the readers came to the conclusion that they were only human.

6. Shri Morarji Desai with his puritanical approach would sometimes deny State Government advertisements to a newspaper because it was hostile to prohibition. He action would be disapproved in many circles, but one in not sure how much the people really cared, even the journalists. Several leaders in the middle or lower echelons would expect that neighbourhood newspapers would promote their factional cause or interests, and the papers would be too happy to oblige. Sometimes the papers would be penalised, or denied favours, but there would be no row, because their circulations were small. The country was being governed through, a consensus, and since newspapers were a part of it, there was no sharp cleavage.

7. The First Press Commission had recommended that a Registrar of Newspapers in India be appointed to collate information and present an annual report. The office was promptly set up, and for the first time, the number and circulation of newspapers in the country began to be entered in a register. Prior to this, even the District Magistrate might have had no exact information about the papers begin published in his area. The Commission had also recommended a price-page scheduled and a news-to-advertisement ratio, and the Government, unhappy at the lack of growth of India language newspapers, genuinely believed that

unfair competition offered by high-paged, lowpriced metropolitan English newspapers was coming in the way. A Price-page Act was therefore promptly passed, but the price-page order came only in 1960. On being challenged, it was set aside by the Supreme Court, and there were no hard feelings.

8. After the Chinese incursion into Indian territory, which came into the open in mid-1959, the Indian Press for the first time became bitterly critical of the Himalayan policy of the Government. V.K. Krishna Menon became a *bete noire* and Panch Sheel evaporated into thin air. Jawaharlal Nehru, liberal to the core, never resented the bitterness which the press was exhibiting towards his policy; because he himself had suffered a great disappointment. The election in Bombay in which Krishna Menon was ranged against Acharya Kripalani became a focus of controversy for the Press, and it foreshadowed many later conflicts. The Government-Press relations in the last years of Nehru's life were perhaps illustrative of the lack of mutual appreciation and understanding which were to emerge more prominently later.

9. The 'sixties had a different texture. It was a decade of instability and turmoil, when the torch was being handed over into the unsteady hands of a new generation. Selig Harrison, calling it the Dangerous Decade, did not give India more than ten years. Editorial columns were full of despair and homilies, but the offensive edge of 1959-64 was gone, because the nation was delicately poised on a cliff. Lal Bahadur Shastri was criticised for being a 'prisoner of indecision' in the earlier half of his prime-ministerial tenure, but the nation rallied round him magnificently in the latter half. When Mrs. Indira Gandhi was elected Prime Minister in 1966, she was acclaimed, because she was modern-minded, and beyond parochialism or obscurantist fads. She began with much sympathy, although newspapers would often speak of her 'ketchen cabinet'. The Press wrote what it liked, and there was no counter-hostility. Newspapers in Bengali, Malayalam and Tamil began to acquire respectable circulations, and in all these States Congress lost the elections in 1967. It lost power in several other States, and under the dispensation of SVD ministries, politics became an amoral game about which sane comment, and the application of logical, normative yardsticks became increasingly difficult. The deeper causes were analysed only later, but that would be hindsight, not journalism. During this decade of turmoil, the Press Council Act was enacted in 1965.

10. The political crisis caused by the great split in the Congress

party in 1969 was a climateric event, and it started a trail which has affected the Press like nothing else before. The major newspapers, steeped in Westminster norms and in the liberal traditions of the fifties, did not altogether share the enthusiasm which the split had generated amongst the young and the Left inclined intelligentsia, and a cleavage developed between the Government and the Press as also between large sections of citizenry and the newspapers. Just as the papers had to yardstick to measure the SVD imbroglios, they had none to assess the processes and techniques which became the stock-in-trade of some political parties in the early seventies. They shared a sense of anxiety with the people, and hoped that everything would turn out right in the end; but many felt concerned about the value world in which these events were taking place.

11. In 1971 the Congress party led by Mrs. Gandhi won a massive mandate in the general election, and it could be claimed with some plausibility that opinion in the newspapers did not properly reflect public opinion. There was nothing extraordinary about it, because such divergences occur in democracies. But influential circles in the ruling party thought that newspapers were hostile because they were being dominated by the vested interest and had little *rapport* with the aspirations of the people. They began to hark back nostalgically to the report of the First Press Commission which had recommended a scheme for delinking newspapers from their owners, and for the diffusion of the divested shares amongst the employees of the newspapers. The draft of a bill seeking to amend the Companies Act for this purpose was circulated in 1971. The reaction it aroused amongst the big newspapers was bitter and furious. But the Government itself was not particularly serious. As a former Union Minister of State in charge of Company Affairs admitted in his evidence before the Press Commission, the bill was not pursued because it was feared that if shares were diffused among employees, some of the newspapers would be controlled by CPI (Marxist) Unions, and others by those of the Jana Sangh persuasion. Another consideration, the former Minister confessed, was that it was far easier for the Government to deal with identifiable owners than with defused worker-proprietors. It was perhaps because of this difficulty that a bill for the appointment of public trustees in major newspapers was drafted in 1974. This too was not taken up.

12. Attempts to control the prices and pages of newspapers were revived, and the price-page schedule, struck down by the Supreme

Court was sought to be introduced in modified form. The newsprint policy for 1972-73 was so framed that no daily newspaper was to be allowed newsprint for more than ten pages. This too was struck down in *Bennett Coleman* case because the Supreme Court held that it was an attempt at newspaper control. The Government also enacted a Newspaper (Price Control) Act in 1972 to enable it to fix the maximum prices which may be charged by newspapers. The Act was never implemented, and in course of time lapsed.

13. Although an atmosphere of confrontation prevailed in Government Press relations ever since the Great Divide of 1969, the conflict became muted after India had played an honourable role in the Bangladesh war in 1971, when the entire nation, along with the Press, stood solidly behind Mrs. Gandhi. People felt their charismatic leader knew what was best for the nation, and had the uncanny faculty of doing the right thing at the right time. Newspapers too wondered whether the people were not after all right, and the great business of ratiocination and discussion which they carried in their columns was not really irrelevant to the running of the country. Being newspapers, however, they could do nothing else.

14. When the country came across another difficult patch in 1974-75, the seam began to grow wide again, and the under-currents of confrontation re-surfaced. As in earlier periods, Mrs. Gandhi and her colleagues strongly criticised the newspapers, and regarded them as prime promoters of political chaos.

15. When the internal emergency was imposed in June 1975, newspapers were a major target. Censorship was imposed, and although the Government seldom undertook the vast and impossible task of pre-censoring the several thousand newspapers issuing from all parts of India, a set of guidelines was issued whose breach was to be censured and penalised with utmost seriousness. At the noise in the newspapers subsided, a great silence prevailed. As later events were to prove, the silence was deceptive and a great chasm developed between the mood of the people and the tenor of the Government during the emergency, which led to the defeat of the Congress Party in 1977.

16. It is not necessary in a Minute of Dissent to go into details about the manner in which the Press was controlled in the emergency. They have been documented in the "White Paper on Misuse of Mass Media during the Internal Emergency" issued by the Government of India in August 1977. Apart from other measures to control the Press, the Government had put on the statute books, a draconian measure,

viz., the Prevention of Publication of Objectionable Matters Act, 1976. The compulsory merger of the four news agencies, brought about by threat of denial of radio subscription and pressures of other kinds, and the manner in which the *Samachar* was organised and controlled, also underlined the dangers to the freedom of the Press that then existed. The Act was repealed after a new government came into power. The *Samachar* was also disbanded and *status quo ante* restored.

17. It was against the background of these events that the post-emergency Government of India decided to appoint the Second Press Commission. Announcing the decision, the then Minister of Information and Broadcasting, Shri L. K. Advani stated in the Rajya Sabha on 18th May, 1978 "A series of steps are already been taken during the last one year to strengthen the freedom and independence of the Press by way of setting right several aberrations of the Emergency. . . . Although these steps paved the way for the revival of a free and independent Press, it is considered that the time has come for an in-depth examination of the entire state of the Press in the country with a view of determining further steps that need to be taken to restore it to full vigour and health. . . . As its role in educating public opinion has been firmly established, it is essential to safeguard the freedom and independence of the Press against pressures of all kinds. All this points to the need for re-examining its place, status and functioning in a democratic set up more so, in view of the recent experience when the Press was subjected to a series of legal and administrative assaults."

18. The Commission, appointed in May 1978 under the Chairmanship of Justice P.K. Goswami, a retired Judge of the Supreme Court, continued to function till January 1980. In July 1979, when there was a change of Government in New Delhi and Shri Charan Singh became Prime Minister after the resignation of Shri Morarji Desai, the Commission unanimously decided to tender its resignation "as a matter of propriety". The Commission wrote that its report "when submitted, will be a charge of the new Government and, therefore, this is the only course fair to the Government as well as to the Commission". The Commission reiterated that it had no intention to embarrass the Government or to shirk its responsibilities for the task assigned to it. It only wanted to establish a healthy convention. But the very next day, the new Government informed the Commission that it would like to continue with its work. The Commission, therefore, continued.

19. When there was another change of Government at the Centre in

January 1980, the Commission again decided unanimously to tender its resignation in the same terms. Two weeks later, the Minister for Information and Broadcasting informed the Commission that "the new Government would like to continue the Commission based on a more comprehensive set of terms of reference. This, you will kindly appreciate, will be possible only if the Commission is reconstituted. It is in this context, that the Government has regretfully decided to accept your resignation".

20. The resignation of the Goswami Commission was accepted at the end of January 1980. The appointment of the New Chairman was announced on April 21, 1980. The names of ten members were announced on June 18, 1980, and the names of another two members were announced on October 16, 1980. The terms of reference of the reconstituted Commission were announced on July 24, 1980.

21. The terms of reference were not significantly different except that there was more stress on responsibility as a concomitant of Press freedom in a developing and democratic society. Some new items were included, viz., the citizen's right to privacy, growth of small and medium papers, the flow of news to and from India, and the proposals for a new international information order.

22. Now to continue our brief resume of Government Press relations, after the Janata Party came to power in 1977, it found that the Press in India was severely critical of its inertia and its internecine quarrels. Leaders were sore that their egotistical perception of their own epochal importance was not shared by newspapermen, and one of them attributed it to the antipathy of the urban-educated middle class against the emerging peasantry in the country-side. One Union Cabinet Minister went to the extent of advocating the burning of the copies of a certain newspaper. Mrs. Gandhi continued to dominate the front pages of newspapers even after her defeat, because of her resilience in returning to the mainstream of politics, and because the Janata Government was having past events investigated. Important sections of the Press opposed the idea of a campaign of vendetta against Mrs. Gandhi, and took up cudgels on her behalf when she was out of power.

23. The confrontationist attitudes of the past have continued unhappily to bedevil relations between Government and the Press after the Lok Sabha elections of 1980. Chief Ministers have compared the Press to snakes and scorpions, and one recently ordered the correspondent of a newspaper he did not like to leave his press conference. The malaise is not confined to any single party. In

September 1981, the Tamilnadu Government amended the Indian Penal Code to enhance the punishment for publication of "grossly indecent or scurrilous matter". The offence has been made cognizable and non-bailable, and fine as well as imprisonment are now both mandatory. Because the offence in non-bailable, hostile journalists can be detained in police or judicial custody for quite some time before the matter is decided in courts. Another order of the Tamilnadu Government forbids Government servants from furnishing any information to the Press.

24. Not to speak of the Chief Ministers and others Prime Minister Smt. Indira Gandhi herself has been critical of the Press. In a recent interview, she said that the Indian Press was not functioning as a free Press. "The Press is the Opposition in India. . . . what is called the National Press. . . . They lead the Opposition. . . . It is not just reporting".*

25. On top of the well-known causes of tension between the Government and the Press in any democracy, some additional ones have arisen in India. There has been a sharp drop in the standards of public morality in public life and the political process is proving inadequate for self-correction. This places a heavy responsibility on the Press which the better sections of it, are trying to perform to the best of their ability and resources.

26. As it happens, intellectual standards have gone down in our public life partly as a result of the rapid turnover in the last decade and partly as a result of the inevitable disappearance of the old guard brought up in the tradition of Gandhiji and Nehru. It will not be an exaggeration to say that, in some quarters, there is a tendency to treat public life as a form of business. This has produced considerable revulsion among the better educated and morally sensitive sections of our intelligentsia. This intelligentsia expects the Press to fill the breach. Again, it is to the credit of the Press that it is trying to do that at its own risk.

27. Witness its role in the recent exposures such as those regarding blindings in Bhagalpur, the cement distribution improprieties and other matters connected with the Trusts set up by the former Maharashtra Chief Minister, Shri A.R. Antulay, existence of bonded labour in many areas and the plight of under-trial prisoners. This list is not

---

* See *Indian Express*, Feb. 15, 1982.

comprehensive and is not intended to be. Indeed, it is only an indication of the evils that would flourish if the Press is not to light up the dark corners of our society. We would go so far as to say that even so big a problem as the atrocities on the *Harijans* and the tribals would not attract the attention that they do but for a vigilant Press.

28. In fact, the complaint should be that the Press has not been vigilant, independent or courageous enough. It is so much easier to fill the paper with reports of what different people say, and what is happening in the corridors of powers in the Central and State capitals. Investigation of what is actually happening in the field, how the economy is faring, how land reforms are being implemented, how various projects are progressing and are being managed, whether various poor and oppressed sections are able to get the facilities that are provided for them, where established groups are misusing their powers – all this requires a great deal of effort, travel in remote areas and even some personal risk. But there has been a welcome tendency in recent years to report on such issues. To an extent, competition has grown among newspapers in investigative journalism and this is all to the good.

29. Such competition can however also lead to sensation-mongering and irresponsible attacks on Government and public authorities and character assassination of public men. This is specially so because criticism sells while appreciation does not. It is seldom that the Press praises the Government where paise is due. Public men and public institutions are often criticised on grounds which are ultimately found to be baseless. It is also well known that, like many other professions, journalists have also not been above misusing the influence and the power which they exercise. These tendencies are obviously not conducive to the growth of a healthy Press and therefore are also responsible for the deterioration in Government-Press relationship.

30. Certain principles need to be firmly kept in view. Free speech, at Emerson had pointed out, is important to ensure individual self-fulfilment; but even more so to ensure the participation of the governed in the process of decision-making. Moreover, free discussion is a method of maintaining the precarious balance between healthy cleavage and necessary consensus. "Suppression of expression merely conceals the real problems confronting a society and diverts public attention from the critical issues. It is likely to result in the neglect of the grievances which are the actual basis of the unrest and thus prevent

their correction".* The truth of these observations was established during the Emergency when those in power found that they were in the dark about what was happening in the country. It was only later that they came to know that vast masses of people had been alienated. President Wilson had pointed out long ago that "the seed of revolution is suppression". It has been emphasised that "nothing adds more to men's hatred to Government than its refusal to let them talk."

31. The desire of those in authority to control the media is reflected in the refusal of successive governments of varying complexions to set up an autonomous body for managing broadcasting. It is possible that the possessive attitude of those in power towards the broadcast media influences their approach to the Press. The official control of the broadcast media further highlights the vital role of the Press.

32. One unanimous conclusion of the Commission is that the present Constitutional provision may not be adequate to ensure a free Press. The case for a Constitutional Amendment in this regard has been made in Chapter IV of the Commission's Report. We are in agreement with the relevant recommendation. Instances of pressures on the Press have been mentioned in Chapter V of the Report the White Paper of 1977 and in the evidence tendered before the Commission. Efforts for example, were made to stop private companies from giving advertisements to newspapers such as the *Indian Express* and *The Statesman*. Power cuts were imposed to create difficulties for certain newspapers. It is true that these attempts happily have been few and far between and, by and large, newspapers, especially in the metropolitan areas, have escaped undue harassment. Newspapers in provincial and district towns have not been so fortunate.

33. In our circumstances, government cannot but be armed with a large powers. A substantial part of the economy is also directly administered through public sector enterprises. It is, therefore, not difficult for those in power to use these instruments to obstruct the working of a newspaper undertaking if they so decide. Vigilance against such abuse is necessary. That is why a Constitutional Amendment, on the lines recommended in the Report or in any other suitable manner to ensure freedom of the Press more effectively is essential.

34. To our mind, the majority opinion is founded on the assumption

* Quoted in Freedom of Speech, ed. Franklyn S. Haiman, New York, 1978, pp. 204-205.

that the more important newspapers have been irresponsible and need to be "disciplined". It is true that there have been occasions where some newspapers have conducted themselves without a proper sense of responsibility. There are instances of aberration. Even so, by and large, the Indian Press has acted in a responsible manner. On matters of national importance, it has exhibited a unity of purpose and exercised commendable restraint. In that context we do not see the need for some of the major recommendations made by the majority which we have been unable to endorse. If implemented, they may easily lead to the destruction of a Press which, despite all its failings, is by common consent, the most competent, responsible and independent in the entire Third World, something of which India can legitimately be proud. It is this basic difference of approach that has obliged us to produce this Minute of Dissent, not without regret.

TABLE 1: *Dailies:* Percentage of space of Display and Classified Advertisements to total space — Category-wise and Language-wise

Language	Advertisements Display						Advertisements Classified					
	V. Big	Big	Medium	Small	V. Small	All	V. Big	Big	Medium	Small	V. Small	All
	1	2	3	4	5	6	1	2	3	4	5	6
English	51.63	40.24	40.24	32.92	26.60	43.96	6.48	3.78	4.47	3.13	—	5.03
Hindi	40.68	45.10	35.00	22.89	38.62	34.72	4.56	2.07	3.33	1.26	0.64	2.72
Assemese	—	—	32.64	18.23	—	23.17	—	—	4.28	4.06	—	4.14
Bengali	48.01	—	19.50	15.25	16.27	27.21	1.10	—	9.46	—	—	1.07
Gujarati	43.42	43.56	31.44	25.06	41.69	36.86	2.16	1.28	0.94	1.00	0.52	1.32
Kannada	38.47	40.00	28.48	27.98	28.95	32.00	0.52	0.10	0.68	—	—	0.93
Kashmiri	—	—	—	—	—	—	—	—	—	—	—	—
Malayalam	42.30	22.54	23.38	50.47	36.18	32.02	6.37	2.86	2.84	1.68	0.79	4.00
Marathi	48.69	46.05	32.87	35.88	—	39.48	2.68	4.98	2.15	1.54	—	2.62
Oriya	—	52.11	49.30	29.34	18.07	49.46	—	1.52	—	0.07	—	1.20
Punjabi	—	—	32.35	14.01	—	21.16	—	—	17.96	11.79	—	14.20
Sanskrit	—	—	—	—	—	—	—	—	—	—	—	—
Sindhi	—	—	—	18.14	—	18.16	—	—	—	4.94	—	4.94
Tamil	33.96	23.75	24.64	17.43	—	27.76	3.92	0.89	1.10	0.86	—	2.31
Telugu	34.40	54.55	31.25	24.81	39.45	35.58	0.19	0.12	0.67	0.09	—	0.37
Urdu	—	45.07	31.20	25.61	18.40	27.17		0.15	0.11	0.28	—	0.21

TABLE 2: Average News Space and Advertisement Space per one paise in Big, Medium and Small Dailies published from Delhi

Sl. No.	Name	Language	Circulation 1980	Price	Total news for 3 days in col. cm	Total Ad. for 3 days in col. cms	News Space per one paise	Ad. space per one paise
				Paise				
1.	*Janyug*, New Delhi	Hindi	12248	40 (Sun 45)	6215.5	2184.5	49.72	17.47
2.	*Nav Bharat Times*, New Delhi	Hindi	346520	50 (Sun 55)	7275	5493	46.93	35.43
3.	*Hindustan*, New Delhi	Hindi	184756	50	7481.5	4502.5	49.87	30.01
4.	Pratap, New Delhi	Urdu	24199	50	5852	1423	39.01	9.48
5.	*Milap*, New Delhi	Urdu	22521	50	7382.50	2274.0	49.28	15.1
6.	*Aljamiat*, Delhi	Urdu	N.S.	45	4848.6	500.0	32.32	3.70
7.	*Tej*, Delhi	Urdu	3471	45	6090.00	1011.50	45.11	6.74
8.	*Qaumi Awaz*, Delhi	Urdu	13775	50	10342.5	940.5	68.95	6.27
9.	*Indian Express*, New Delhi	English	121644	60	10875	7781	57.23	40.95
10.	*Times of India*, New Delhi	English	195381	60	11560.0	13227.00	60.84	69.61
11.	*Statesman*, New Delhi	English	33374	50	10538	8822	70.25	58.81
12.	*Patriot*, New Delhi	English	32617	50	12356.00	5452.00	82.37	35.01
13.	*Hindustan Times*, New Delhi	English	262334	60 (Sun 70)	9951	13857	52.37	79.93
14.	*National Herald*, New Delhi	English	17259	50	13671	5033	91.14	33.55

TABLE 3: Dailies: Cost of Display and Classified Advertisement

(In thousand rupees)

Language	Display						Classified					
	V. Big	Big	Medium	Small	V. Small	Total	V. Big	Big	Medium	Small	V. Small	Total
1	2	3	4	5	6	7	8	9	10	11	12	13
English	21671.8	1292.1	5197.4	730.1	15.3	28906.7	2594.9	122.7	547.4	70.4	—	3335.5
Hindi	1522.4	2494.5	1889.7	610.6	53.8	6570.9	179.1	116.8	169.2	33.7	0.9	499.7
Assemese	—	—	69.8	49.7	—	119.4	—	—	9.4	13.2	—	22.6
Bengali	3056.1	—	431.5	81.6	88.8	3658.0	127.0	—	1.8	—	—	128.8
Gujarati	2730.3	678.5	1208.6	169.6	99.5	4886.6	126.3	20.0	38.8	7.1	0.3	192.5
Kannada	95.9	76.4	177.1	39.0	36.8	425.2	6.2	0.4	8.4	0	0	15.0
Kashmiri	—	—	—	—	—	—	—	—	—	—	—	—
Malayalam	308.8	77.9	151.4	27.1	32.2	597.4	363.3	31.2	45.9	0.8	0.5	441.7
Marathi	1344.7	587.0	496.0	219.4	14.0	2661.1	65.0	58.2	33.1	9.1	0.6	166.0
Oriya	0	230.4	83.4	70.3	5.2	389.3	0	6.7	0	0.1	0	6.8
Punjabi	0	0	103.7	69.6	0	173.3	0	0	57.7	56.3	0	114.0
Sanskrit	—	—	—	—	—	—	—	—	—	—	—	—
Sindhi	0	0	0	25.8	0	25.8	0	0	0	7.3	0	7.3
Tamil	1299.8	68.8	87.5	20.0	0	1476.3	178.2	3.0	3.7	0.9	0	185.8
Telugu	364.0	886.6	316.4	54.3	18.8	1640.1	2.0	2.2	7.4	0.2	0	11.8
Urdu	0	144.5	304.9	547.7	38.7	1035.8	0	0.2	1.3	4.7	—	6.2
Total	32393.8	6536.7	10517.4	2715.0	403.1	52565.9	3642.0	361.4	924.1	203.8	2.3	5133.7

TABLE 4: Value of display advertisements of various categories in English dailies by size

	Total amount (in Rs. hundred)	Very Big	Big	Medium	Small	Very Small
		(in per cent)				
1	2	3	4	5	6	7
1. Central	25,404 (9.81)	9.14	7.74	12.08	17.29	17.99
2. State	23,145 (8.94)	8.23	13.78	10.50	9.70	34.53
3. Local	3,081 (1.19)	1.15	0.45	1.41	2.14	0.72
4. Private	38,406 (14.84)	16.05	14.25	9.63	17.6	5.76
5. Foreign	1,142 (0.44)	0.43	0.70	0.41	0.5	—
6. Industrial	33,617 (12.99)	13.69	17.20	9.28	11.40	—
7. Consumer	60,664 (23.44)	22.75	28.29	25.42	20.93	7.91
8. Farm	601 (0.23)	0.25	—	0.21	0.3	—
9. Entertain-ment	26,623 (10.29)	8.43	8.36	18.47	10.19	5.04
10. Employment	46,159 (17.83)	19.87	9.23	12.60	9.94	28.06
Grand total	2,58,842 (100.0)	1,93,756 (100.0)	11,815 (100.0)	46,761 (100.0)	6,368 (100.0)	139 (100.0)

Note: Figures within brackets in column 3 and also in the last line of columns 4 to 8 indicate percentage

TABLE 5: Value of classified advertisement of various categories in English dailies day size

	Total amount (in Rs. hundred)	Very Big	Big	Medium	Small	Very Small
		(in per cent)				
1	2	3	4	5	6	7
1. Central	4,582 (18.09)	18.82	16.39	15.29	16.61	—
2. State	7,034 (27.7)	26.48	35.07	31.53	33.05	—
3. Legal	1,039 (4.10)	3.72	2.29	6.06	4.97	—
4. Private	2,291 (9.04)	8.73	9.66	9.92	11.99	—
5. Foreign	—	—	—	—	—	—
6. Industrial	681 (2.69)	2.37	6.99	3.49	0.19	—
7. Consumer	642 (2.53)	1.83	5.72	4.79	4.97	—
8. Farm	—	—	—	—	—	—
9. Entertain-ment	1,912 (7.5)	7.28	6.73	9.02	7.02	—
10. Employment	7,151 (28.23)	30.77	17.15	19.89	19.52	—
Total	25,333 (100.0)	19,639 (100.0)	787 (100.0)	4,323 (100.0)	584 (100.0)	

Note: Figures within brackets in column 3 and also in the last line of columns 4 to 8 indicate percentage.

TABLE 6: Value of classified advertisements of various categories in Hindi dailies by size

	Total amount (in Rs. hundred)	Very Big	Big	Medium	Small	Very Small
		(in per cent)				
1	2	3	4	5	6	7
1. Central	405 (9.46)	9.60	14.82	7.16	2.41	—
2. State	1,479 (34.55)	32.88	53.81	24.38	29.9	100
3. Legal	496 (11.59)	9.99	5.18	15.91	20.27	—
4. Private	275 (6.42)	7.85	0.91	8.26	8.59	—
5. Foreign	—	—	—	—	—	—
6. Industrial	158 (3.69)	6.87	0.61	2.62	3.09	—
7. Consumer	242 (5.65)	2.98	1.42	11.16	6.37	—
8. Farm	15 (0.35)	0.32	—	0.62	0.34	—
9. Entertain-ment	655 (15.30)	9.73	12.28	20.59	26.12	90.0
10. Employment	556 (12.99)	19.78	10.96	9.30	2.41	—
Grant Total	4,281 (100.0)	1,542 (100.0)	985 (100.0)	1,452 (100.0)	291 (100.0)	10 (100.0)

Note: Figures within brackets in column 3 and also in the last line of columns 4, 5, 6, 7 and 8 indicate percentage.

TABLE 7: Value of display advertisements of various categories in Hindi dailies by size

	Total amount (in Rs. hundred)	Very Big	Big	Medium	Small	Very Small
		(in per cent)				
1	2	3	4	5	6	7
1. Central	6,730 (11.30)	11.43	9.98	10.90	16.67	23.54
2. State	11,027 (18.51)	15.08	19.95	19.77	18.18	6.70
3. Local	2,679 (4.50)	2.63	3.58	6.40	7.23	3.24
4. Private	2,860 (4.80)	6.45	3.55	4.58	6.67	3.67
5. Foreign	31 (0.05)	—	—	—	0.23	—
6. Industrial	3,992 (6.70)	7.60	8.30	4.09	5.47	10.80
7. Consumer	19,659 (33.0)	39.35	36.69	28.25	17.50	22.03
8. Farm Related	912 (1.53)	2.34	1.44	1.31	0.6	1.30
9. Entertain-ment	7,698 (12.92)	8.58	9.53	18.08	20.72	27.65
10. Employment	3,986 (6.69)	6.53	6.97	6.58	6.73	1.08
Total	59.574 (100.0)	13.666 (100.0)	23,014 (100.0)	16,802 (100.0)	5,633 (100.0)	463 (100.0)

Note: Figures within brackets in column 3 and also in the last line of columns 4, 5, 6, 7, and 8 indicate percentage.

Appendix A to Minute of Dissent

The Enquiry Committee on Small Newspapers (1965), which was appointed specifically to look into the difficulties and problems facing small newspapers and to suggest measures for assisting and improving them, was vertically split over the price-page schedule, and it could recommend this measure for a period of ten years only with a five to four majority. The Chairman and Vice Chairman of the Committee were both opposed to the measure.

In his minute of dissent, the late Shri A.D. Mani, the then editor of *Hitavada* (Nagpur and Bhopal), both small newspapers run by the Servants of India Society, and a member of the First Press Commission, argued the case against the schedule powerfully. "The question arises whose view should prevail now, that of the Press Commission or the Supreme Court of India, "he asked, and answered: "My answer is clear and without reservation. The Supreme Court's judgment should prevail."

Shri Mani was not convinced by the arguments about monopoly in the Press: "The arguments of the majority that the present state of the

Press has encouraged the trend to monopoly is yet to the proved by statistical evidence. It would have been desirable for the Committee to have pointed out in what manner monopolies have been created in the country. It is because concentration of ownership in the U.K. had led to distortion of news that the Royal Commission of U.K. had commented on these trends. In my humble view such a situation had not arisen yet in India.

"I have had experience of newspapers in Nagpur and Bhopal which are primarily small newspapers' regions", Shri Mani wrote, "And my experience shows that whatever effort may be made by newspapers in this region, they cannot go beyond a certain optimum circulation; and that even in respect of advertisement revenue, their chances of competing with big newspapers of metropolitan cities are limited on account of the fact that the consumer market in this region is restricted. It is also noteworthy that throughout the enquiry that the Committee conducted, it came across *no case of a newspaper having been forced to close down on account of other newspapers publishing more pages at a lower price*." (italics ours).

And again: "If the Committee had shown as a result of a statistical study and analysis of evidence that a certain point of view which could have been presented and should have been presented in public interest was not allowed to be presented on account of the larger number of pages which a big newspaper was in a position to print at what the Committee considered a low price, then the question could have been considered whether the number of pages that the big newspapers published had resulted in the shutting out of a valid point of view. . . . If it could have been shown that small newspapers had set up a superior standard of performance in the matter of serving public interest that big newspapers, and that they would be in a position to increase the quality of their performance if they were given statutory protection in the form of an amendment to the Constitution, that position also could have been understood."

Shri Mani also pointed out that the implications of a Constitutional amendment providing for a price-page schedule would not be confined to newspapers: "Any amendment to Article 19(1) (ii) dealing with printed matter will *ipso facto* apply to other forms of printed matter besides newspapers and periodicals. There are books and pamphlets, there are big publishing houses in the metropolitan cities, there are small publishing houses in other parts of the country. The economics of the larger publishing houses in the metropolitan cities help them to sell books at lower prices than those published by small publishing houses which have to content themselves with only printing a limited number of copies of publications at a higher cost than big publishing houses. . . . If the price of books is to based not on their quality but on the number of pages they print, should it be necessary for example, for a History of India to be sold at a fixed price of Rs. 2 per 200 pages or Rs. 4 for 300 pages? Would not any such regulation of the trade in books make a mockery of freedom of expression? Further why should the equalisation of opportunity in the matter of a rigid price-control be limited only to newspapers? . . . . Would it be unreasonable to ask that other Constitutional amendments should be made to ensure a price-fixing machinery for all categories of manufacture which is for sale so that equality of opportunity enshrined in the Constitution can be achieved?"

Shri R. R. Diwakar, Chairman of the Enquiry Committee agreed with this logic, and wrote: "The logic would be, if there can be a curb on newspapers and periodicals, why not on books, Cinema, radio, painting, and why not".

Regarding the argument that statutory news-to-advertisement ratio would lead to more advertisements being diverted to small newspapers, Shri A.D. Mani wrote: "The Commission has not shown any-where in the report that by taking such drastic steps there would be a diversion of advertisements from big to small newspapers. From the evidence that was tendered before the Committee by the Indian Society of Advertisers and the Advertising Agencies Association of India. It was clear that the scope for advertisement in small newspapers was limited. . . . I fear there would be a diversion of advertising revenue from small newspapers to other forms of publicity, like posters and cinema slides." (Radio and television were not seen then as potent advertisement media, which they have become now).

In conclusion, Shri Mani wrote: "The recommendations, if accepted by Government, would send up the cost of living of the citizens in respect of their resources to buy newspapers. They would further amount to acceptance in principle of the Government's right to interfere, influence, and control the economy of newspapers; once that principle is conceded, it may be possible for the Governments of the future to extend the field of interference to bring into existence a State-controlled Press and such a Press would undermine democracy in the country. On these grounds, I regret I cannot be a party to these recommendations."

Another dissenting member of the Enquiry Committee on Small Newspapers, Shri M. Yunus Dehlvi, had this to say: "There has been no evidence before the Committee that during the period a price-page schedule was in operation in England and during the short period it was imposed in India before being struck down by the Supreme Courts as *ultra vires* of the Constitutional guarantees of freedom of Expression, it helped in growth of small newspapers."

"Shri A. R. Bhat, the chief exponent of the price-age scheduled, told the Committee that the restrictions when they were enforced in India had the effect of reducing the circulations of some of the bigger metropolitan papers and of restricting moral growth in the circulations of some other newspapers of the same class. In my view, it was not one of the functions of this Committee to work for restraints on the growth of any section of the Indian Press or even to recommend the growth of one section of the Press at the cost of the normal development of another section. Ours is a developing country and acceleration in the growth of one section of the Press can be achieved out of the additional growth potential instead of circulation or advertisement revenues being diverted statue, as it were, from one section of the Press to the other".

Dissenting note of Shri Prem Chand Verma relating to Chapter II entitled 'Retrospect 1952-1982'

Hindi Language Newspapers

1. The First Press Commission's Report in 1935 examined the problems relating to the development of newspapers as they existed at that time. Now, after a lapse of 28 years the Second Press Commission is to make recommendations in the situation obtaining at present as well as keeping in view the next fifteen years.

2. It is my considered opinion that the question of development of Hindi newspapers should in no case be dealt with at par with the newspapers of regional languages. I fully recognise that all languages included in the schedule attached to the Constitution should be given equal opportunities to develop for which all encouragements needed be provided and their problems resolved with sympathy and understanding.

3. However, Hindi language has a pre-eminent position in as much as it is the Official language of the country and is ultimately to replace English language. It is, therefore, only fair that its problems and

extension programme are treated entirely on a different and special footing. In other words effective steps should be taken to bring it to an equal position with English with a view of providing it the status of National Press in the real sense of the terms within a reasonable period of time.

4. According to 1981 census the population of India was more than 68 crores. The total circulation of newspapers was estimated at 4,64,49,000. The population of six Hindi-speaking States and one Union Territory was 29,02,00,687. In addition the population of Punjab, Jammu and Kashmir, Gujarat and the Union Territory of Chandigarh, where Hindi is read, written and spoken extensively is 5,69,63,321. Taken together the population of Hindi knowing people comes to 34,71,64,008 or a little above half of the total population. Further in Maharashtra, Andhra Pradesh, Karnataka which together have a population of 16,02,70,184 nearly 50 per cent of the people can read, write and speak Hindi/Urdu well. If these 50 per cent people (nearly 8 crores) are also taken into account, the number of Hindi knowing people would come to 43 crores. Apart from it, considerable number of people in the remaining States also are Hindi knowing. These facts make it abundantly clear that Hindi is truly our national language and the necessity of its development and extension cannot be overemphasised. It should be brought to a level that it should be possible for Indian people in all the State in the North, South, East, West and Central to read national and international news and information through Hindi Press.

5. At the time of First Press Commission daily newspapers comprised 41 in English and 76 in Hindi with circulation of 6.97 and 3.79 and lakhs respectively.

The position in 1980 was as under:

	No.	Circulation
1. English dailies	98	32.80 lakhs
2. Hindi dailies	333	46.10 lakhs

The above figures would show that the readership of Hindi newspapers is growing at more than double the rate of English newspapers.

6. At present, it may be that thousands of newspapers and

periodicals are published in the country, but their total circulation is only 4,64,49,000. This means that circulation is 14 copies per 1000 persons or only 1.5 per cent people read newspapers, which is indeed too low.

7. On the other hand, while the Hindi knowing population is 43 crores, the circulation of Hindi newspapers is only 1,02,59,000. In other words, for every 42 persons, one copy is published. This position of the national language indeed calls for a stupendous effort for its development. The figures quoted are true and reveal the problem in reality that we have to resolve.

8. In the light of above, I recommend the following measures for the development of Hindi newspapers:

(i) The Government of India should make arrangements through P.I.B.'s offices in each State for release of Press material in Hindi also in addition to English and regional languages;

(ii) All State Governments should treat Hindi language on equal footing with local regional languages and should make necessary changes in their policies for all purposes;

(iii) Government of India should continuously examine the progress and development of Hindi language newspapers published in Non-Hindi States and Union Territories. An Expert Committee should be set up for this. The Secretary of the Committee should not be of a rank lower than Joint Secretary. This Committee should be made responsible for sorting out the problems, removing of obstacles and fulfilling the needs of Hindi newspapers. The Committee should keep a watch on advertisement and other policies of State Governments and Governments of Union Territories with a view of ensuring that Hindi newspapers are not ignored or suffer disadvantages. The Committee should make suitable recommendation from time to time to the Government or India for the speedy development of Hindi Newspapers; and

(iv) In order to improve the standard of Hindi journalism and for its further promotion suitable curriculum and training facilities be organised in the Universities and training institutes.

Supplementary note of Shri Prem Chand Verma on small and medium newspapers

Under Term No. 13 of its Terms of Reference the Press

Commission was required to examine and make recommendations on the development and growth of small and medium newspapers. Unfortunately, however, the Commission has failed to apply its mind to the problems of this section of the Press.

2. A large part of the report of the Commission deals only with the larger and relatively prosperous, newspapers. Some of the problems of small and medium newspapers have come in for mention in different parts of the report but they have not been brought into sharp focus anywhere.

3. On my suggestion, the Commission had carried out a survey of small and medium newspapers. An analytical report of the survey was also prepared bringing out their financial problems and need for assistance for acquiring land, buildings and machinery. However, apart from mentioning the results of the survey (the report has been given in Appendix II. 17), the Commission has not come out with specific recommendations to meet the needs of small and medium newspapers.

4. The role of the small and medium newspapers in the development of the country as a whole cannot be played down. The majority of the Indian population even today live in rural areas. But their level of development is low compared to the urban population. The need for the flow of information to and from the rural people is, therefore, all the greater. The larger and more well-known daily newspapers which have, by and large, monopolised the attention of the Commission are all published from the metropolitan and other large towns. They are produced by big industrial houses and other business concerns who give no thought to the well-being of the rural population. Most of the editors and journalists of these big papers are city-bred people who have little or no sympathy for the rural people. The result is that the big dailies cannot and do not reflect the problems and aspirations of the rural population.

5. It is the small newspapers, both dailies and news periodicals, who have the potential to bridge the communication gap. Small newspapers are brought out by people with small means, they come out from the smaller towns and carry local news and cover problems concerning the local people. These newspapers speak in the languages of the people in the villages and are read and understood by them. These papers alone are capable of influencing or building up public opinion. They serve as a bridge between the people living at distant places in the interior of the country on the one hand and the local administration, State Governments and the Central Government on the

other. They bring to the notice of the authorities the sufferings, difficulties and needs of the people while carrying to the people the type of information from the Government which they need. These papers are the best vehicles for building up unity and communal harmony among the people and promoting the process of development by strengthening the roots of democracy.

6. It is said that the growth of the small and medium newspapers in the country has been very slow as compared to the growth of the larger papers.

7. According to the records of the Press Registrar, the average circulation of a small daily (circulation up to 15,000) was 4,100 in 1952. Twenty-seven years later in 1979, the average had gone up just to 4,900. The average circulation of medium dailies (circulation 15,000 to 50,000) went up from 25,900 to 28,100. Against this, the growth of the big dailies has been nothing less than phenomenal. From an average circulation of 71,800 in 1952, they achieved an average circulation of 1,22,800 in 1979. Taking into account newspapers of other periodicities, the average circulation of all small newspapers has in fact come down from 2,700 in 1960 to 2,300 in 1979. Medium newspapers have shown only a marginal improvement from an average circulation of 24,600 in 1960 to 27,100 in 1979. As against that, the average circulation of big newspapers, dailies and periodicals together, rose from 84,600 in 1960 to 1,17,200 in 1979. Looking at the situation from another angle, in 1952, small and medium dailies accounted for 83 per cent of the total circulation of daily newspapers in India. Today they account for only a little over 43 per cent. Taking dailies and periodicals together, small and medium newspapers accounted for 82 per cent of the total circulation of all newspapers in 1960 but in 1979 their share in the total circulation had come down to 56 per cent.

8. It is often contended by the protagonists of the bigger papers that small newspapers indulge in yellow journalism and black mailing, that they lack business acumen and hanker only after government advertisements. It is said that such newspapers do not maintain professional standards and do not deserve to be assisted. While some of the small newspapers may, indeed be, practising yellow journalism it should be appreciated that the large circulated newspapers are no paragons of virtue. On the other hand, while a few rags with negligible circulation can hardly affect the society, a large paper that violates the unwritten code of ethics of journalism can do incalculable harm.

9. As regard the lack of business acumen among the owners of

small newspapers and the lack of regularly of some of the papers, it will be wrong to blame them for the same. If a newspaper which can make a positive contribution to the developmental processes but cannot make itself a financially viable proposition for the owner, it is for the state to see that the paper does not fold up. If a small newspaper cannot come out regularly because it cannot buy newsprint in the black market or because it cannot afford to take the supply of newsprint allotted by the Press Registrar from a distant depot of the State Trading Corporation, it is not the fault of the newspaper, it is the fault of the system. It is the duty of all of us to see that such papers do not die.

10. According to the techno-economic survey of small and medium newspapers done by the Commission, a large number of dailies and periodicals in the small category earned less than 15,000 rupees in a year from either sales or advertisements. Some papers did not have any income from advertisements. The survey of newspaper contents carried out by the Operations Research Group, Baroda had also revealed that big newspapers gather more than 75 per cent of the money spent on advertising through newspapers.

11. The small newspapers' share in the total advertisement revenue was found to be only 6.2 per cent. Based on this the Commission's Secretariat made an estimate according to which all big newspapers got advertisement worth Rs. 12,340 lakhs in 1980 of which all small newspapers got only Rs. 4,376 lakhs. It is nothing less then unfortunate that only 174 out of 17,168 newspapers should corner 56.6 per cent of the total advertising revenue, while nearly 17,000 small newspapers should get only 20 per cent. Ending of such injustice cannot be left to the mercy of the so-called market forces as contended by the spokesmen of the bigger newspapers. If the small and medium newspapers have a role of play in the development of the country they should get their share of advertisement revenue. There is nothing wrong or immoral in assisting small newspapers through advertisements so long as it is not used as a lever to influence the policy of the newspaper.

RECOMMENDATIONS

(i) *Specific Advertisement Share Allocation*

In my opinion the Government should treat the small and medium newspapers in the same manner as it treats the scheduled castes and backward classes in the country. The Union Government as well as the Governments in the States including public sector undertakings should allocate at least 50 per cent of their advertisement expenditure to small and medium newspapers of which at least 60 per cent should be allocated to news periodicals. Of course the basis of release of advertisements should take into account the circulation, the standards of journalism and the quality of production of each paper. No newspaper found guilty of yellow journalism should be assisted. Even the advertisers of consumer goods should recognise the growing importance of the rural market. They should stop patronising only the big newspapers particularly those in English, and start releasing advertisements in the good small dailies coming out from the districts.

(ii) *Subsidy on Newsprint and other Facilities*

I have repeatedly drawn the attention of my colleagues in the Commission to the fact that only a very small section of the Indian Press has monopolised the consumption of newsprint. Newsprint as we all known, is an imported commodity for which the country spends large amounts of precious foreign exchange. In my opinion it will be a criminal waste of public money if the in justice in the allocation of newsprint is continued. It should be noted that 25 big newspaper concerns were allotted more than 2,34,000 tonnes (68.3 per cent) of newsprint out of the total of 3,42,000 tonnes allotted to newspapers in 1979-80.

As brought out in the survey of small and medium newspapers, a large number of such papers were being printed on white printing paper which is costlier than newsprint. Ironically, it is the small papers which are more in need of cheaper paper. The total demand of newsprint of the small and medium newspapers is not very substantial and Government should see to it that each such paper gets its requirements of newsprint before the demands of the bigger papers are met. The official price of newsprint in recent years has recorded a steep increase. It is beyond the reach of most of the smaller newspapers. Keeping in mind their limited demand and in view of the positive role they play in the development of the country, it will not be asking too much of the Government to demand a subsidy on the sale of newsprint to small newspapers.

Newsprint to small and medium newspapers should be subsidised by Government to an extent that brings its price within the means of such papers.

(iii) *Facility for Import of suitable Printing Machinery*

The Commission in its report has recommended the import of re-assembled second-hand printing machinery for the use of small newspapers. While endorsing this, I would like to point out that the needs of the small newspapers are not confined to printing machinery only. As brought out in the survey of small and medium newspapers, a large number of such papers are in need of metal types. Government should make a survey of the existing facilities with regard to the manufacture and supply of metal types for printing press and take necessary steps to help the small newspapers. Such newspapers should also be given finance to get other equipment required by them.

(iv) *Provision of Land at Nominal Cost and Loans for setting up Press and Office*

The survey brought out the fact that almost two-thirds of the dailies and other periodicals who responded had their offices in rented buildings. A large number of such newspapers said that they would like to have their own buildings. In terms of value of the land and the cost of construction, the need of most of the newspapers was less than Rs. 1 lakh each. On a rough estimate the total requirement of small newspapers for purchasing land and buildings will not be astronomical. The Government provides land at a nominal cost to small scale industries. Similarly, it helps them to build their factories at liberal terms. Similar facilities should be extended to the small and medium newspapers. All Governments should allot plots of land to such newspapers to meet their minimum requirements in terms of setting up of press and office.

(v) *Accreditation Facilities for Weeklies*

In order to be able to provide the necessary information, small newspapers need to have easy access to the sources of information. Accreditation enables the journalists to have direct access to government departments. I think it is necessary to give accreditation to small newspapers coming out from the districts. Since most of the newspapers published from rural areas are weeklies, accreditation should not be confined to dailies only, but should also be given to editors of other small news periodicals.

(vi) *Machinery to Monitor Growth and Developments*

Government should take up on a priority basis the task of helping small and medium newspapers to grow. They should try to minimise the unhealthy competition faced by small newspapers from the bigger newspapers. The Ministry of Information and Broadcasting of the Government of India and the State Governments should simplify their policies to help the small and medium newspapers and streamline the machinery for its implementation with a view to helping the small and medium newspapers. A joint committee consisting of Government officials and representatives of genuine national newspaper organisations should be set up to monitor the proper implementation of such policies and to make recommendations from time to time on the basis of its findings.

I would like to reiterate that all my recommendations with regard to the small and medium newspapers should aim at the growth of the genuine papers which have the potential to make a positive contribution in the development of the country. Assistance should not be given to the small time rags which come out from time to time with the sole purpose of getting money from the Government. No help should be given to papers which resort to blackmailing and other unethical practices. While assisting the small and medium newspapers the Government should ensure that only genuine newspapers benefit from such assistance.

Upgrading the Quality of Indian Language Dailies

A SUPPLEMENTARY NOTE
P.V. Gadgil

If Indian language newspapers are to fulfil their role of mass awakening and nation-building, planned efforts should be directed to raise the quality of the regional language dailies so that they, each of them, aspire to match the first-rank English dailies.

The present position in India is a travesty. In France the first-ranking daily newspaper is in French; in Germany it is in German. The first-ranking daily newspaper in terms of quality in each region in our country should therefore be a paper in the language of the region. But in India, with many regional languages spoken by populations as large as each of the West European countries, the first-ranking daily newspaper, in point of quality, is everywhere in English, while the next-ranking regional language daily is, in point of quality, far behind.

The argument often advanced is that no regional language of the country is rich and developed enough to deal adequately with the problems of modern society. This is not a tenable argument. If, say, on the midnight of 15th-16th August 1947 all the English daily newspapers in India had ceased publication, most of the brilliant writers of today's English dailies, 99 per cent of whom have some Indian languages as their mother-tongue, would have naturally started writing in their mother-tongue and would have done their job as brilliantly as they do in English today. The could have, of course, continued to enrich their intellect by means of learned books and journals in English but would have formulated and assembled their thoughts in an Indian language which would have, as a result, developed strength enough to deal adequately with modern problems. After all, languages develop with the development of intellect, skills and culture of society through the media of expression on the part of workers, thinkers, narrators and preachers who in turn develop their cultural powers along with the general development of society.

I am not for expulsion of English from India. The predominance of English in India was historically inevitable and has also proved beneficial to this country as it has helped India intellectually, culturally and emotionally to join the mainstream of world thought and world events. Also, during the foreseeable future we shall have to take the help of all developed languages in the world including English for the development of our languages.

When the language of courts or universities or political or financial administration will become non-English is beside the point here. I am confining myself to elevation of the quality of Indian language dailies so that they not only match but even surpass the best English dailies. The emergence of high-quality Indian language dailies will lead naturally to the respective regional language flowing to courts and universities. After all, common people mould a language through the daily newspapers now-a-days.

During the last twenty-five years, readers of daily newspapers in all the regions of the country have multiplied many-fold. There has been tremendous awakening in the masses who feel provoked and have become unmanageably astir to get their grievances removed and secure their demands. Regional language news dailies which reach the general reading public, and through them the masses, have played the key instrumental role in this awakening. But these language dailies suffer from lack of adequate quality in terms of proper information, thinking and criticisms, for the reason that an undue volume of scarce resources in the form of intellect, skills, finance, materials and opportunities are attracted by the English dailies which are rapidly rising in quality and size, leaving the language dailies deficient in resources and therefore far behind in quality. The most brilliant and incisive English writers, of today, who could have moved millions in the right direction are allowing themselves, without reaching the common people, to be folded in the arm-pits of the elites.

The contradiction in the situation is glaring and highly detrimental to national interest. Barely five per cent of the public who are wealthy and well placed, the elite who are mentally as also physically far removed from the masses, are catered for by the high quality English dailies, while the general public constituting 95 per cent have directly or indirectly to gulp the not very high quality stuff offered by resource-poor language dailies. The contradiction is painful because the resource-poor language dailies cannot produce the sober, thoughtful atmosphere pervaded by knowledge and a sense of responsibility. There is, thus, no shared body of information, insights and attitude as between the top crust of the elite and the common people below. It is true that in single-language countries in like those Europe, high-quality papers are not read by the masses. But because of the homogeneity of thought process resulting from a single-language situation, high thought sprinkled on the top soil percolate to the bottom. This cannot happen in India.

There is in our country a new danger. Daily newspapers in Indian languages are thriving in terms of circulation because of demand arising from general awakening. If the level of quality is not promptly and quickly lifted by vastly adding to the resources of the Indian language dailies, low culture and low taste will thrive.

I beg to state that the Commission has devoted very little time and attention to the problem of improving the quality of Indian language journalism. Let me show what should be, and what is, the situation today, rather figuratively. The tallest mountain in India pours the purest water from its sky-high head on the lowly lands below. The holy flow in turn makes holy the lakhs of water currents that rush into it from both sides and mix with it on its way. The flood takes in its flow all the dirt, all the sewage from miles upon miles of habitation, fertilises thereby the soils that sustain and nourish millions, and ultimately merges in the sea – only to be resurrected by the blazing sun to run the cycle of its holy ministry of fertilising the earth. But, in our world of journalism in India, writers in English, though English is not their mother-tongue, take pride in the fact that the Gangotri flowing from their brains directly pours into the Mahasagar (which is after all just a dead sea) without polluting itself in the dirt and sewage of thousands of miles of the lowly landscape. They should realise that they are missing a mission of awakening the masses. The significance of why Nehru wished his ashes to be immersed in the Ganga and other holy rivers and of India has yet to dawn on these brilliant brains. Man's intellect, as life-giving water, is his maker's noblest and mightiest gift. Like the water from the highest mountain going down to the lowliest landscape to spread nourishment and joy among the children of the soil, the intellect of the loftiest brains should with to rush down to the lowliest to spread intellectual and emotional nourishment and energy and to urge for self help. The day on which this happens will be the turning points in India's current history. No Government, no political parties, no universities, surely not English journalism, but only Indian language journalism developed by the best brains can bring salvation to the nation through mass awakening.

The task is so vast as to be mind-boggling in a country which is seeking to achieve rapid development within the democratic framework. There are sober-minded experienced, elderly journalists and statesmen in India, who have developed an analytical mind and detached judgement and are asking the Indian journalist to adopt a detached, balancing role as between the economic classes and other groups contending for shares in the cake of national development. This would have been adequate if it was only an economic conflict. But the burst of conflicts in recent years all over India, in the rural as well as the urban spheres, has not come about only on the economic front as 'capital *versus* labour' or 'landlord *versus* peasants', as the theorists of socialist doctrine had visualised as inevitable in the modern era all over the world. We have in our country an unfortunate historic heritage of multiple castes, multiple religions, and multiple sect. It is a tall sociological, emotional, psychological hierarchy, almost a skyscraper, of strata upon strata erected on the philosophy of dumb and unquestioning submission to a system of inequality. This structure has now been shaken and its is breaking to pieces and is getting pounded to rubble by mighty and noble Western ideas of democracy and equality. Once the political bondage of the country was ended, people at large were awakened to these ideas by Indian language papers almost percipitately. The sudden awakening of the downtrodden millions was and is, naturally unsettling and confounding to the upper strata. They in turn started violently suppressing what seems to them an illegitimate revolt against what had been for centuries an edifice designed by God with inequality as the cementing essence.

It is there that the Indian language journalist has to play an educative role of great importance. He can and must speak to the masses at large and convince them that though the burst of violence resulting from sudden awakening might be understandable, it is not the way to mend matters. Violence breeds and leads to utter destruction. The path of constructive, peaceful and dedicated effort preached by Gandhi is the only way for a poor country to achieve progress within the democratic framework. The Indian language journalist in the present Indian situation cannot be a passive and detached onlooker. He must reach the masses and preach a half to hatred, violence and destruction, and advocate a mutual-help effort to build a cooperative commonwealth on the basis of equality, peace, tolerance and harmony.

The circumstances of the emergence of democracy in India dictate such an active role for the Journalist. The founding fathers of our Constitution chose for India a parliamentary democratic constitution of the British type, but, unlike Britain, based on adult franchise from its very start. The British parliamentary system grew over centuries, first through bloody struggles and later through hot debate in parliament and outside. Half the adult population, i.e., womenfolk, were not given the right to vote even as late as after the first World War when Britain was already fully industrialised, highly educated and technologically advanced. On the country, India, an industrially, technologically and educationally backward and agriculturally poor country accepted a full-fledged adult franchise democracy from the start of its free existence. This step was not taken thoughtlessly. Throughout the decades of the freedom struggle the leadership had affirmed that nothing less than a free and democratic Constitution based on adult franchise would be acceptable to India, and when the time came for fulfilling the assurance, the Indian Constituent Assembly, freely debating in detail for three long years, forged the constitutional instrument on the assured pattern.

This meant that the long and hard period of preparation of the people, in countries like Britain or France, for exercising rights and bearing responsibilities owing from the establishment of a full-fledged democracy was abridged in our country to a quick one-time instalment. This necessarily implies that leaders and educators of the people have to undertake, vigorously and methodically, the task of educating, enlightening and preparing the people for carrying on the onerous responsibilities suddenly falling on them as citizens of a newly born full-fledged democratic republic.

The above is only the political side of India's free and democratic existence. The other and more important side is that of economic democracy. While in the hay-day of British imperialism in the 19th century, exploitation of the British labouring population and their factory working conditions were horrible, here in India with the very advent of independence, despite an underdeveloped economy, trade union rights, improved working conditions and conciliation-machinery have been with us in the industrial sector in our growth effort.

On the economic side, there is another important aspect to note. We have accepted economic planning with the object of establishing a socialist form of society. Surely in a resource-poor country's backward economy, progress cannot be made on the basis of individualist competition and/or class conflict. A planned economy with socialist ideology and peaceful methods is dictated in our circumstances by the needs of an immature economy and the foundational system of full democracy laid down by a far-sighted and wise leadership.

Here is at once a disadvantage and an advantage both of which must be carefully noticed. This disadvantage is that, while the developed countries of today could effect their growth in relative international isolation in a leisurely way by improvising trial and error methods over periods of decades or even centuries, undeveloped countries of today, like India, in a world rendered small by rapid transport and communications, have to compete with the already developed countries. But the advantage is that the lessons of the long, hard and experimental efforts of the developed countries are available to us as ready instruments for us to forge our destiny in a narrow

What will Indian journalists do in this situation? Will they go on extolling class-struggle as a 'religious' economic dogma, or obstructionist political methods as the dictate of political ideology, or will they explain and teach peaceful constructive action, individual and collective, so that people may help themselves and one another in the national growth effort? Just as minority rule, whatever might be its deceptive form, is undemocratic and outrageous, surely a majority rule which is unmindful of minority opinion or minority interests, is equally undemocratic and outrageous. Journalists must support first and last the cause of justice and humanity, whose-so-ever the Raj Peaceful and rapid progress is only possible in our present context by resort to established democratic institutions and methods ushered in our day-to-day life by our far-sighted forbears immediately on the achievement of freedom. To explain and preach this is the role of journalism, especially Indian language journalism, in India today.

The immediate problem for India is, therefore, how to elevate the quality of the Indian Language dailies so as to raise them to the level of the highest quality dailies in their respective regions. The best English dailies should continue to thrive and move all over India. But they should also divert adequate resources from their profits to Indian language dailies so as to see that the regional language dailies not only match but even surpass their English counterparts.

My prayer is that the best quality English dailies in India should play the role of *Dhanastra* and *Sandeepani* to their Indian regional language youngsters. The tradition of our *Sandeepanis* was that they aspired to be defeated at the hands of their disciples. SHISHYATICHET PARABHAVAM was the motto of our ancestral *Sandeepanis.*

(x) *Indian Legislatures and the Privileges Issue – Dissenting note by Shri P.V. Gadgil relating to Section (7) on Contempt of Legislature in Chapter IV entitled "Constitution and Laws" (A study of powers, privileges and immunities of Indian legislature, of members and of Committees thereof).*

The Indian Government system, and therefore legislature system also, is a two-tier structure. At the Centre is Parliament (or Sansad) with two Houses, Lok Sabha and Rajya Sabha. At the State level there are a Vidhan Sabha in each State and a Vidhan Parishad in some of the States. Article 105 and Article 194 deal with powers, privileges and immunities, respectively, of Central and State Legislatures and of members and committees thereof. The two Articles are exactly identical in terms except for their reference to the particular tier they apply to. The complete text of them is given below with state legislature reference put into bracket of this kind (.).

"*Article* 105 (194)(1) Subject to the provisions of this Constitution and to the rules and standing orders regulating the procedure of Parliament (the Legislature) there shall be freedom of speech in Parliament (the Legislature of every State).

(2) No Member of Parliament (the Legislature of a State) shall be liable to proceedings in any court in respect of anything said or in respect of any vote given by him in Parliament (the Legislature) or any Committee thereof, and no person shall be so liable in respect of the publication by or under the authority of either House of Parliament (a House of such a Legislature) of any report, votes or proceedings.

(3) In other respects, the powers, privileges and immunities of each House of Parliament (the legislature of a State) and of the Members and Committees of each House shall be such as may from time to time be defined by Parliament (the legislature) by law, and until so defined (shall be those of that house and of its members and committees immediately before the coming into force of Section 15 of the Constitution (44th Amendment) Act 1978)*.

(4) The provisions of clauses (1), (2) and (3) shall apply in relation to persons who by virtue of the Constitution have the right to speak in, and otherwise to take part in the 'proceedings' of a House of Parliament (a House of Legislature of a State) or any committee thereof as they apply in relation to Members of Parliament (Legislature of a State)."

The wording and content of Arts. 105 and 194 being identical, as is obvious from the text given above, the Articles will be considered together.

There are two controversial issues arising out of their contents. One, freedom of expression in a Legislature, which is covered by clauses (1) and (2), and two, privilege, which is covered by clause (3). Clause (4) is non-controversial and needs no discussion. The two

---

* The words in bracket ( ) in clause 3 were substituted by the 44th Amendment for the words "shall be those of the House of Commons of the Parliament of the United Kingdom and of its committees and members thereof before the commencement of this Constitutions".

issues will be discussed in separate parts.

PART I

Freedom of expression in the Constitution is a Fundamental Right, but it is not unrestricted, which is made clear by reading Articles 19 (1) (a) and 19 (2) together. But the freedom of expression given in 105 and 194 to a member of a legislative House is fully unrestricted and absolute under claluse (1) of each of the two Articles. The only exception, under Articles 121 and 211, is discussion about judicial court proceedings. The freedom of publication of Legislature speeches and proceedings is, however, circumscribed by clause (2) of the same which lays down that legislature proceedings and speeches if published by or under the authority of the Legislature, cannot be challenged in a law court.

The legal implications and consequences of this provision have been authoritatively laid down by Calcutta High Court (Suresh *v.* Punit A. 1951)* where the Court has indicated that a newspaper is allowed to publish without legislative authority a report of a legislature speech, but if it contains allegations involving breach of any law, the newspaper will have to face a likely prosecution. On this issue, the position in England differs from that in the Indian Constitution. In England, parliamentary proceedings are freely published with impunity. In India the position in Act. 105 and in Art. 194, as explained by Calcutta High Court and which is contrary to the position in England, holds the ground. The reason is, in England there is no written Constitution: common law and usage govern Parliament there. We in India are governed by a statutory Constitution.

This position is not liked by many political leaders in India. Ever since the Constituent Assembly started debating the issue there has appearred to be a resentment against this position in the minds of the leadership.

---

* The immunity conferred by cl. (2) of Art. 105 or 194 of the Constitution was confined to publication 'by or under the authority of the House', and there was nothing else to except a newspaper report from the criminal law of defamation as codified in s. 499 of the Indian Penal Code. Hence, a newspaper report, however fair or faithful, would be under criminal liability for defamatory statements in such report, even though it merely reproduced a speech or other proceedings in the Legislature, or even though in civil proceedings the English Common Law rule in Wason's Case might be applicable.

But the dispassionate and far-seeing among the Constitution-makers realised the harm that unbridled freedom to publish legislature proceedings could cause. In this speech in the Constituent Assembly on clauses (1) and (2) of Articles 105 and 194 (Sections 85 and 169 respectively at that stage), Shri Ananthasayanam Ayyangar declared that while legislators had to be given unrestricted freedom to open their hearts and preach even violence, sedition or rebellion to persuade other Members to their view (this he regarded as an essential part of Parliamentary freedom and democracy and not even the presiding officer could stop the speech-making member from uttering what he liked), such speeches inciting crimes and offences could not be make available to the public with impunity.

The said Articles were later passed in the same form as was defended by Shri Ayyangar, and as they as to this day.

But agitation against restriction on newspapers' reporting of legislature proceedings has continued all the three decades and more, after the commencement of the Consitution. What is amazing is, without amending Articles 105 (1), (2) and 194 (1), (2) legislation land even constitutional amendment, crept into statute books though they are contrary to the content and implication of those Articles. This has resulted in difficulties and risks to the good name and decent life of the citizens.

The first Press Commission which published its report in 1954 seems to have taken the lead in this aberration. The Calcutta High Court's decision mentioned above was the main roadblock. How to remove it? The Commission did not recommend amendment or Articles 105(1), (2) and 194 (1), (2) of the Constitution, but suggested amendment of the Indian Penal Code. In the Defamation Section (499) of I.P.C., there is permission to report with impunity court proceedings involving defamation. The Press Commission recommended that this permission should, by suitably amending S. 499 of I.P.C., be extended to Legislative proceedings also. The Commission failed to notice the important difference between the two situations. While in the case of publication of court proceedings resulting in defamation, the aggrieved party cannot sue the publisher under S. 499 of I.P.C. but surely has remedy under the same section against the defamer, in the case of publication of legislature proceedings, if freedom is given to the publisher by amending Sec. 499 of I.P.C., the publisher as well as the defamer would escape the clutches of S. 499 of I.P.C., leaving the aggrieved citizen helplessly smarting under a grievious wrong. Besides in accepting the Press Commission's recommendation, the defficulty was that without amending the Constitutional provisions in Articles 105(1), (2) and 194(1), (2) of the Constitution, amending the Penal Code was not possible.

A new device, therefore, was adopted which sought to bypass the need of amending the Constitution and the Penal Code. A new legislation was formulated which permitted newspapes to publish Parliamentary proceedings to the extent of being substantially true. This legislation was passed in both Houses of Parliament by simple majorities in 1956. It was limited to the Central legislature only. This was regarded as an answer to the Calcutta High Court's decision mentioned earlier.

There were many flaws resulting from this new device. The Calcutta High Court had interpreted Articles 105 and 194 in the Constitution. The difficulty created by it could be removed only by an amendment of Articles 105 and 194 of the Constitution. Ignoring this, an ordinary legislation was passed as a measure to remove the difficulty. The new law, with transgressed the Constitution and was therefore illegal, remained on the statute book and in operation from 1956 to 1975. The law, as said above, was confined to Parliamentary proceedings only. It did not apply to state Legislature proceedings. But an impression spread somehow all over the country that this applied to the State Legislaturer also.

Central and State legislature then began to be used for character-assassination of rivals or enemies. Newspapers took part in this nefarious business enthusiastically and 'impartially' by publishing 'substantially true' reports of legislature proceedings. Anguished cries and complaints from people who found their character maligned through reporting of legislature proceedings became the order of the day, but the cries were derided or ignored.

In the wake of this legislation the Constitution was mauled in more than one way. An ordinary legislation was, here, used to thwart a constitutional effect, as I have already mentioned above. Therefore, the law was void. What is more, the House of Parliament extended, without constitutional authority, a privileged freedom to newspapers – to the exclusion of other citizens – to publish, without legislature's authority, legislature reports with impunity. This violated the fundamental right to equality (Art 14). This illegal measure was repealed after 19 years, in 1975, not because it was illegal, but because it had been misused.

But the politicians's obsession, that legislature orations must be published freely in India as in England, was not calmed down. In 1978, in the 44th Amendment, a new article – Article 361A – was added to the Constitution. It purported to be an improvement, because the privilege given to newspapers for publication of Parliamentary proceedings in the 1956 law was now enlarged to include publication of State Legislature proceedings also. Besides, it was now not an ordinary legislation but a constitutional amendment to counter a constitutional difficulty.

Did it, however, improve matters? No ; the constitutional confusion became worse confounded. First, the new Article 361A, like the 1956 measue, continues to stand in contrast to Articles 105(1) (2)and 194(1) (2) (as interpreted by Calcutta High Court). Between Article 105(1) (2) and Article 194(1) (2) on the one hand and Article 361A on the other, the contrast is so clear and precise that no harmonious construction between the two is possible.

If a newspaper is given a privilege to publish legislature proceedings without authority, such a privilege given to a newspaper is unconstitutional under Article 105(1) (2), under Article 194 (1) (2), under entry No. 74 of 1st List and under entry No. 39 of 2nd List of the seventh schedule, because by adding Article 361A to the constitution Parliament has transgressed limits put on Parliament's power to extend privilege under these provisions. Also, to extend such a privilege to newspaper while denying it to ordinary citizens goes against the fundamental right of equality (Artical 14). Here also harmonious construction between Article 361A and Article 14 is impossible.

To remove this difficulty, an authority is quoted which is said to lay down that when a previous existing clause in the Constitution or in a law and a subsequent amendment are in conflict, and no harmonious construction is possible, the subsequent amendment stays and the previous clause becomes void. If this is accepted, are we also to accept as a consequence that Article 14 as also Articles 105(1) (2) and 194 (1) (2) became void in order to keep Article 361A alive and in an operative position? The legislators are silent on this question.

The judgment in the Keshavanand Bharati case lays down that any amendment of the Constitution of India which goes against any of the 'basic features' of the Constitution is itself void. Arts. 105(1) (2), 194 (1) (2) and even more so, Art. 14, surely have elements of 'Basic Structure'. This is conveniently ignored.

The reader should recall here Shri Ayyangar's plea in the

Constituent Assembly, as to why, in the interest of democracy, unrestricted freedom of expression must be given to a legislator in a legislative House, but on the countrary, why newspapers should not be granted the privilege of publishing legislature proceedings without authority. If that is accepted, than it calls clearly for the repeal of Article 361A.

There is a moral point also. Fame and good name are some of the unpronounced birthrights of a citizen. If one citizen defames another in public, the aggrieved party has a judicial remedy. But in a legislature speech, a legislator can with impunity defame any citizen [Articles 105 (1) and 194 (1)]. Now before Art. 361A was put in the Constitution the position was that if that defamation was published without authority of the concerned legislative House the aggrieved party could sue against the publisher in a court of law and could get his name cleared according to Calcutta High Court's interpretation of Articles 105 (1) (2) and 194 (1) (2). Now Article 361A comes to the rescue of the defaming publisher and paves the way for permitting assassination of character through the back door of legislatures. Article 361A therefore deserves to be repealed – the earlier the better.

To keep important provisions on the statue book and to reduce them to a dead letter by contrary provisions and contrary practice is derogatory and disastrous, in the extreme, to constitutional (not a conventional as in U.K.) democracy.

PART II

This part will deal with Articles 105(3) and 194(3). They are, as stated at the beginning of this statement, identical in terms and content except for one difference that the former applies to the Central legislature and the latter to the State legislature.

The text as it is before us is the text amended in the course of the 44th Amendment. From the day the Constitution commenced (26-1-1950) to the day when the 44th Amendment came into effect (20-6-1979) the words "shall be those (powers, privileges and immunities) of the House of Commons of U.K. and their members and their committees at the commencement of this Constitution" existed in the text. These words were replaced (from 20-6-1979) by the words "shall be those of that House and of its members and its committees immediately before the coming into force of Section 15 of Constitution (44th Amendment) Act of 1978". But this elaborate changing of words did not change the content. For almost thirty years, free India's legislatures have continued to enjoy the powers, privileges and immunities of the House of Commons. The 44th Amendment only deleted the explicit reference to House of Commons while continuing the same position, by suggesting that things will continue from 20-6-1979 as they were until 20-6-1979.

So while considering this clause we must ask ourselves the question, "What were the powers, privileges and immunities of the House of Commons at the commencement of our Constitution?"

A few extracts from the Constitution Assembly debates will indicate the doubts and difficulties that were expressed about these powers, etc., in those days by some of our leaders and constitutional experts.

Naziruddin Ahmed: "Clause (3) of S.85 (Art. 105) has been bodily lifted from Government of India Act 1935. . . . . We should have our powers, privileges and immunities clearly and specifically defined. In fact the privileges of the members of the House of Commons are not statutory. They are embodied in the Common Law to be found in the text books which are many. They are also contained in case laws which are scattered. . . . . But these should all be collected and defined, not left vague as at present. I suggest that at the end of the Constitution-text, there should be added a schedule defining powers, privileges and immunities, pending our Parliament making adequate laws in this respect".

Pandit Thakurdas Bhargav: "Not that I am ashamed of the reference to the House of Commons; but in a matter like this, it will again be shelving of an important question which is whithin the scope of the Constituent Assembly. After all, if we cannot find a solution to this difficult question may I know when the solution will be found? If today our jurists and leaders cannot define the privileges of the members of Legislatures I do not see at what point of time this would be possible."

Dr. P.S. Deshmukh: "What we want to know is whether it is not possible to embody them in the Constitution".

Dr. B.R. Ambedkar: "It is not easy to define what are the acts and the deeds which may be deemed to bring Parliament into disgrace. That would require a considerable amount of discussion and examination. That is one reason why we did not think of enumerating these privileges and immunities. . . . . As I said, if you want to categories and set out in detail all the privileges and immunities it will take not less than twenty-five pages."

The above extracts are fairly representative of the mood, anxiety and doubts of the makers of the Constitution and the difficulties in their way. It is also necessary specifically to note Pandit Thakurdas Bhargava's prophetic exclamation: "If today our jurists and our leaders cannot define the privileges of the members of our legislature, I do not see at what point of time this would be possible".

Once, at that time, the enumeration of privileges was avoided by the Constituent Assembly, it was never done afterwards, and of late people who claim to know, tell us that not only will it never be done but that in important circles of all political parties there is a thinking that any kind of identification and enumeration of privileges is not necessary and must never be done.

Dr. Rajendra Prasad who presided over the Constituent Assembly had expressed his confidence that the new Legislatures which would be born would surely undertake the task of formulating the privileges. But in his two innings as President of the Republic he and the elected Governments at the Centre, and the Governments in the States consigned the issue to oblivion.

Later in a U.P. breach-of-privilege controversy the dispue was submitted by the then President of India to the Supreme Court (under Article 143) for 'opinion'. This 'opinion' delivered by the Supreme Court (1964) did not say anything about whether the Legislature should or should not formulate their privileges. The Supreme Court, however, expressed a view that House of Commons privileges can be accepted by Indian legislatures subject to the provisions of the Indian Constitution and hinted also that since the privileges of the House of Commons arose out of a bloody civil was history, Indian legislatures with a completely different historic background should search into their Constitution itself for a way out of a deadlock arising from privileges issue.

What is more, the Supreme Court supplied a guideline derived from the provisions of the Constitution for all citizens and Legislatures to follow.*

---

* Article 212(1) seems to make it possible for a citizen to call in question in the appropriate court of law the validity of any proceedings inside the legislative chamber if his case is that the said proceedings suffer not from mere irregularity of procedure, but from an illegality. If the impugned procedure is illegal and unconstitutional, it would be open to be scrutinised in a court of law though such scrutiny is prohibited if the complaint against the procedure is no more than this, that the procedure was irregular.

But this 'opinion' and the particular breach of privilege issue that caused it were all left where they were and quietly forgotten. Thereafter it appears that there has been developing a consensus on the part of leaders and legislators of all parties that privileges of Indian legislators need never be formulated. If the leaders and legislators had also agreed to avoid the exercise of any of the supposed powers arising out of their privileges, the citizens of India would have had nothing to complain or worry about. But the legislators have always desired to use those powers: They have admonished, prosecuted, arrested and convicted the victims of breach-of-privilege accusations. A high-raning elected members of the Lok Sabha was, on being so convicted, also imprisoned and was deprived of her seat in the House and disqualified to stand as candidate for any election for a certain period, though there is no authority for all this in our written Constitution.

Every citizen of India is now in danger of being so treated but, so far, mostly journalists have been the victims of these prosecutions.* This has spread so much fear in the journalist' world that breach of privilege cases are reported scantily, and the defence of the accused is scarcely reported or supported. In a case where the accused made a reference to this 'resign-of-terror' atmosphere, his prosecutors retorted that "this attitude on the part of journalists indicated their support to the prosecution."

Legislatures have their own rules and regulations which govern their internal administration. Breach of privileges arising in this sphere, i.e., arising out of a breach of regulation, cannot be inquired into by law courts and this is an exclusive sphere of the particular Legislative House to deal with (Articles 122 and 212), There is no quarrel with this position. However, if an alleged breach of privilege is not on the ground of violation of any rules and regulation of a legislative House, then the legislature has no jurisdiction to try the case. If the impugned action should be violative of any law, it will be for the courts to deal with it.*

That against is another indication which may afford some assistance in construing the scope and extent of the powers conferred on the House by Article 194(3)" — 'Opinion of the Supreme Court' (1964).

* [On 16th November, 1973 the Maharashtra Legislative Assembly committed to imprisonment for 30 days Shri Pradeep Dalvi, Editor, *Prashasti*, a Marathi weekly as he was held guilty of breach of privilege and contempt of the Assembly. On 18th November, 1973, I wrote an editorial in the Marathi daily, *Lokmat*, which contained some comments on the manner in which the decision to imprison Shri Dalvi was taken

Even in regard to alleged breaches of privileges of the latter kind – not involving violation of any rules and regulations of a legislative House – my quarrel is not in regard to the prosecution as such but to a procedure which abides by no law. It is conducted thoroughly lawlessly.

To convey to the reader a fair idea of the lawlessness involved in prosecution for supposed breach of privilege, not entailing violation of any rules and regulations of a legislative House, I beg to enlist and explain some of the major faults which the accused has to encounter.

(i) *Constitutional Requirements*

Article 20(1) of the Constitution requires that if a person is to be accused of an offence, that offence has to have been named and defined by a law. It has to be shown that the accused, by his impugned act or behaviour, has violated that law. He should know which act or

---

by the Assembly. A motion of breach of privilege was moved by a Member of the Assembly against me and the matter was referred to the Committee of Privileges. The Committee came to the conclusion that the editorial as a whole, prima facie, constituted breach of privilege and contempt of the House. Issues were framed and I was asked to comment.

I contended that while it is true that the Assembly had correctly followed the procedure laid down by the rules made by itself, that would not satisty the needs of justice as Shri Dalvi was not heard personally by the Assembly before awarding the punishment. The procedure followed in trials before the Law Courts should have been followed strictly by the Legislature also. Shri Dalvi should have been given the list of privileges as they were in vogue in the House of Commons at the time of commencement of our Constitution. The Legislature, I maintained, could not take on all the three rols of the prosecutor, the judge and the executioner while affording no ordinary privileges to a citizen. I said that the codification of privileges should not be delayed any further.

The Committee found that the editorial produced an effect in the minds of the public so as to belittle, or to cast reflections on, or redicule the Assembly. It held that there is a distinction between a quasi judicial body and the law courts and the provisions of Criminal Procedure Code are not applicable to matters before quasi judicial bodies. The Committee referred to my plea for codification of privileges and said that it has been a subject matter of debate in the Press and outside. It expressed the view that "the main reason behind this agitation for condification is obviously to invite judical interference in the domain of legislature — a situation which was incompatible with the repugnant to the supremacy and independence of the legislatture". (Report of the Privileges Committee, Maharashtra Legislative Assembly, August 1974, page 7). The Committee accordingly recommended that I be called before the Assembly and be admonished.]

behaviour of his amounts to that offence, so that the accused knows what he has to defend against.

The law defining the offence must also have laid down the penalty. A penalty more severe than this punishment or sentence may not be inflicted on the accused if convicted.

A breach-of-privilege prosecution, however, relates to no offence named or defined by any law. The accused is not told, in terms of law, how his impugned action or behaviour constitutes what offence, of which category.

The accused therefore is completely at a loss to know what wrong, in terms of law, he has committed. And he is at a loss to know how he must defend himself against what.

(ii) *Procedure*

Now let us see that procedure. When a Legislative House passes by a majority a resolution that 'x' has insulted the House by a certain writing or behaviour, the case is by another resolution handed over to a Privileges Committee or the House.

The Committee has to summon the accused before itself and to ask him to explain his side. The accused may be cross-examined. Other evidence may be examined.

If as a result of this proceeding the accused is found not guilty, he will be declared innocent. But it the accused feels that he was put to all this trouble for a frivolous purpose or malicious motive, he has no authority available to appeal to.

If the accused, on the other hand, is pronounced guilty by the Committee, the Committee is also authorised to recommended a penalty of its own conception: no law defining an offence and prescribing a penalty is taken as the basis for prosecution, and the law relating to evidence does not apply.

Article 21 lays down that no person shall be deprived of his life or personal liberty except according to procedure established by law. In the breach-of-privilege prosecution proceedings no procedure established by any law is followed.

(iii) *No Competence*

The point to be noted here is that while the Privileges Committee undertakes what in fact are criminal prosecution proceedings, it has no criminal investigation competence, no investigative apparatus, and no authority conceded by the Constitution or by a law passed under the Constitution to undertake criminal trials. The only difference between a street mob arresting a person and handling him over to a select few in the mob for trial, on the one hand, and a Legislative House handing over a person to its committee on the other, is that the mob is not elected and the members of the House out of whom the Privileges Committee is formed are elected.

But the legislators are not elected to undertake criminal trials, nor elected because they possess such a competence. Even literacy, not to speak of higher education, is no part of the qualification for being accepted by the Election Commission as a candidate for being elected to a legislature. Before such a tribunal, the helpless and puzzled accused is forced to appear.

There is nothing to stop this illegal tribunal from recommending that the accused be flogged or be hanged from the nearest lamp-post.

(iv) *No Right to Appeal*

Further, the accused has no right to appeal to any authority, or even to the accusing House of a legialature. The Privileges Committee's recommendation is only placed before the House. The decision has to be arrived at by a majority. This means and implies that every member must form his own opinion and must therefore have an opportunity to hear, see and take evidence himself and to know at first hand the accused's mind and his plea. But the accused is not called before the House as of right to enable him by stating his case, to canvass minds and votes to his side when even a single vote may tilt the balance for or against him. A majority vote or minority vote in the present procedural system is a blind and deaf vote.

(v) *Separation of Powers*

There is further fault in this procedural system which results in breach of 'basic structure' of the Constitution. The accuser and prosecutor becomes the judge and the executioner, making nonsense of the spirit of the Constitution which requires that the Legislature, Judiciary and Executive must each of them occupy separate sheres and exercise strictly divided and defined authority.

If we seek guidance from our Constitution on this point, Article 61 serves our purpose best. There, in the resident's impeachment proceedings, if one of the two Houses intends to accuse the President, the other House is exclusively authorised to undertake investigation proceedings, examine evidence and give judgment itself by a two-thirds majority wihout delegating any of its deciding powers to a committee.

That the current breach-of-privilege-prosecution procedure completely ignores this important and precise guidance in the Constitution is a great pity. It is in fact an insult to the Constitution.

(vi) *One offence – Two Prosecutions*

Article 20(2) of the Constitution lays down that no person shall be prosecuted and punished for the same offence more than once. And the breach-of-privilege-prosecution proceedings undertaken by legislatures and not recoĝnised by the regular judiciary. So the victim of the proceedings continues to remain liable to be assailed again by the regular judiciary. Here he faces a new situation rendered difficult because off being prejudiced, himself having been convicted and sentenced by a body which has not been given a judicial status by the Constitution or by any law.

The Way Out

It there a way out of this absurb and cruel situation?

The ex-imperial British Government has given a clue to that end, which few or none may have noticed. It is mentioned in one of the above quoted Constituent Assembly speeches that clause (3) of Art. 105 was bodily lifted from the British Parliament's Government of India Act 1935. That was only part of Section 28 of that Act, i.e., Sec. 28(1) (2). Clause (3) of Section 28 of that legislation which was not taken went on to say:

> "Nothing in any existing Indian Act, and, notwithstanding anything in the foregoing provisions of this section, nothing in this Act shall be construed as conferring, or empowering the Federal legislature to confer, on either Chamber or on both Chambers sitting together, or on any committee or officer of the Legislature, the status of a court, or any punitive or disciplinary powers other than a power to remove or exclude persons infringing the rules or standing orders, or otherwise behaving in a disorderly manner".

The view of British Parliament as is clear from this is not only that contempt of legislature prosection must be lodged in law courts, but also that Indian Democracy can adopt House of Commons Privileges only to the extent of their fitting in the Indian Constitution.

The Constituent Assembly while bodily lifting Sec. 28(1) and (2) from Government of India Act 1935, did not pick up Sec. 28(3). They may have or may not have intentionally avoided incorporating Sec. 28(3) in Articles 105 and 194. But its historic significance cannot be ignored. This omission cannot be understood to confer on free India's legislatures the status of law courts, unless in can be shoown that such a status is given in specific terms in our written Constitution. That 'Indian legislatures have never been given the status of law courts' has been emphatically maintained also by the Supreme Court in its 'opinion' referred to above.

The Supreme Court in its 'opinion' also clinches the whole issue in a nice and precise way which I have referred to above, as 'guideline'. The Supreme Court in its 'opinion' was thrashing out a breach of legislature privilege issue. But instead of giving guideline directly to the legislature they have supplied a way out to a citizen accused of contempt of legislature by seeking relief from judiciary in the first instance.

The Supreme Court has also laid down that it is the duty of law Courts to entertain complaints from citizens who feel aggrieved by accusations of breach of privilege of legislature or contempt of legislature. The court should examine by legitimate and lawful procedure whether the accusation involved a breach of law of the land or a breach of regulation of the legislature House. In the former case the court should ask the legislature to come to the court as prosecutor and in the latter case the court should advise the accused that for the desired relief he must go to the accuser.

This sage guidance from the Supreme Court has never been looked into and propagated even by prominent newspapers. But it is yet not too late to do it, because unless people awaken and assert their rights, the ruling powers will not refrain from humiliating and insulting those whom they want to curb or wreak vengeance on.

The legislators at the Centre and the state level should heed the advice indirectly given by the Supreme Court in its 'opinion' by pointing to the contents of Art. 212 (As also Art. 122).

If Article 122 (1) and (2) [also Article 212 (1) and (2)] is carefully analysed, one comes to understand that legislatures surely have regulatory powers with regard to their own proceedings in which the judiciary cannot interfere. They can also make laws, but cannot undertake coercive or penal action for enforcement of these laws. They cannot take the law into their own hands, because they lack judicial authority.

If and when the legislators define their powers, privileges and immunities by codifying them in a law, according to Article 105(3) [also 194 (3), then they with be the law of the land (not just rules and regulations for legislature proceedings)] and all proceedings for breaches of privileges will have to go to the judiciary for inquiry, trial decision and final order. The legislators cannot arrogate to themselves the powers of a court of law.

Amendment of Article 105 (and Art. 194)

The above interpretation and argumentation indicate the correct understanding as I see it, of Art. 105 (and Art. 194). It may not however, remove the doubts of the hesitant and obstinacy of those to any change from the present position. This hesitancy and obstinacy however have proved dangerous and iniquitous. The straight and right way out of the difficulty is to amend Art. 105 (and Art. 194), on the lines of Clause (3) of Sec. 28 of the Government of India Act 1935. Accordingly I beg to propose that the following be inserted as (3) (a) between clauses (3) and (4) of Art, 105 (also Art. 194):

> "Nothing in any existing law and, notwithstanding anything in the foregoing provisions of this article, nothing in this article, shall be construed as conferring, or empowering Parliament (State Legislature) to confer, on either House or on both Houses sitting together, or on any committee or officer of Parliament (a State Legislature) the Status of a court, or any punitive or disciplinary powers other than a power to remove or exclude persons infringing the rules or standing orders, or otherwise behaving in a disorderly manner."

(xi) *Dissenting note of Shri Ram Chand Verma relating to Chapter VI)*

Right to Privacy

In any democratic society a citizen is the most important primary factor and to the extent his freedom independence and privacy is respected and protected does democracy become more relevent and functional. This freedom is guaranted by the Indian Contitution.

2. If is therefore necessary that a citizen is not noly entitled to have freedom of information but his personal life is properly protected. Just as it is necessary to protect him from physical harm by any member of the society, similarly it is necessary to protect his reputation and character from being harmed or destroyed.

3. It is a well accepted moral code of journalism that before anything adverse and damaging the character of any member of the society is published the onus of taking care to ascertain the facts is on the person who publishes the same. While by and large this principle is observed there have been instances where newspapers and periodicals ignore it and indulge in character assassination. Such practices constitute breach of Code of Ethics.

4. Whenever a derogatory item regarding an individual is published the well accepted norms is that in case the individual involved sent a contradiction in his defence, the publisher, if he is satisfied that the affected party had a point to make, should publish the same fairly prominently. Not to publish it or to publish it in a manner which did not provide sufficient means of clarification or to publish it at a place where it would go unnoticed is considered a breach of Code of Ethics.

5. In order to seek redress of his grievance against violation of such individual freedom, by any newspaper or periodical, he should be able to represent his case to the Press Council of India or a similar authority. Such an authority should have the power and means to take corrective or compensatory measures. Such a provision is necessary not only for protecting in individual freedom but in the interest of fostering healthy journalism. But protection under the right to privacy should not extend to those individuals when their actions are related to their public life or to their duties as Government servants. In such matters Press is the only effective agency to inform the public of true facts. Another danger in not providing effective means of redressal of such grievances can result in some individuals resorting to retaliation through extra-legal methods and violence to vindicate their sense of honour.

6. It is also important that the procedure laid down by the Press Council of India or any other authority that may be set up for this purpose, should be such that a final decision is taken within a period of six months as otherwise the grievance would deem to have been perpetuated.

(xii) *Dissenting note of Shri Prem Chand Verma relating to Chapter VII*

I recommend the following additions in Chapter VII of the Press Commission Report entitled "Freedom and Responsibility: Role of the Press Council":

(i) *Foreign Money in the Indian Press (Para 37)*

Large sums of foreign money are being brought into India clandestinely and are being used against the interests of the country. A part of this money is being given to newspapers. It is, therefore, necessary that the Press Council of India or some other agency keeps a constant watch on it and devises such steps that foreign money is not able to corrupt the Indian Press, newspapers and journalists. The following measures may be adopted for thtis purpose:

(a) The newspapers which own printing presses and undertake printing work from foreign missions, trade commissions, and other foreign institutions and organisations should be required to file annual returns indicating the rates charged for printing work and the total amounts received from each party, with the Press Registrar and the Press Council of India. The return should also include information with regard to printing machinery imported for setting up of new printing presses or for expansion of existing printing presses together with true copies of invoices, and documents showing clearance through banking channels. Details from all printing presses installed or expanded during the past five years should be called. Newspapers should be required to include above details in their balance sheets and profit and loss accounts.

(b) The journalists who go abroad on foreign hospitality should be required to file a return with the authority appointed showing details of gifts, etc., received during such trips.

(c) The Press Council should be competent to entertain and inquire into any complaints against journalists regarding undue financial or other gain from a foreign country and to take action against those found guilty.

(ii) *Composition of the Council (Para 48)*

The Press Council need ensue that it approves for representation on the

Council only such Associations which have an all India character and cover sizeable membership from at least 75 per cent of Indian States and Union Territories and that their rates of subscription are reasonable. Highest Membership and revenue should be taken into account.

(xiii) *Dissenting note of Shri Prem Chand Verma relating to Chapter X – The Press as a Public Utility*

Chain Newspapers

In a democratic country, particularly a vast country like ours, where the number of literates is comparatively small and that too comprises largely lower middle class, the importance of media in influencing the public opinion becomes rather significant, among which newspapers media counts most. If this mass media happens to be at the beck and call of a few industrialists or some other rich people for achieving their personal gain and influence and opposes progressive policies day in and day out in order to bring failure to them, can there be anything more dangerous than this for the people and the democracy?

2. While the Report deals with the issue of delinking of industrial houses from newspapers elsewhere, in para 25 under the heading 'Chain Newspapers' the recommendations made do not appear to be either suitabe or adequate. I therefore record my dissenting note as under:–

The figures given below will show circulations of newspapers with common ownership (8 chain newspapers) indicating the percentage they reppresent of total circulation in the country:

Name of group	No. of papers	Total circulation	Newsprint allocation (1980)
1	2	3	4
1. Express Newspapers (*Indian Express* Group)	25	15,76,071	41,452 M.T.
2. Bennett Coleman and Co., (*Times of India* Groups)	25	27,96,991	37,194 M.T.
3. *Hindustan Times* Group	10	9,44,398	18,363 M.T.
4. Kasturi and Sons Ltd.	6	2,64,519	16,143 M.T.
5. *Malayalam Manorama* Group	4	8,76,742	13,221 M.T.
6. *Ananda Bazar Patrika* Group	18	11,12,485	11,766 M.T.
7. *Amrita Bazar Patrika*	7	5,10,737	10,688 M.T.
8. *Statesman* Group	2	2,49,998	9,382 M.T.
	97	83,31,941	1,58,289 M.T.

1. Total Number of Newspapers	No. of newspapers in 8 chain groups of newspapers	Percentage of total
5694	110	1.70%
2. Total circulation of all newspapers	Circulation of 8 chain newspapers	Percentage of total
4,64,49,000	83,31,941	18%
3. Total newsprint allotment for 2039 newspapers	Allotment for 8 chair newspapers	Percentage of total
3,42,901 M.T.	1,58,239 M.T.	46.47%

The figures mentioned above will show that the 8 chain newspapers (110 newspaper) are merely 2 per cent of 5694 newspapers in the country. But they take away 46.47 per cent of the total newsprint on which the country spends nearly as 65 crores in foreign exchange. The allotment of the total newsprint of 3,42,901 M.T. is done by the Government as under:

Big newspapers	2,34,685 M.T.	68.44%
Medium newspapers	78,124 M.T.	22.78 %
Small newspapers	30,092 M.T.	8.78%
Total	3,42,901	

3. The *Express* Group alone gets 1ł times newsprint of the total allocation to small newspapers all over India. *Times of India* group too gets more than the total allocation of all small newspapers. The story in the matter of release of advertisement is no different and almost the same ratio and pattern obtains.

4. If the above-mentioned chain newspapers and some other groups are permitted to go to bringing out more and more editions, there is no doubt whatever that only the views of a very small group of people would influence the public opinion and only such news as they would wish would be published.

5. Thus the chain newspapers are a define source of danger to the freedom of Press on the one hand and a big factor in weakening the

roots of democracy on the other hand. In this manner the large industrial houses which have already acquired considerable control on the economic resources of the country, would also gain undue influence on political and social life of the country. The freedom of Press and democracy would then exist in name only and far removed from reality.

6. The chain newspapers shift their existing machinery to smaller cities, establish big printing presses, thereby gradually eliminating the existing newspapers on the one hand, instal sophisticated and modern imported equipment in larger cities for ousting medium newspapers there on the other. A process has been set in motion which is extremely dangerous for the existence of small and medium newspapers particularly language newspapers. I, therefore, make the following recommendations to prevent the hold of chain newspapers on the Indian Pess:

(i) No newspapers should be permitted to bring out more than 3 editions throughout the country and not more than 2 editions in a single State.

(ii) The Government of India and State Governments should not release more than 2 sets and one set of advertisements respectively to chain newspapers.

(iii) In order to control the monopoly trend of chain newspapers suitable changes be made in MRTP Act.

(iv) All edititons of a chain newspaper in the country with the same name even though each edition may have different Board of Directors, should for all purposes be treated as one newspaper.

(v) A company of chain newspapers publishing dailies, weeklies and other periodicals should be treated as a single unit for the purpose of newsprint allocation and for determining its classification as big, small or medium.

(vi) Specific measures be taken to ensure that chain newspapers are not able to unduly influence the political, economic and social life of the country on the one hand and do not hinder development and growth of small and medium newspapers on the other.